Introduction: My Journey – Past and Present

If you're reading this, you're probably familiar with my work from YouTube. How long this will remain on that site is anyone's guess - the climate has changed a great deal since I started making videos all the way back in 2010. Political repression has continued to grow, as the powers that be have begun to realise the influence of alternative media such as video production and written online communication, be it social media, blogs or websites. As a result, it's entirely possible that the hundreds of videos I've uploaded to YouTube could disappear overnight, and by the time you're reading this, that may well have happened.

This brings me onto the purpose of this book – my aim is to preserve the wealth of knowledge I've catalogued over many years. Though my YouTube journey began in 2010, I was a philosophical or critical thinker long before that. This has gradually resulted in me questioning and challenging everything I once believed, reaching conclusions I would never have expected. Not only does this involve unravelling a global conspiracy that has become impossible to dismiss, but it also involved questioning the political and spiritual beliefs I was raised in, from socialism to Christianity. Who I am today is a reflection of this journey.

The writing style of this book will be true to this journey by explaining what I've learnt from a first-hand perspective, each chapter presenting a new realisation, in the chronological order it took place. Every effort will be made to stick to this format, wherein I will actively avoid academic and pretentious language whenever possible. This will be done for several reasons - the first; I want this book to be readable by people that do not have an academic background in philosophy, history and politics – the core subjects I cover in great depth. I myself have no background in any of these areas, other than the autodidactic knowledge I have acquired over years - enough years, in fact, to constitute a Ph.D. While I do have an education based degree, and some experience with academic writing and teaching, it was tireless study, and of course development of my writing style, that truly shaped my ability to communicate and learn the ideas expressed in this book.

Second, we cannot underestimate the extent that modern degrees have been rendered useless by ideological repression. Peer-review, the crisis of replicating scientific research,[1] and the subversion of academia by the far-left, have made degrees economically [illegible] not to mention extremely expensive. Th [illegible] an

gatekeepers of truth and knowledge – a library (like the internet) was supposed to be a way to circumvent this. As a result of this gatekeeping, there are many people who see their higher education as much more valuable than it is in practice, though their employment prospects upon completing their degree highlight a state of denial that makes them defend this education system, rather than question it. When it comes to subjects where higher education is a necessary route for the demonstration of competence - maths, architecture and science, for example, there are exceptions. But that degree in social science isn't going to give you much more than a great deal of student debt and a completely warped view of society. You do, however, become a textbook example of the Dunning-Kruger effect.

I've come across this delusion of competence many times when I've presented my arguments in my videos online. There are those that immediately dismiss anyone that has no education background in a particular subject area. But the truth is quite the opposite. For instance, if you have a degree in economics, you'll be fed a diet made up of very little aside Keynesianism, Monetarism, and other forms of central planning, at the expense of any other schools of thought. Is this a balanced education? Absolutely not! And this is where we begin to see how I was able to escape this intellectual plantation, by going on an independent intellectual journey.

The rise and fall of internet freedom

The internet has made it easier to gather new information and knowledge than ever before, and being a natural autodidact, I have taken full advantage of that. Ironically, as the nature of the internet changes, it's become necessary to return to old-fashioned mediums of communication and information, since rising censorship could well make it nigh on impossible to continue this journey on the same road.

Websites like Wikipedia have been an absolute godsend in the earlier years of the internet, especially prior to these sites being incrementally co-opted. Many disingenuously scoff at the notion that Wikipedia was ever valuable, but the way you could easily acquire knowledge on so many subjects in one place allowed me to voraciously consume information at a level that could never be achieved with books. Not only does it take time to read books, but if you don't know what to look for you don't know what to read. Hyperlinking revolutionarily transformed this by allowing you to traverse in-depth topics, accessing new information with the click of a button.

From here, you can figure out what books you should read, once you've learnt about the basics online. Without some sort of formal education, this scale of learning would have been extremely difficult in years gone by, if not impossible, and the traditional alternative to the internet – a library, was an endeavour that only the most time rich individual could take advantage of due to the sheer length of time it takes to browse through the pages of a book, and search endless shelves. Even encyclopaedias (which Wikipedia virtualises) are limited not only by the expense of purchase, but storage space for every volume of a certain edition. To top it off, the information can become quickly outdated, making it necessary to purchase new books, to say nothing for the amount of time it takes to read a whole book when you want to learn the basics before developing more advanced knowledge. Certain books are more helpful with these problems than others, but you'll find no better medium than the internet for browsing information quickly, making it an invaluable resource.

Don't get me wrong, reading books can be invaluable, too. But in the age of the internet, it's often far more efficient to watch videos or read websites that summarise complex subjects in a quick and condensed manner. Naturally you must be cautious of sources and bias, but this works both ways. Books can also suffer with the same problems due to publishing houses, and much like mainstream media, are riddled with gatekeepers that can stifle free speech and truth. In prior decades, the circulation of information was so concentrated into traditional media like radio, TV, and of course written form, that it was impossible for someone like me to be heard. All that changed when YouTube came along - but those days are increasingly behind us.

There is no putting the internet genie back in the bottle, but I seriously doubt it will ever be the same again after the purge that began after 2016. Although the establishment was dealt a heavy blow when people in the UK voted to leave the EU, the hysteria really ramped up when Donald Trump was elected. There were other attempts to control the internet before this happened, and I actually believe it was the transfer of internet control to ICANN,[2] under the Obama presidency, where the real damage was done. Without getting into too much technical jargon, this means that DNS (Domain Name System) is no longer under the jurisdiction of the first amendment of the United States that protects free speech. Hence, we now have the European Union pushing for link taxes and upload filters that prevent the internet from being the place of free speech and expression that it once was. We're basically seeing a move towards China style censorship of the internet akin to the Great Firewall of China.

These are modern day book burnings, and with Amazon now controlling the ebook market, not even this medium is easy to break into anymore. A growing number of books are being banned from Amazon, too, meaning that this medium is becoming just as restricted. How you will be able to read this book may therefore be subject to change, since I may need to become very creative in the way I make it available to the public. I cannot rely on conventional publishing, and alternative publishers may not be interested in this title. Obviously I can only speculate about the future, but based on current trajectories, the internet is becoming a very different place to what it was when I started making videos in 2010, and we must think outside the box in the era we're entering. It's possible that a new form of internet will emerge to counteract this tide of censorship, but these things take time, and aside from the potential of blockchain technology, there is nothing that can escape the walls of censorship closing in around us, as yet.

My journey before YouTube

Before I move onto the first chapter I'd like to take some time to talk about my past, which certainly shaped my future, as one might expect. I mentioned I was a critical and philosophical thinker long before 2010. But it wasn't until my twenties that I could really explore this side of who I am. School was not exactly the most stimulating time for me - I spent a great deal of it bored to a stupor, and sports didn't come naturally to me due to my smaller stature as a child. I also had to deal with bullying until around 14, when weight training and karate helped me turn this around. As you can imagine, I didn't like school much. Teachers wrote me off as a child of low intelligence by the time I was 8. When I was in school during the 80s and early 90s, children that struggled were allowed to fall between the cracks by being dismissed as remedial or badly behaved.

A good example of the damage this did is in the subject of mathematics. Until my twenties I believed this was beyond my comprehension because this is what I was led to believe by teachers. Thus, I just gave up trying because I thought the subject was too hard. Bar a few exceptions like history, I just didn't feel cut out for school at all. Then in my twenties I resat maths because I needed this qualification to enter a degree course. Not only did I achieve a 'B' grade in a course where this was the highest grade possible, but I suddenly realised that I was actually quite good at it.

What changed, you might ask? Apart from bullying and rigid state education leading to my utter apathy towards education, I started learning guitar when I was 16. This was the turning point that helped me realise I could succeed if I applied myself. From here I remember becoming increasingly hungry to learn and achieve, but though I always had an intellectual curiosity when I was interested (I could recite the rules of Warhammer roleplay and tabletop games with ease), I never really realised my potential until my twenties. I started with a Higher National Diploma in my late teens. I then got a degree in my twenties, and it was around this time that I started getting more interested in politics.

Admittedly I was much more left-wing at this time of my life, which is hardly surprising when you consider the culture we live in. I was also a bit of a rebel in my late teen and twenties, and once again this is hardly surprising when you consider my youth. Though my love of music was about much more than rebellion or conformity to politics, it's not exactly difficult to become influenced by left-wing politics when you listen to artists like Rage Against the Machine and Marilyn Manson. That being said, I've learnt to appreciate a wide variety of music over the years, and as a composer of music I was always looking for new styles to inspire me. In my younger years it was 80s rock and metal that caught my attention the most, but searching for new music is probably something I'll always do.

Then along came Michael Moore, a man that showed me a way of expressing politics I never thought possible, and to read a book about political commentary was completely inspiring. Today I'm as far away from Michael Moore's far-left politics as humanly possible, but he nonetheless made me aware of the potential for political commentary. Moore's influence coincided with the most left-wing point of my life, once again hardly surprising. Socially I was very left-wing; I did some volunteer work for Amnesty International and was passionate about human rights. As part of this volunteer work I got involved with various events, including Mardi Gras. Being raised orthodox Christian, this was a big deal, since I previously questioned the morality of same-sex attraction.

By now I was in a co-habiting relationship with the woman that would eventually become my wife, and mother to my children. Like me she was also in a left-wing part of her life, not least because her university course was in humanities. She took a module in politics, which made her more interested in the subject, and the Michael Moore book's I read belonged to her. For my birthday she bought me The Communist Manifesto, although I'm happy to say that despite all my socialist beliefs, I never bought into communism as an economic system - socialist regulation of the economy, yes - but that's as far as I went.

All these influences led to me writing my first commentary book in 2006 – no, not this one – a book I called The Undertone, because it dealt with the 'undertone' of society. It was the left-wing version of what I do today – my younger, more naïve self, inspired by Michael Moore, Amnesty International and socialism, laid out in book form. This never got published (thank God!), but it did help me develop a style of investigation and commentary that would lead to what I do today.

And then there was atheism. Though I was brought up Greek orthodox Christian and attended an Anglican high school, ever since my early twenties I was wrestling with my faith due to my prior negative experiences having a knock-on effect on my outlook. Going to church slowly but surely became an empty and meaningless experience as a result, especially as I was dealing with so much frustration when God never seemed to answer my prayers. During his sermons, the priest at my local orthodox church would scold people for not attending, and not being generous enough when making church donations. This seemed excessively critical, all adding to me questioning the belief in God, not quite accepting atheism until I read The God Delusion by Richard Dawkins in 2007.

Last but not least, there's YouTube. By 2007 I was listening to a whole host of atheist commentators on this site – Christina Rad, ThunderF00t, Richard Coughlan, Laci Green, and other less notable YouTubers that led to the formation of an online atheist community. Admittedly, this had a significant influence on my desire to finally call myself an atheist, and I found the entire concept of making videos fascinating. Though I was tempted to try it, I was worried about how it would affect my employment. It was thus around 3 years later when this would finally happen.

In 2010, about 6 months after the birth of my first child, my wife went back to work. Due to circumstances in life I became completely self-employed, working from home in the evenings as I looked after my baby daughter in the day. I guess you could call me a stay-at-home Dad, but since I've always worked, the label gives the wrong impression. Once per week my mother would look after my daughter, and these were the days I recorded and edited videos for my YouTube channel. The research that went into my videos allowed me to go on a journey of discovery that formed the basis of the book you're now reading.

With this introduction, I hope this helps to establish the scale of the journey that I went through in the earlier years that followed 2010, outlined in this book. Each chapter opens with a statement that summarises the crux of the chapter, followed by a detailed analysis and breakdown. As a whole, the book will concentrate on three key subjects that connect and develop into various other areas, these being feminism, socialism, and the nature of freedom. The latter was influenced by what I learnt about feminism and socialism, and the direction I took as I began to question how to resolve the problems that come when freedom is suppressed. As I'm pulling back the curtain with each chapter, learn what philosophical truths I come to learn about the world, and how this would inspire me to me questioning everything we think we know.

Chapter 1: The First Red Pill of Feminism

Feminism is a form of reproductive and economic control.

When I first came across YouTube commentary in around 2007, I was a firm believer in feminism. Like everyone else immersed in mainstream society, I learnt about the positive contribution that feminism had made to society from a young age. I certainly learnt about the Suffragettes in the first few years of high school, but I vaguely recall learning about it in earlier years of schooling, too, albeit not in the same depth. So if we learnt about this in school it must true – right? Oh the number of times I would realise this was false when I started doing research for my YouTube channel.

I recall a day in primary school, as my class sat on the floor listening, that our teacher asked how many of our dads helped their mums clean. I then recall the teacher, dissatisfied with the replies, lecturing the class about how dads should help out more in the house. Many more incidents like this would come to mind as I slowly began to question what I thought I knew about life. Feminist theory speaks of female objectification – the simplistic notion that women are turned into objects that have no value in their own right, as they serve a role in society that prevents them from achieving their personal ambitions. Though most people aren't aware of this academic description, this is pervasive in our modern culture, trickling down from academics in their ivory towers to the culture at large – including schools.

Something happened to me in around 2009 that helped me break this programming; I came across an article on MSN written by Kathy Lette, an Australian-British author. It was nothing but a mean-spirited attack on men, packaged as something comedic. The article tried to couch feminist talking points in low-tier humour that was really just an excuse to be spiteful about men. It was the first time I saw a negative side to feminism that previously I never thought existed. Like most people, I was led to believe feminism was all about equality, and that it was right for women to have the same rights and opportunities as men. But this article seemed to fly in the face of that, painting modern men as terrible, despite generally embracing tolerance and opportunities for women in society.

It wasn't the first time I'd seen this derisive attitude towards men as a sex, but somehow my perception had begun to change. Michael Moore was known for praising feminism and scorning men, too, but not only did I feel no sense of anger or sadness about this in my earlier twenties, but Moore actually made me more sympathetic to the feminist movement. In chapter seven of Moore's book, Stupid White Men (called The End of Men), he talks about how nature is killing off males because they're so destructive - not exactly a positive representation of the human male.

There was one thing that was different, however. Around the same annual timeframe that I came across the Kathy Lette article, I recall watching a Channel 4 documentary about fathers being denied access to their children when they separated or divorced. I couldn't believe how tragic it was. It showed men that hadn't seen their children for extended periods of time (sometimes years), who had to go to court to get permission to see their children once per week in supervised visits, and legally arranging to have visitation rights or go on holiday with their children, only to have the mother violate the court agreement and face no consequences. Was this the country I lived in? How could such injustice take place in a free and democratic society?

It wasn't long before I started learning about fathers' rights and, of course, Father 4 Justice, a well-known activist group in the UK. Similar groups exist all over the Western world, written off by mainstream society as misogynists that want to put women back in the kitchen. Once you start noticing the biased way fathers are treated in modern society, it won't be long before you start to question feminism, if you're an inquisitive person, that is. Learning about the plight of fathers really changed my perception of men in society. Thus, the next time I came across veiled animosity masked as activism or comedy, i.e., Kathy Lette's MSN article, I did not take it well.

No longer did I merely see men as the misogynistic pigs that feminist activists and apologists purport them to be. I realised that men experience social problems in society, and that in spite of men like me that were passionate about women's rights from a feminist perspective, not only were feminists still really unhappy at men as a whole, but they acted as though most men were still as bad as the stereotype of the 1950s sexist pig who only treated women like sex objects, unpaid nannies, and housemaids.

Taking my first red pill

After reading the Kathy Lette article, I recall immediately feeling the urge to figure out why feminism would lead to such hostility. So I did some Google plus YouTube searches, and soon came across some enlightening and insightful YouTube videos that opened up a whole new world of commentary. At this point my only real experience with commentary on

YouTube was related to atheism. But now I found another subject that was even more fringe than that – criticism of feminism.

In 2009, feminism certainly wasn't as widely criticised in countercultural circles as it is today. One video I came across was called 'How Feminism Screwed My Generation', where a young man explains how feminism has made it impossible for men to find a decent woman to settle down with, partly due to serial dating and sex leading to females having multiple male partners, therefore corrupting their desire to settle down with one man. He explained that, thanks to other cultural issues related to feminism (like more divorce), he was going overseas to find a wife. Having somehow recalled the name of this video from memory, I searched for it online at the time of writing. I discovered some sites and forums discussing it, also featuring an old embedded link to the video. It was, however, unavailable when you clicked on the player.

There were only a few more notable voices talking about this subject back then, one being a channel by the name ManWomanMyth. It featured a series of videos breaking down feminism extensively, addressing everything from the pay gap and rape statistics, to father's rights and bias against men (otherwise known as misandry). The series included interviews of notable commentators like the late Angry Harry, and Erin Pizzey, all names I would grow to know well as I learnt more about men's rights. However, I will not delve into this further here because this is the subject of chapter 5.

Feminism was the first time I'd really begun to question left-wing politics, and feminism is most certainly left-wing, as I would further realise. My whole life I was raised to believe that the Right was responsible for everything wrong in society, and that the Left stood for noble endeavours such as equality, opportunity and progress. Like the very idea of feminism itself, I would grow to understand that these words mean very different things to different people, and are just meaningless buzzwords when they lack context. If we question the motive of an ideology tirelessly pushed by the state in an openly authoritarian or totalitarian country, many people would accept that it could easily be indoctrination designed to indoctrinate the masses, making them easier to control. If you asked the same question about an ideology pushed in the Western world, most people won't accept that this may be indoctrination because they believe we live in a democratic and free society that might not be perfect, but at least you can work towards making it better. Is it really that simple, though?

Some people that manage to shake off brainwashing have described how it's a bit like picking away at wallpaper or a picture, until you realise there's something else underneath. Once you start picking, it's almost impossible to stop because you've already found the motivation to pick away. Before long, you've picked so much that the entire wall or picture reveals something very different peering out at you. This ability to pick away at the truth is precisely why tyrannical ideologies and governments are so repressive. The only way to stop people questioning (or picking), is by making the punishment so harsh that they're too afraid to do it. With enough conditioning, especially at a young age, you can convince people that certain lies are true, and certain truths are lies.

There are those who, no matter how dangerous, will seek the truth. As you can imagine, this drives tyrants and despots crazy – it's something they've had to deal with since the dawn of civilisation. Every time they think they've created the perfect open air prison for the masses, corruption and truth corrodes it. It doesn't stop them trying again, but as you can imagine, the techniques are becoming more sophisticated over time.

So what's this got to do with feminism? Well, it's actually no surprise that feminism was the first 'red pill' I took on my journey (referred to as a red pill due to the film, The Matrix, where the character, Neo, must choose between the red pill of truth or blue pill of ignorance). Why is this no surprise? Because if you want to take over society, the first place to start is the relationship between men and women. Absolutely nothing will function well if you drive a wedge between them. You'd imagine the reason for this would be rather obvious at an exterior level, but I'll endeavour to explain it in more depth.

For one, if men and women don't get along there can be no families, or at least no stable families. There's a reason why totalitarian states and cults deliberately try to break families apart. The aim is to make the collective the centre of the individual's life, not only at the expense of individual free will and liberty, but at the expense of all other group association. Hence, people find themselves alienated from everyone around them when they're being manipulated in this fashion. I imagine that many people will agree that this takes place, but they're often very selective about where they notice it.

Given that I plan to break down the roots of feminism later in the book, I won't go into that here. It certainly helps to understand this if you want to grasp why feminism is a sinister ideology designed to control people. For the purpose of this chapter I want to focus on how feminism fundamentally manipulates and controls people. Besides, my understanding of the roots of feminism would not only come later in my journey, but is something I continue to learn about to this day, therefore going beyond the early years of discovery set out in this book. However, at its most fundamental level, we can break feminist control down into two forms of manipulation and control – one; reproductive, and two; economic.

Reproductive control

On the reproductive level, feminism is used to take control of child rearing in society. If this sounds far-fetched, ask yourself this simple question; would a totalitarian state or cult control reproduction? Remember this question whenever you start to have any doubts. Note it down if you have to, because it's a pertinent thing to ask if you're struggling to accept what you're reading. Also, be aware that I'm breaking down my journey in a way that reflects my own gradual realisation over the years. If you're patient, every chapter will therefore make things clearer.

There's nothing new about authoritarians wanting to control reproduction. As far back as ancient Greece, Plato talked about it in his book, Republic. In his vision of society, it would be ruled by philosopher kings that decide who reproduces, based on eugenics criteria.[1] No child would know their parents in this society, and no parent would know their children. Plato argued that this would create greater social cohesion. Many people blame Plato for the totalitarianism of the 20th century because his ideas were often foundational. It's not as though Plato was the only inspiration in this regard, but it's certainly true that he had a far-reaching effect.

Controlling human development from birth inevitably becomes the method of creating model citizens under totalitarianism. So it's hardly surprising that, even as far back as Plato, totalitarians aspired to achieve this. It's for this reason that totalitarian societies are well known for replacing the family with the state. Organisations like the Hitler Youth indoctrinated children with Nazi ideology. Mao's Red Guards made young people so fanatical that they terrorised adults during the Cultural Revolution. The Young Pioneers of the Soviet Union, started by Lenin and the Bolsheviks in 1922, only ended in 1991 when the Soviet Union came to an end. These organisations might give the impression of being similar to the scouts, or other innocent childhood clubs and groups, but this was far from the case. How do you create adults that unquestioningly follow the totalitarian state? Aside from using repression to terrify people into submission, you indoctrinate them into loving their servitude, which starts from as young an age as possible.

But can we really lump feminism in with totalitarian indoctrination and repression? Even without an insight into where feminism originated, the answer is yes. Consider this; without the support of men in history, women would never have survived. It's easy to look at our modern world and say that women don't need men, or that men treated women badly. Automation makes everyday tasks easy - from washing machines cleaning our clothing without the need to do it physically, to vacuum cleaners quickly removing dirt and dust. However, everyday chores formerly required a great deal of effort to complete, so unless you could afford a servant or a slave, someone had to do it, and inevitably this was women. Why not a man, you might ask? Because being a provider was often back breaking work, completely unsuitable for the physical capabilities of a woman.

Setting aside the poorest in history (like medieval peasants or industrial era factory workers), women therefore had no interest in being in the workplace unless this was either compulsory, or essential for their survival. As time progressed, this changed. But it wasn't because women were being kept down by men in a system feminists refer to as patriarchy. When it's impractical (sometimes impossible) for women to work, society is inevitably shaped around men at the forefront, with women in supporting roles. I certainly don't want to suggest there was no injustice in history. Hereditary hierarchies and caste systems were common practice, but it's easy to blame this all on men when they took the majority of the risks that kept women safe, otherwise too many female deaths would lead to a catastrophic drop in the birth rate.

Economic control

This brings me onto the second level of feminist manipulation and control; economic (economics defined as the study and analysis of consumption, distribution and production of wealth in society). Once technology made it safer for women to enter the workplace en masse (and I must explicitly clarify that I do mean en masse, given that some women have always worked), that's exactly what they did. That being said, I cannot honestly say this happened organically because they were coaxed into abandoning their natural proclivities to stay close to the nest. Warm and comfortable office spaces made the workplace more attractive to women, and factories became much safer than the early industrial era, meaning that many more women could now work (industrial era being the period in history beginning around the middle of the 18th century, where new technology led to the proliferation of mass manufacture in factories – also known as the industrial revolution). There is, however, a practical limitation to women in the workplace given that they still need to give birth to children, and children are much better off being at home with a biological parent until at least 3 to 4 years old, at which time they're ready to appreciate socialising with other children.

Speaking as a parent, I can attest to this dynamic. I was home with my two daughters while my wife worked full-time - if anyone is going to suggest that my attitude to family life is somehow archaic, they should bear this in mind. It worked for my family because I like the flexibility and independence of being self-employed, and I cherish being around my children more often, something fathers missed out on in the past. If feminism was truly sincere, it would have encouraged this kind of flexibility for modern family life. Instead, women were pressurised into leaving the home because they were told they weren't reaching their full potential, and much of this took place through a barrage of media propaganda that made women feel inadequate if they didn't work.[2]

Women subsequently joined the workforce in droves, giving in to peer-pressure from female family and friends, as well as social conditioning by feminist propaganda. Conversely, men weren't told that staying home or that working part-time is an acceptable alternative, leading to a growing number of children who were put in childcare, something research has repeatedly warned against[3][4] – like everything else relating to feminism, the warnings fall on deaf ears. I can think of nothing more anti-family than making mothers feel inadequate or ashamed if they stay at home to look after their children, and keep a good home. This most certainly does not make a woman a failure. What I can personally attest to is the feelings of isolation that come when most people are working during the day, and what this does for the once thriving communities that women formed in the background of society, while men brought home a wage. To be a stay-at-home parent now is to learn to do things alone, and this isn't something most humans are very good at doing on a regular basis.

Is it therefore any surprise that evidence repeatedly proves that women are unhappier after 40 years of feminism?[5] It's as though women have been pressurised into denying their nature, leading to non-instinctive lifestyles that not only make them more miserable, but makes family life unnecessarily stressful. As you can imagine, these factors have increased the divorce rate right across the Western world, something that hardly needs a study or research to prove.

The first video I ever made on YouTube was called The Negative Effects of Feminism. It wasn't exactly a masterpiece, and I've since removed it. I uploaded it in late October 2010. Looking back, a better title for that video would have been The Negative Economic Effects of Feminism, because that's what it fundamentally addressed. Although I really didn't possess the scope of economic understanding I have today, even then I could see that the feminist insistence on more women in the workplace equals lower wages and fewer jobs. There are those that will quibble about this because human desire is infinite, but resources aren't. You can't expect to infinitely create more economic activity - there will always be limits in a finite world.

The impact that far more women in the workplace had on the family cannot be understated. It had a devastating effect on family life because it gradually led to the requirement for both parents to work, partly through the deflationary effect of wages, and partly because the cultural influence of feminism meant that people were staying single for far longer. More single people equals less jobs for families, coupled with fewer homes for married people. Particularly during the 1950s - which feminist supporters generally insist was not the golden era of family life that many traditional and conservative people suggest - the father could provide a good standard of living for his wife and children. Those days are now long gone, and feminism was the first significant blow to the wider cultural deterioration that has accelerated in subsequent decades, something I will explain further as this book progresses.

Well known feminist 'icon' Gloria Steinman once said that "A woman needs a man like a fish needs a bicycle." Like oh so many quotes the exact origin is debated, though it really doesn't matter. What matters is the meaning, which is crystal clear: women don't need men in their lives. But is this really true? Can society function when men and women see themselves as autonomous beings that don't need to live as couples? The answer is a resounding no. When you put your own self-interest above everything else, it won't be long before everything begins to unravel, and the reason why this would be desirable to the powers that be will become clearer in subsequent chapters.

Before I end this chapter I'll leave you with this; Gloria Steinam, founder of the magazine 'Ms', received funding from the CIA for her feminist activism.[6] Why would a government intelligence department be interested in pushing an ideology that destabilises the family? Unless the government was in the business of engineering control over society, much like Plato described over 2000 years ago.

Chapter 2: Bankers Rule the World

Banking is at the heart of all modern tyranny.

A quote attributed to Mayer Amschel Rothschild, part of the world renowned Rothschild banking dynasty, is "Permit me to issue and control the money of a nation, and I care not who makes its laws." His son, Nathan Rothschild, is attributed with saying that "I care not what puppet is placed upon the throne of England to rule the Empire on which the sun never sets. The man who controls Britain's money supply controls the British Empire, and I control the British money supply." Although we cannot substantiate whether these quotes are attributed to these individuals, the premise still stands; if you control the supply of money, you control everything else. You can call these quotes myths. You can call them 'conspiracy theories'. But it really doesn't matter when you know how banking works in actuality. They truly do sum up the world we live in.

It's strange how quotes like this can never be substantiated, however, like so much about who runs the world. Many of us have that nagging feeling that something isn't right - so we start digging. But no matter how much we dig, there are some things we'll never be able to prove because the trail goes dead after a certain stage. And yet everything will still point in a certain direction. So I want you to ask yourself this question; if you had absolute power, would you rule from the forefront or from the shadows? History demonstrates how much more effective it is to do the latter.

If you had absolute power it would be better to quietly dispose of the evidence of your existence and motives, so even if someone did find out what you were doing they would never be able to prove anything. All they'd be left with is the deductive certainty that you're guilty, without enough evidence to convict you, like a detective that doesn't have enough proof to convict a culprit, even though he knows full well that all the signs point in his direction. It's the missing link, so to speak – that one piece of evidence that a court would need to convict someone beyond a reasonable doubt.

Hence society appears to be based on democratic accountability, but only to those that don't ask any questions, or those that lack the insight to figure out how they're being duped. Banking is by and far the biggest piece of this deception of false choice, and without it, all the chains that bind us would disappear, at least when it comes to state power. With this in mind, whatever I talk about in this book, or whatever political, social or economic problem you can think of – everything starts and ends with the monetary system. If this is corrupt or flawed in any way, shape or form, you can only effect change as far as the system allows, and that system is banking.

So what exactly is 'banking'? Put simply, banking is a system of monetary exchange that can involve a vast array of transactions - from lending and investing, to saving and spending. The definition of money is subject to debate, but usually involves something of value that people use for everyday transactions like buying, investing and selling. People are familiar with money as notes and coins with official seals that provide legal status in society. But money has changed a great deal over thousands of years, and it's still changing today.

The 2008 Financial Crisis

Before I explain how this took place, allow me to turn the clock back to 2007. That year I decided to try running a small business, drawing on several years of experience I had in the retail sector. I was running a clothing stall in the indoor market of my home city of Cardiff, which was initially doing pretty well, despite extremely high rents because the council were charging so much that no one succeeded in that particular stall. That being said, this was the best option in the short to medium term because I only needed to give one week's notice if I wanted to close or relocate.

As Christmas approached, I began to realise that something wasn't right. Business was eerily quiet and trade was inexplicably evaporating. With all the experience I had in retail, I knew this wasn't normal for this time of year. Given that the high council rents made the stall far more expensive on a square foot basis than a standard commercial unit, I started to have second thoughts.

What's more, I couldn't find an appropriate high street unit that was available. Thus I decided to close the business with no financial loss – possibly restarting the business later on (this never came to fruition). I just couldn't shake a gut feeling that the economy was about to go south, and sure enough as Christmas drew closer, there was news abound of a so-called credit crunch. Banks were no longer lending money to each other, and in turn they weren't lending money to the public, hence 'credit crunch' (credit being another word for your available funds). Then something unprecedented happened on the 14th September of that year - something that hadn't occurred in Britain for over 150 years - there was a run on a British bank. No, that doesn't mean that people ran over a bank. It means that lots of people were trying to get their money out of a bank at the same time. That bank was Northern Rock.[1]

Now this is where the switched on might notice that this doesn't make sense. Why would it matter if everyone took their money out of a bank at the same time? The money's all there, right? If it wasn't that would be criminal - wouldn't it? Well, banks don't actually have enough money for everyone to withdraw their full balance in cash. Let that sink in for a moment because there's a special name for this kind of system. Some call it a pyramid scheme. Others call it a Ponzi scheme. In other words, the higher up the pyramid you go, the more likely you are to benefit. Conversely, the further down you go, the more likely you are to lose everything.

The fact we're living in a society where such a system is in existence really should ring alarm bells. There are two reasons why this is justified; one: people have no idea how banking actually works behind the scenes, and two: economists have all sorts of fancy theories about why this is a good idea. That's right – a system where not everyone's money actually exists is best, apparently. In a better time and place this would have been called fraud.

Northern Rock was the first sign that something wasn't right with the financial system. After going bankrupt, Northern Rock was later nationalised on the 22nd February 2008. But by September of that year, people were quite literally crying Armageddon, as bank after bank became exposed to toxic loans known as subprime mortgages in what became known as the 2008 Financial Crisis.[2] On the 7th September 2008, US backed mortgage lenders Fannie Mae and Freddie Mac were placed into 'conservatorship' by the US government. But it was the bankruptcy of US Bank Lehman Brothers that led to utter panic. Many were saying that the entire economy would collapse if governments didn't intervene. This fearmongering is the reason the US Emergency Economic Stabilisation Act of 2008[3] was passed, since becoming known as the 'bank bailout'. Initially it was voted down on the 29th September 2008. Two days later it passed with an amendment, after politicians were scared senseless about the prospect of total economic collapse if they didn't act. How did things get this bad, and why was the economy so vulnerable to such catastrophe?

To be perfectly honest, I had no idea how banking really worked until late 2010, after I started my YouTube channel. Though feminism was the first subject I tackled, banking was the second. In 2010-11, we were only 3 years into the biggest economic downturn since the 1930s. I, like so many others, was trying to figure out what caused this crisis. I found the answer to that question when someone sent a video series to my YouTube inbox. Like so many videos on YouTube, the series was later removed, but it allowed me to take the first steps to understanding the banking system we live in.

Fractional-reserve banking

I discovered that our financial system is based on fractional-reserve banking.[4] What this means is that only a fraction of the funds from banking comes from money that you and I carry around in our daily lives, thus explaining why this system is called 'fractional' reserve banking. The vast majority of money is therefore merely digits on a screen, taking no real world form at all. Banks are only required to keep a certain amount of real-world money in 'reserve', which allows them to create substantially more digital money. An agreed formula allows banks to multiply the amount of money they can literally create out of thin air, as long as they have a small fraction of real world money in reserve on their balance sheet. These reserves come from real world money that people deposit into their bank accounts, explaining why this money is referred to as 'deposits' in economics.

It's no surprise, then, that a run on a bank is so catastrophic. Having only a small percentage of physical money is justified by its defenders because it supposedly stimulates lending (as though this is necessarily a good thing). Which brings me onto the next part of this scam; most money is brought into existence via said lending. Every time you borrow money from a bank, whether it's a mortgage, business loan, or anything else, this is created out of thin air by the bank, limited by the amount of physical money it has in reserve. The loan becomes mere digits on a screen that would lead to economic collapse if we all decided to conduct our transactions with real world money, rather than electronically. Creation of this money is approved by the central bank of a particularly part of the world, like the US Federal Reserve, Bank of England, or European Central Bank.

Now we get to the heart of why this system is favoured by the higher-ups in society; loans are secured by collateral we purchase with debt. So if we buy a house, car, furniture, or anything else, the bank can seize those assets if you fail to repay the loan. Consider this for a moment; your bank can seize real-world assets if you fail to pay for a loan created by nothing of real-world value! Isn't that the perfect win-win situation for a bank? It doesn't matter either way to them – it can continue to make interest on the loan it gave you, or it will seize your real-world assets if you can't pay the whole loan back.

Principle and interest

The logical conclusion of this system is diabolical. It means that the financial elite can slowly but surely acquire more and more, merely by waiting for economic downturns to take place, at which time they'll be able to seize assets from people they loaned money to. If that doesn't sound like a rigged game to you then perhaps what I'm about to say will change your mind; there is never enough money in circulation because only the loan itself is created, called the 'principle'. The other part of that loan is the interest that you and I pay back to the bank for lending us the money. To keep up with the fact that there's never enough money in circulation, the economy must constantly grow. As soon as this stops, we experience an economic downturn like a recession or depression. Taken far enough, this can cause an economic collapse because this system is so precarious.

We now see why there's so much obsession with growth in the economy. Without it, we wouldn't just experience the natural ebb and flow of everyday economic life. We'd suffer societal collapse as the banking system fails us. These predatory lending practices were once kept in check by basing money on something tangible like gold and silver. This meant that you could only have so much of it, therefore limiting economic instability. People kept their precious metals in vaults, but vault owners figured out that they could loan this at interest, without people realising it was gone. Eventually the gold owners found out that this was taking place, but asked vault owners to give them a percentage of the interest in return for lending their gold. And so modern banking was born, where depositors would expect a certain amount of interest if they stored their money with banks.

The concept of money has evolved over time into something based entirely on nothing, to the extent that most money is nothing more than digits of a screen anymore. Paper money came about as a claim cheque for gold stored by a bank. People started using these cheques in everyday transactions because it was much more convenient than using gold. Today, paper money has no value in its own right, other than pure consumer sentiment. If ever this is shaken, the results are far-reaching, as we saw in the 2008 financial crisis. To arrive at this place, the financial elite gradually moved us away from money as a real world store of value. Gold, for example, is one of the most durable precious metals, used in a myriad of industrial applications, not to mention jewellery or even tools and weapons. It's this that led to it being considered so valuable that people would use it to trade with – your gold for my food produce being a demonstration of such trade.

In certain times and places in history, states would emblazon their official seal on gold, silver and copper because people were accustomed to using precious metals as a convenient way to trade. Once claim cheques became guarantees for precious metals, it was the beginning of what we have today. The state started using paper money that was backed by gold, and this became known as the gold standard. Various reforms took place over the last few hundred years, until the Nixon Shock in 1971 ended the gold standard across the world.[5] Now all we have is a system of money backed by nothing but your assets as collateral.

Taking this knowledge into consideration, let's revisit the social effects of feminism from chapter one. Can we honestly say that women were encouraged to go out to work because it was in their best interests? Or was it to fund a debt based system? Bear in mind that this doesn't just include personal and business debt, but government debt as well. Therefore it's in the best interest of the state to have as many tax payers as possible to fund national debt. In the 1950s it was mainly men going out to work – just one tax payer per family. But that radically changed once feminism convinced women that they would be more liberated if they worked for a boss, instead of supporting their families at home. We've already seen that more job seekers equals lower wages, also explained in chapter 1. The other side of the economic manipulation I mentioned in chapter 1 is the benefit to the banking system, now addressed in chapter 2.

We now know that without continual growth that keeps up with an ever expanding money supply caused by paying interest, the economic system will completely collapse. This means that the monetary system must have an ever increasing supply of debtors in the form of tax payers and borrowers. Former economic wisdom elevated saving, and investing some of these savings was encouraged, to help grow an economy. But this investing was based on savings as opposed to debt, which made an economy far more robust and stable. When everything is based on debt, the slightest change in interest rates can be disastrous, further explaining why the modern economy is so fragile.

I once had someone say to me that "savers are losers," a person sucked into the kind of mantras encouraged in our debt based system. Prior to the 2008 financial crisis, people were creating huge property portfolios by remortgaging each and every time their property went up in value. For example, if the property went up by £40,000, they would get the bank to give them a loan for this amount. Can you imagine what happened to these people when the financial crisis hit? Many lost everything! One of these individuals I was aware of was driving a Porsche. Not anymore! The person that said to me that 'savers and losers' is using this precise tactic to get rich quick, as though it hasn't been done before. Alas, people never learn.

Don't get me wrong, I don't think people should hoard everything they have at the expense of any material enjoyment. We should strike a balance that absolutely must come with the ability to save (and invest) income, for the sake of long-term stability. But I return to what I said at the start of this chapter; everything starts and ends with the monetary system – there's only so much we can do when this is designed to benefit the wealthiest financial elites, lending us paper and digital money backed by nothing of real-world value, unlike when money was backed by precious metals.

There's also something else that people all too often fail to consider – inflation. The less people save, the more of this there is. Being encouraged not to save is having an adverse effect on all sorts of market prices, not to mention property prices that were a major contributing factor to the debt behind the 2008 financial crisis. When people have easy access to debt this creates the kind of inflation we saw prior to 2008, when housing prices were rising at a ludicrous rate, pricing many people out of a market that was once affordable on an average income. The only people that win in an economy this precarious are those who already own a great deal of assets outright, not to mention banking elites and their guarantees of interest payments or the seizure of assets. For those prepared to weather a high risk to reward ratio, you may do well in this environment with a bit of luck, but you have to embrace economic decisions that could ruin you for years, even the rest of your life.

There's no point trying to blame this system on bankers alone, who've often become the scapegoats for the perverse incentives we're given within this loose credit system. There are others to blame - the ones insisting that fractional-reserve banking is the best monetary system. Nothing could be further from the truth! It's actually the worst of all because it encourages irresponsibility on a gargantuan scale. It's even the catalyst for destructive social policies, like the feminist narrative that being a housewife is oppressive, as though this is worse than being obligated to an employer. There's nothing less oppressive than raising the next generation, and it should now be easier to see why feminism is a movement designed to break down this maternal instinct, without women realising they're being manipulated by a ruling class using social movements to gradually push us towards their objectives.

There's absolutely no way anyone can fathom these objectives unless they understand it from the bottom-up. As we can see, banking is the economic foundation for a system of control, explaining why our society is becoming increasingly materialistic. We can see two aspects of this agenda via feminism and banking, although banking is where it all starts. Once ruling elites were in charge of money, they had an infinite access to funding backed by nothing, fuelling their machinations into a centrally controlled society.

Chapter 3: Moving Away from Socialism

Those who depend on welfare will be enslaved.

Allow me to briefly define what left and right-wing conventionally means before proceeding in this chapter because it's very important to the wider context of this book, and I won't assume that the reader knows the difference; we're led to believe by mainstream politics that left-wing denotes people that lean towards socialism and liberalism, often called 'The Left', those on the Left called 'Leftists'. Likewise, right-wing denotes capitalism and conservatism in mainstream politics, often referred to as 'The Right', people on the Right less commonly called 'Rightists'. That's as far as I'm prepared to go for now because these definitions and terms are mired in flaws that I'll revisit later on. Let's just assume, for the time being, that they're correct.

I've already explained that I was very much a creature of the left before I started my YouTube channel. This made me a big believer in the government helping the most vulnerable in society, and making sure that fairness reined supreme. I've since addressed how my political beliefs affected me on social issues like feminism, and what made me start to question this. In this chapter, I'll explain why I moved away from the economic side of my formerly socialist way of thinking.

I come from a family of predominantly small business owners that had no experience working for the public sector (this being a term for government workers, contrasted to the private sector, where people work in privately owned industries). They were model immigrants that came from very humble origins in Cyprus – they integrated, worked hard, paid their taxes, created jobs, and did a great deal of charity work over the years. All things considered, it's surprising that more of my family weren't sympathetic to right-wing politics given that many of them worked in the private sector, who were always pretty evenly split between left and right, at least in my parent's generation. This demonstrates how deeply people have been indoctrinated into believing that the government can solve every problem, even if they work for the private sector (myself included).

My youngest political memory is another situation where I was sitting on the carpet in primary school when I was around 7 years-old. Along with my fellow classmates, we sat there as the teacher criticised Margaret Thatcher. I recall many of the children agreeing with her, as though 7 year-olds know anything about politics, or should know anything when you consider the priorities that children ideally have at that time in their lives – such as playing and learning core skills like reading, writing and numeracy. When I asked my mother about Margaret Thatcher when I got home, I remember feeling that I shouldn't like her because most people at school didn't, either. I now know that I was being socially conditioned by teachers to feel a certain way about politics from a very young age, and it comes as no surprise that many teachers are sympathetic to socialist policies when you consider this early experience.[1][2]

My late father was someone that didn't conform to this thinking, voting for Thatcher and being against Labour his whole voting life, to the best of my recollection. He wasn't an openly political person, and came from a generation that said you shouldn't talk politics, especially in public. I now know why people say this because the price you pay when you don't support the Left is very high, not only socially but financially. Why? Because the Left target anyone that isn't like them – they'll ostracise and lecture you, boycott your businesses, try to get you sacked, and seek to prosecute you.

It's much easier to see what that results in today because this process is so far along, especially when you consider what I said in the introduction about growing online censorship. For example, the Left dominates Silicon Valley, turning Big Tech platforms like YouTube, Facebook and Twitter into echo chambers that censor anyone that doesn't conform to their ideology.[3][4][5] At the same time, left-wing protests about corporate exploitation have gradually faded away as corporations become dominated by Leftists. It's not hard to see why when you realise that the true purpose of these protests is consistently to co-opt, rather than reduce, power.

When it comes to working for the public sector, it's much easier to see why left-wing bias is so much more naturally prevalent than even the corporate world. Whereas a process of co-option is actively required in the latter, this is generally not the case for the former. It's said that you should never bite the hand that feeds you. When you work for the government, it's therefore in your best interest to have more government intervention and control in society (at least in the short to medium term), but this is hardly altruistic when a government worker is only demanding more government because it helps preserve their employment.

Justifying socialism

What, then, do you need to say if you want to justify your government job without looking self-interested? The easiest way would be to make it look as though you're not self-interested at all – quite the opposite, in fact. You'd make it look as though you're genuinely interested in helping the poorest in society (the main argument during the early years of socialism). You don't want people to starve or become deprived of basic needs like a home and healthcare, because that would be cruel and inhumane. Furthermore, you'd say that greedy bosses and 'robber barons' are exploiting everyday working people by taking more than their fair share from society, turning into rich fat cats. So supposedly we need the government to step in to stop this terrible injustice.

There's one big problem with this narrative; con-artists don't all run away into the night after they've swindled or defrauded you. A truly diabolical con-artist wraps in a cloak of compassion, maintaining this pretence even after they've left you penniless or totally enslaved to their will. History clearly demonstrates this bait and switch. People once claimed that slaves were helping society by serving their masters, and that if they were freed it would lead to economic or social collapse. Ancient Greeks like Aeschylus and Plato argued that slavery was natural,[7] while people in the South of the early United states postulated that it was a "positive good" or "necessary evil".[8] Thomas Jefferson once said of slavery that, "We have the wolf by the ear, and we can neither hold him, nor safely let him go. Justice is in one scale, and self-preservation in the other."

But the Left aren't trying to enslave or swindle anyone, you may reply. You might go as far as calling me cynical or dishonest to suggest such a thing. Why would helping the poorest in society be a bad thing? Wouldn't it be more obvious that rich people are the real bogeymen? Such questions require nuance to answer, but it's certainly not true that malevolent intentions are as black and white as the Left suggest. Due to the typical experiences of young people today, overwhelmingly indoctrinated to believe that socialism is a moral good, it's hardly surprising that many would accept a simplistic explanation of economic exploitation and poverty. Conversely, it's not as though I was trying to economically exploit anyone when I was at the socialist period in my life, and I don't deny that a lot of socialists have very good intentions, but the problems arise when denial of reality takes hold.

Socialism comes in many different forms historically and theoretically, but socialism as we know it today is basically the belief that government should provide a basic standard of living alongside legal protections from the injustices of inequality. What many know as capitalism today is the buying and selling we experience on a daily basis – from buying groceries, food and clothing, to investing in stocks and shares. To understand why the Left goes so wrong, we need to look at the facts in this regard. Does socialism make people wealthier as a whole? The answer is a resounding no. The more socialism you have in society, the poorer people become, to say nothing of the entitlement this breeds. When you look at every key indicator of wealth in society, the answer is very clear – the more economic freedom you have, the easier it is to eradicate poverty. There are some caveats given that there is no genuinely free economy, which I'll address later in this book. But the reason socialism is so bad at eradicating poverty is easy to see when you look a little deeper; socialism is a system that takes money through taxation, fees and tariffs, redistributing it across society in various ways. Much of this is eaten up by bureaucracy, and it creates absolutely no wealth in the process.

Capitalism, on the other hand, is the only way to create real-world wealth, which takes place by buying and selling goods and services. Not only is it the only realistic way to establish what people actually want or need, but it's the only realistic way to figure out how to give it to them. Consider this; you open up a greengrocer. At first you can only estimate what people want based on your own experiences or market research. Over time you figure out that there's more demand for oranges and potatoes, so you supply more of these than other products. You also figure out that you can make 100% more than the price it costs to supply oranges and potatoes, meaning you can decipher how much profit you make, and how much it costs to supply these products. These are 'price signals' that you acquire from interacting with consumers in the marketplace, and this cannot be done under pure socialism because no buying and selling takes place.

Such a purely socialist system is better known as communism, but I don't suggest this is the only name it goes by because the Left has a habit of giving new names to old ideas. Pure socialism is based on establishing what people need and want through central planning, but there's no way to do this efficiently without direct interaction with consumers in the marketplace, otherwise known as a market economy. There are those that realise how futile pure socialism is in practice, therefore advocating some capitalism in a so-called mixed economy. However, though you won't experience the kind of utter economic catastrophe under communism, you will experience an increased cost of living and a decline of productivity over time. There lies the rub; if you listened to the mainstream consensus, it's capitalism that causes these problems, while only a pure socialist system is widely condemned.

The reality of socialist economics

In reality, socialism leads to gradual economic decline that culminates in a complete halt under communism. To explain why, let's take a moment to establish how socialism acquires wealth, and how it's spent. We've already established that socialism creates no wealth. So where does wealth come from under this economic model? The answer is taxation and debt, meaning that you're subtracting wealth from individuals and businesses. Some argue that by doing this you can create wealth through investment, or at the very least break even in the long run. This is known as the broken window fallacy. In true economic terms, this money creates no growth in wealth because you're merely spending what you already have. In other words, it's just like fixing your broken window instead of buying that new item that would have increased what you owned, hence broken window fallacy.

This is further compounded by the fact that socialism can only truly divide wealth up among society, known as 'redistribution'. Returning to our greengrocer, we generate wealth by making more money than it costs to supply products, using this profit to maintain our business and make a living, therefore adding and multiplying wealth. We can also take out a loan we can afford to repay after covering expenses and making a living, or we use savings we've amassed previously. You cannot, however, do this under socialism because it generally involves using divided and subtracted wealth to pay wages, provide supplies, service debt, or pay for other infrastructure costs.

For example, some 60% of the National Health Service (NHS) in the UK goes on paying staff, 20% goes to drugs and other supplies, with the rest split between buildings, equipment, training costs, medical equipment, catering and cleaning.[9] Consider, now, that over 98% of NHS funding comes from taxation, and 10% of the UK's total economic production (known as GDP) is taken up by this government funded healthcare system. There is absolutely no profit in that equation, so is it really so hard to accept that economic catastrophe is the result of ever increasing socialism? Imagine what would happen to a society with an economic model 100% based on dividing and subtracting wealth in this fashion. Without the ability to add and multiply, you'd quickly end up with mass poverty.

These are basic mathematical principles, but to call them obvious would seriously underestimate the way the Left completely indoctrinates people into denying reality. What this results in is people that think only in terms of ideals. When they're faced with the economic truth about socialism, people sympathetic to the left side of politics will quickly fall back onto the moral arguments for welfare (welfare being the term for government support like unemployment benefits, food stamps, council housing, etc.). They'll argue that it's wrong to let people suffer when they're falling on hard times, inhumane to let people starve or remain homeless, cruel to keep more than you need when others go without, and so on and so forth until you feel so terrible for your average to above average quality of life.

There are a couple of problems with this line of thinking, however, that must be acknowledged in an honest discourse. First, where is the personal responsibility in this narrative? Is there ever a point where a person is responsible for their actions? Yes bad things can happen to any of us, through no fault of our own. But does that mean we get to live off welfare for the rest of our lives, and it's wrong to make welfare a safety 'net' rather than a 'hammock'? In other words, welfare is not a way of life, no matter how much people are struggling.

It would be ideal to think that there are no people out there looking for ways to avoid working (for the rest of their lives if they can help it), and that there aren't people exaggerating or lying about their inability to find work – or even lying about their disabilities. The truth of the matter is that at least 20% of UK GDP is taken up by welfare spending.[10][11] When you add that to around 10% of UK GDP taken up by the NHS, government spending is about 30%, give or take fluctuating figures over time. And that's before we talk about other government spending like roads, street infrastructure, military spending, prisons, courts – the list goes on and on! And don't think that other countries in the world don't have the same problems – we're drowning in GDP being swallowed up by divided and subtracted wealth!

When you add all government spending up, we can deduce that around half of GDP easily goes on government spending in many countries, crippling ordinary people through high taxation and public debt. And what happens when people take steps to reduce welfare spending, because they realise how unsustainable this is? Armageddon, to put it lightly! No one wants to cut back on their government job or welfare cheque because they feel entitled to receive it. Are they really entitled to this much of what people earn, all on the false premise that the government does so much for us by dividing and subtracting our wealth?

Feeding the pigeons

The second problem is the sheer demagoguery of this system. It allows elites in society, particularly those closest to government power, to redirect government money towards policies that benefit their wealth at the expense of the majority (think bank bailout from chapter 2). They then hide their greed behind political and economic propaganda that makes this look sensible and compassionate. To end this deception, the culture of involving government in every aspect of our lives would need to be stopped. But this would affect people at the top of society as much as those at the bottom because they feed from the same government trough. The poorest in society defend this system because they're given scraps off the table of those that keep them down. They have no idea that they're being conditioned to become dependent, but neither does the pigeon being fed breadcrumbs in Trafalgar Square, or the bear eating left over picnic food in Yellowstone Park.

Ironically, we're told not to feed pigeons because their excrement is corrosive to structures. Likewise, bears are nuisances that will attack and kill humans. It's therefore advised that we don't teach these animals to associate human beings with easy to acquire food because they'll make less effort to look for it on their own. Let's not pretend that this behaviour isn't present in human beings, and let's not pretend that people on welfare aren't used as a wedge issue to make people vote for anyone offering the most 'free stuff', although it's not really free when we the tax payers are the ones paying for it.

When anyone tries to reform this system, the conditioned dependants are turned against them. This can results in harassment or attacks from mobs of activists and protesters, not to mention elites in society that use the media to protect their influence in government. The poorest welfare recipients are like modern day slaves that defend their masters. Slaves were regularly fed and clothed. Many would have grown to love their masters because it was all they knew, or they were conditioned to see no other way to live without them. You could argue that people who depend on welfare aren't slaves in the literal sense, but in terms of their mentality they're similar because they see no way to live as free and independent individuals - free range animals on a farm may be able to walk around, but there's still a fence to prevent them from leaving, and a farmer that owns them.

Politicians are, of course, very much involved in this demagoguery. It's easy for them to make promises with tax payer money, in return for votes from people on welfare that pay little to no taxes. Many politicians see it as beneficial to increase the number of voters on welfare that they can bribe, because it keeps them in power. Try cutting the pay and employment benefits of politicians, though, and you'll soon see how self-interested they are. If you're someone that doesn't work for the public sector and doesn't receive a penny of welfare, it's becoming tougher to make a comfortable living, and this is entirely the fault of absurdly high taxes to fund government debt and bureaucracy (another major area of government spending). You get bureaucracy in the private sector, too – accounts, middle management, human resources, etc. But the private sector very quickly teaches you that without a revenue stream greater than bureaucracy, you'll inevitably go broke. It's therefore essential to keep bureaucracy under control, while remaining mindful of revenue generation, if you're to make a profit.

It's easy to be blasé about wealth in the public sector because you rely on government funding, not profit in the market. Does this encourage personal responsibility? Most certainly not! We're already at a point where it's common for around 50% of GDP in Western countries to go towards programmes funded by dividing and subtracting wealth, with whatever's left going towards real-wealth generation that genuinely adds and multiplies. What happens to society when this creeps closer to 100%? The answer is social and economic collapse, just as we see in every communist experiment. Margaret Thatcher once said that 'The trouble with socialism is that eventually you run out of other people's money'. How right she was!

Chapter 4: Discovering Libertarianism

True freedom is a birthright.

In 2009, I picked out an old book up from my bookshelf that belonged to my wife. She bought it when she was a student taking a module in politics, in the first year of her university degree. I'd seen the book sitting there for some time, and my wife kept saying to me that I'd enjoy reading it. Sure enough, I didn't have anything to read at that moment in time, so I decided I'd give it a try since I had an inkling that it would be something I'd find interesting, although I hadn't gotten round to it. The book was called An Introduction to Political Philosophy, by Jonathan Wolff. I wasn't aware at the time that the author was a far-left academic with Marxist sympathies, writing for (surprise, surprise) the far-left Guardian newspaper.

Despite his Marxist background, the author presented many parts of the book without giving his ideological opinion, although as it progressed his views became more suspicious. That being said, he wrote the book in the nineties, a time when academia was much more open to free speech and debate. Once totalitarians are in control, however, all this inevitably goes out the window, even if people like Jonathan Wolff are more sincere (and pawns to be discarded once they serve their purpose). But although I've alluded to the fact that it is, at times, obvious that Wolff himself is a leftist, the book is still a good summary of the fundamentals of political philosophy. By this point in my life I was hardly unfamiliar with politics, and I'd already gone through a series of experiences which were making me more 'right-wing'. I wasn't aware that this was what was taking place, but once I read this book I became exposed to ideas I'd never come across before, further shifting me in this direction. One of the first things you learn about if you study politics is the social contract, and when I read about this I began to realise that I was sympathetic to liberal ideas in the classical sense.

There are three foundational thinkers you learn about when you begin delving into politics, who all shaped our understanding of a social contract. Other thinkers tend to expand on these thinkers, rather than come up with completely new thoughts, the first of which is Thomas Hobbes. The second is John Locke, and the third is Jean-Jacque Rousseau, appearing in this order historically. Before I talk about what these thinkers believed, I'll briefly explain what the social contract is. The social contract is the theory that we're all bound to an unsigned contract that we consent to by living in society. However, people have radically different ideas about what this contract is, or whether it exists at all.

Absolutism versus limited government

Thomas Hobbes released his seminal work on the social contract in 1651, called Leviathan[1]. It was written during the bloody and drawn out English Civil Wars that lasted between 1642 and 1651, fought between the Cavaliers (Royalists) and the Roundheads (Parliamentarians). This led to tens of thousands of dead combatants and civilians, and tore England apart for almost a decade. The effects of this war still exist today within the British political system, and in his lifetime, Hobbes was principally concerned with the way that Parliamentarians wanted to weaken the control of the monarchy, Charles I ruling during this period.

Hobbes argued that, due to the selfish nature of human beings, life without government, which he called a state of nature, would be "solitary, poor, nasty, brutish, and short." [2] He therefore believed that human beings should sacrifice all their freedoms to a sovereign via a social contract, allowing the sovereign to severely punish anyone that breaks the law. Clearly the English Civil War had a significant effect on Hobbes' pessimistic views, and he obviously didn't have much faith in people at all. It's certainly true that selfishness is a particularly destructive aspect of humanity, but it's by no means inevitable or universal. Pessimism made Hobbes believe that order was worth any price. He stems from a long historical tradition known as absolutism, where absolute power equals supreme authority, and nothing can limit this power in any way. The English Civil War was an attempt to temper the power of absolute monarchy in England, and though it had some success, totalitarianism has a way of creeping back up on us when later generations forget the sacrifices of their forebears.

The second thinker is John Locke, who was far more optimistic about human nature, and much more inclined to value freedom over security. In 1689 he wrote his seminal work, The Two Treatises of Government,[3] a very dangerous time for him to argue for the 'right of revolution', thus explaining why it was first published anonymously. Even though the English Civil War led to a parliamentary democracy and the dethroning of the king, Royalists used this system to re-establish a monarchy, ultimately leading to the parliamentary monarchy we have in the UK today. We tend to refer to this as a constitutional monarchy, despite the fact that the constitution of the UK might as well not exist when it's regularly ignored and undermined, its very existence repeatedly denied. We can see this blight on the state of modern government, where absolutists constantly and insincerely manoeuvre themselves into a position of advantage by undermining any moral limits put in place. This process of subversion, however, is not something I'll elaborate on until later in this book.

In stark contrast to Hobbes, Locke believed in limited government, with power restrained by unalienable individual rights. His ideas would be pivotal in the creation of the Bill of Rights in 1689, after the Glorious Revolution prevented yet another attempt to re-establish Royal and Catholic dominance in England. This later became the blueprint for the American Bill of Rights, not to mention the US Constitution itself. Locke had a very different view of the state of nature to Hobbes, believing that it was "a state of perfect freedom of acting and disposing of their own possessions and persons as they think fit within the bounds of the law of nature. People in this state do not have to ask permission to act or depend on the will of others to arrange matters on their behalf."

Natural versus legal rights

Locke did not, therefore, see a state of nature as some sort of miserable existence (as Hobbes did), but a natural state of freedom that only others can violate. To understand why, consider what it takes for murder, theft or slavery to take place. This doesn't happen unless these things are physically inflicted upon you. Logically speaking, our default state of existence in nature is freedom, and this comes with what Locke referred to as 'natural rights'. A right is one of the most misunderstood terms we come across today, but there are actually two ways to interpret this that adds to the confusion; legal and natural.[4]

A legal right is shaped and defined by those in power. Those advocating this believe you have no real rights without said power, generating a system of 'might makes right', where no real freedom exists without being granted. This is further complicated by the arbitrary way that rights shift and change from one moment to the next under a legal definition of a right, due to the whim of those in power. Conversely, natural rights are the opposite, where instead of rights being granted, they're part of your birthright. How do you establish what rights are on this basis? The best way to explain this would be your ability to act in a state of nature, without harming others. Locke described this in terms of ownership; you own the product of your actions that don't violate the property of others. Your life is the main example of this; you don't harm anyone by the mere act of breathing. Thus no one has a right to murder or enslave you, just as you don't have the right to do this to others.

As living and breathing entities, we need to acquire certain resources to exist. If we pick an apple from a tree to eat, the act of picking the apple makes it our property. Even if we gathered apples that fell on the floor, our effort made this possible, also making them our property. "Aha," you may add, "but how do you know who owns the tree that the apple came from?" The answer is that if it's a tree that isn't on private land, then anyone can pick the apples. If it is a tree on private land, then you can't pick the apples without the permission of the property owner. To become the owner of private land you need to claim it through your labour, by mapping out a boundary, maintaining and improving the land, plus defending your ownership from those that would contest this. Due to the effort this requires, there's a natural limit to how much property you can lay claim to in nature, because you can only maintain and defend so much at a time.

This principle is known as the labour theory of property,[5] and this is how property is created in a state of nature. The only way to dispute this is physical aggression, and while I've philosophically described natural property here, this is something widely endorsed due to the golden rule of "Do unto others as you would have done unto you." This is an ancient axiom that transcends cultural boundaries, due to an innate sense of fairness. People twist and deny this rule to justify transgressions against the individual. They never admit this, but tyrants and criminals will inevitably try to defend their actions.

Locke referred to natural rights as unalienable. When rights are unalienable, this means you can't separate, give or take them away, which is crucial for the prevention of tyranny. If you give your rights away, you create an authority that uses this transference as justification to rule over others. Initially this authority may be too small to cause much trouble, but the larger this authority becomes, the more power is acquired, making it capable of forcing ever more people to recognise and obey whatever this authority commands - exactly how totalitarianism seemingly comes out of nowhere. First people are promised that if they give up some or all of their natural rights, they'll be better off, like greater safety or economic prosperity. There will always be those that favour security over freedom, but this is a deal with the devil. Once your freedom depends on the whim of a tyrant, you'll be no better than a slave, even if this does come with some form of security. What's more, tyranny is a greedy entity that voraciously consumes, until all that is left is misery and poverty.

As history demonstrates, it will only be a matter of time before absolute authority becomes so powerful that no one can challenge it peacefully. The only option left will then be some sort of physical conflict like war or revolution, both of which are very costly and risky - hence the reason true rights must be unalienable. Unalienable natural rights therefore stop false prophets from promising people the earth, only to use this as a springboard for a dictatorship. Even if these promises are initially sincere, absolute power will always attract megalomaniacs that will do anything to acquire this, sooner or later sweeping everyone aside. The only real protection against this is the unalienable natural rights that John Locke advocated.

Forced to be free

The third social contract thinker is Jean-Jacque Rousseau, a Genevan philosopher who was pivotal in the development of the values of the French Revolution. John Locke's ideas would become the bedrock for the American Revolution from 1765 to 1783, undoubtedly a core reason why it was so much more successful than the French one from 1789 to 1799. Rousseau's seminal work was written in 1762, under the title of The Social Contract.[6] Being an anti-monarchist, he wasn't exactly on a par with Hobbes. Nonetheless, he's very much a founding thinker of the poor substitute that's slowly but surely replaced absolute monarchy in the Western world.

Pre-revolutionary France was last ruled by Louis XVI, and people were growing restless due to widespread poverty and discontent. The story goes that the monarchy was so disconnected from the people that Marie Antoinette said "Let them eat cake," when she heard that peasants had no bread. Some deny she said this, but if there's one thing I've learnt during my research it's that quotes are invariably contested by people sympathetic to an opposing point of view, so always keep this in mind. Most historians do agree that pre-revolutionary France was highly taxed and verging on bankruptcy, which led to the French Revolution that followed. How people forget the extent to which people fought against taxation over the centuries.

Both previous social contract thinkers had a great deal to say about a state of nature, and Rousseau was no different. Rousseau is affiliated with the idea of a noble savage, and though he didn't use that term specifically, he was pivotal in shaping it in The Social Contract, and in Discourse on

Inequality[7] (full title: Discourse on the Origin and Basis of Inequality Among Men) that preceded it in 1754. The theory of the noble savage has had far-reaching effects since the Enlightenment era that began in the 18th century, especially in a post-colonial world. It purports that human beings are happier and more peaceful in a state of nature, whereas civilisation has a corrupting influence. Rousseau referred to a 'natural' or 'savage' man, and while he didn't believe we can return to primitive societies, he argued that human beings in a state of nature had a "natural repugnance" to suffering.

Rousseau argued in Discourse on Inequality that self-preservation was the main concern of man in a state of nature. In it, he states: "Now savage man, being destitute of every species of intelligence, can have no passions save those of the latter kind: his desires never go beyond his physical wants. The only goods he recognises in the universe are food, a female, and sleep: the only evils he fears are pain and hunger." [8] To protect against the passions that led to more than "physical wants", Rousseau proposed a "general will" in The Social Contract that binds humanity together. Despite being a favoured philosopher of the French Revolution, Rousseau was not necessarily against monarchy. Rather, in The Social Contract he states that the executive of the state is "An intermediate body set up between the subjects and the Sovereign", and that "The sovereign can limit this power, modify it or take it back, just as it wishes; because the alienation of such a right is incompatible with the nature of the social body, and contrary to the goal of association". [9]

This is all well and good until you ask yourself how you establish a general will. While Rousseau was an advocate of direct democracy (directly voting for laws, not political representatives), and a highly educated citizenry that knows how to make political decisions, democracy has a habit of turning into mob rule, where groups fight for dominance. Thus without Locke's limits on power, a vote at a ballot box can be just as dangerous as a single tyrant. Education being heavily regulated by the state is also a dangerous notion, since this makes society vulnerable to indoctrination. To top it off, Rousseau argued that those disobeying the general will would be "forced to be free". [10] Suddenly it's not hard to see why the French Revolution was so disastrous, resulting in tens of thousands of executions alone.

Hobbes, Locke and Rousseau have become the foundational thinkers of modern civics because they each embody the core values of the main schools of thought we encounter today. Hobbes is the quintessential totalitarian who justifies tyranny through pessimism. Locke is the realist that elevates freedom above security, and Rousseau is the idealist who refuses to accept that his utopian views lead to tyranny. Personally, I've always struggled to see how anyone would think Hobbes' totalitarian views are desirable (although tragically, many do). Rousseau had some ideas that resonated with me when I was more left-wing, like the romantic notion of living in a state of nature, where only the passions corrupt the human character. Equally, if democracy is going to exist, I would argue that a direct version is more appealing. A thorough state education is also something I valued greatly when I was more left-wing, and this is ubiquitous to people on this side of the political spectrum. Finally we have Locke, and though elements of Rousseau appealed to me, I was always drawn more to Locke due to his elevation of unalienable freedom.

It took me some time to realise that Locke's ideas are anathema to the Left, but it was only when I started exploring libertarianism that I really began to realise this. I first came across libertarianism not long after I started making YouTube videos in 2010. Many commentators on the 2008 financial crisis were strong critics of central banking, and these people tended to be very libertarian. Libertarian can mean many things to different people, but at its core it's associated with less government. In the American sense it aligns with John Locke's philosophy - not surprising considering his influence on the US Bill of Rights and constitution. As you can imagine, I was drawn towards these content creators because I was already attracted to John Locke's ideas. Initially this was a ragtag selection of YouTube channels of small to medium audience sizes, talking about everything from the banking crisis, to prepping and 2nd amendment gun rights. It wasn't long before I discovered people with larger audiences, like Stefan Molyneux, Peter Schiff, and Adam Kokesh.

Many libertarian content creators have disappeared over the years. Others lost influence because they became too idealistic. Encountering these content creators introduced me to philosophical thinkers like Friedrich Hayek, Murray Rothbard, and Ludwig von Mises of the Austrian School of Economics. I also discovered Ayn Rand, writer of The Fountainhead and Atlas Shrugged, as well as the founder of the Objectivist school of thought. What I realised as I explored libertarian ideas in my videos, is that people on the left aren't actually interested in freedom at all. What they really want is security. But the balance between freedom and security is precarious, and usually ends with so much security that you're no better than a prisoner in a cage. There may be people guarding your house, but those guards could also stop you from leaving. Those guards could even eventually become the enforcers of your own slavery!

Little by little I began to realise that I'd misdiagnosed the problems that I saw around me when I was in my twenties. What I thought was corporations causing so much strife in the world, was quite simply the corruption of centralised power. When I started leaning towards libertarianism I was more inclined to blame this on the state, but even this is merely a symptom of any centralisation whatsoever. Many of my early YouTube videos were deeply inspired by secular libertarian philosophy that truly became the foundation of who I am today. While I don't have any particular attachment to libertarianism as a term anymore, because all labels are rendered meaningless by constant redefinition, I still value the principles I took from this aspect of my research and development.

When I first came across John Locke, I didn't know I was turning away from left-wing thought. But I was ultimately taken aback by the hostility I received from Leftists when I started exploring libertarianism, which would only accelerate my journey of discovery.

Chapter 5: Patriarchy and Men's Rights

Feminists gain power by lying about men.

As I explained in chapter 1, my first red pill was feminism. I began to realise that this was not the movement I thought it was, and is actually employed by the rich and powerful to shape society. This is called 'social engineering', feminism being an early onset of this process that takes many forms. In the earliest period of my channel (2010-2011), most of my videos would delve into feminism to some degree. It was a shock to find how wrong feminism was on practically everything, although it's probably more accurate to say feminists are wrong about everything, when you aren't looking at history through the rose-tinted lens of absolute egalitarianism.

Due to the time I gave this topic, I would attract the attention of the men's rights movement. People in this movement call themselves 'MRAs', short for men's rights advocate. I had no idea such a movement existed, and while I never technically called myself an MRA, for a time I did find a great deal of support and camaraderie from those that did. A de facto bible of this movement that I would go on to read is The Myth of Male Power by Warren Farrell, a book that examines the dynamics of male power, minus the bias of feminist theory. This book did a great deal to help me see just how wrong feminism is.

If we take the feminist perspective, men treated women unjustly because they wanted power over them. This is hyperbolic to say the least, since most men had very little power in most historical instances, and were usually as much victims of power as women. It's important not to get caught up in 'us and them' politics that paints any single group as inherently oppressive, not least because many men worked tirelessly to reform society for the benefit of women. Sometimes this is well considered. Sometimes it isn't, especially when masculinity is now treated as inherently bad. To understand why, allow me to relate this to how societies worked historically.

Hunter-gatherers

Earliest societies emerged from tribes. There were males and females of various ages that had corresponding roles, limited by technological and environmental mastery. These tribes were hunter-gatherer in nature because there was no better way for them to survive. Therefore they would gather vegetables, fruits, nuts, and any other edible food they could get their hands on. They would also hunt animals for meat, depending on what animals lived in their habitat. Being nomadic, these tribes would move around, giving them more access to food and making it easier to survive the colder times of the year. Hunting has always been the domain of males because they're biologically stronger and more physically able than women. Denying this is where feminists and their supporters utterly lose touch with reality.

There's just no point using outliers to deny this when even professional female athletes are average compared not only to their male counterparts, but sometimes even male amateurs. There are countless examples of how women aren't physically as capable as men, but if we refer to Olympic records, this is easy to prove,[1] especially in weight lifting.[2] Likewise, we can demonstrate this with the 2015 Women's FIFA World Cup winners, the United States, who lost 5-2 to the FC Dallas under-15s academy team.[3] In tennis, women play best of 3 sets, instead of best of 5 like men (and yet still paid the same). The Williams sisters, supposedly two of the best female tennis players ever, both lost to the 203rd male seed in 1998, Karsten Braasch.[4] Playing single set matches, he beat Serena 6-1, followed by 6-2 against Venus, and all after a light game of golf in the morning, and a couple of shandies.

One must understand that these differences between men and women do not make either sex more important, but problems arise when we expect males and females to be the same, leading to tyrannical policies that seek equality of outcome. Equality of opportunity is one thing, but not at the expense of common sense, and certainly not for the benefit of social engineering to make men and women exactly the same. In practice, men and women are often very different, despite claims to the contrary, and when women do outperform men in the aggregate, this often occurs by making it harder for men to succeed. Bear with me if you find this hard to believe, because I will prove that this is so.

Before that, let's return to early societies. As tribal hunter-gatherers, the increased strength of men would lead to them being the hunters - bringing home the proverbial bacon, so to speak. The women would stay close to camp, gather food in the surrounding area, and help each other take care of the children. If these roles were reversed, this would potentially lead to hunger and malnourishment because women do not have the same physical acumen for hunting as men (it's easy to get side-tracked with vegetarian/vegan claims that discount the importance of meat, but meat is a good calorie source that's particularly essential when food is harder to come by).

When a species population is small, very little in-species conflict exists because there is no competition. Day to day living is still tough, but when humans stuck to their male and female roles, they generally thrived. Make no mistake, if conditions became similar once more, humans would soon return to these sex based roles. Equality would be thrown out of the window in a heartbeat, and females would realise that they need males to survive. Equally, men would need to protect and provide for females if they want to reproduce, and the supportive role of females is essential to the success of this dynamic. Alas, so many assumptions are made about equality that the mere suggestion of male and female roles in early primitive society is denied and maligned by feminists and their egalitarian contemporaries.

For humans to reproduce would require good relations with other tribes, thus avoiding the risks of inbreeding. As you can imagine, good relationships with several surrounding tribes would be advantageous, creating alliances that almost certain laid the foundations of early civilisations. In this setting, both males and females would be obliged to reproduce with people from friendly tribes, creating multi-generational bonds – remaining childless is a luxury that only flourishing modern societies could truly entertain.

As populations grew, competition with surrounding tribes became more commonplace. Any tribes that did not have established bonds with other tribes were more likely to risk destruction, and this danger made a warrior class necessary. Naturally this fell to the men, and if you aren't convinced of this necessity when looking at the sporting world, it's doubtful anything else will. The advantage males gained from becoming warriors was the prestige of heroism and bravery. It's no accident therefore, that warriors and hunters have always been celebrated in history for their bravery and prowess, given the risks these men took. Such males would often become the most high status individuals that received the most attention from the opposite sex. They would also become the leaders of tribes because they gained the respect of other males as well.

With competition and tribal bonds, it would only be a matter of time before the earliest civilisations formed, but it's not as though we went from primitive to industrial societies overnight. This was a slow and arduous journey of incremental developments. A critical part of this process was monogamous pair-bonding, which allowed males to know who their children were. Females benefitted from this because the male would bond to the female (hence pair-bonding), and he would also bond with their offspring, therefore ploughing resources and time into raising them. Even today, males all over the world want to know that they're raising their own children. Various social experiments or outliers have existed here and there, but in the aggregate they're never on a par with biological parenting from a pair-bonded couple. The sheer consistency of this pattern, from time immemorial, tells us that this is something innate within the human species. Raising someone else's child comes with all sorts of complications, even if you're altruistic enough to sacrifice time and resources with your own biological children for this endeavour. Without digressing, there's no point denying that we don't have a closer bond to those we're related to, even if adoption can be a noble endeavour.

People on the left side of politics are inclined to think that this is an antiquated family structure that represses women and minority sexual lifestyles, but this absurd. It works because we're wired to behave this way – and for good reasons that I've already outlined. However, that's something I'll go into more depth with in the next chapter. For now, let's continue to explore the idea that the greater power of men represses women.

The myth of patriarchal oppression

The term that regularly comes up to explain this alleged oppression is patriarchy. The best lies take a glimmer of truth and distort this so much that it's very difficult to unravel, since an underlying truism makes people believe the lie. Feminists are very good at this technique, and indeed the entire ideology of feminism is based on such distorted truisms, one being the myth of patriarchal oppression. For example, the idea that men historically had more power in society is technically true. But let's put that power into context. Who always takes the greatest risks – men or women? The answer is almost universally men. The biggest objection that people come up with, when all other avenues are exhausted, is giving birth. This was indeed a much bigger risk before medicine progressed, but this didn't generally come with such a high risk of death or injury because women have the biological anatomy to cope with labour. Modern medical procedures like epidurals have made us forget just how resilient our ancestors were. If we weren't capable of surviving in the arduous conditions of our ancient predecessors, we would never have gotten far enough to invent the modern luxuries we now take for granted.

Thus when people say that men had more power than women in history, they cannot exclude the way that this dynamic emerged out of ancient customs, where males and females adapted their roles to their nature. Slowly but surely this was relaxed, but not without significant technological advances making it safer for women - particularly indoor workplaces like offices and hospitals. If we look at the workplace today, we quickly see how this plays out. We can break this down to people and things[5]: women generally like to work with people. Men generally like to work with things. Consistently you'll find that even in the most 'progressive' countries, like those in Scandinavia, women work in the nurturing professions. This generally consists of teaching, medicine and social services. We can break this down further by pointing out that most primary level teachers are consistently female, as are most nurses, also explaining why psychology is such a popular profession for women. All these professions are generally very safe places to work, but the other common denominator is people – females today still have an innate attachment to the social skills they developed in ancient societies, where they worked closely with other females as gatherers and nurturers.

Likewise, males have an innate attachment to skills they developed as hunters and warriors, gravitating towards high risk to reward. Hunting, for example, could lead to being killed, but the potential for high calorie food was a reward worth risking for our ancient ancestors. Even in these emasculating times, males still gravitate towards activities, tasks and employment that reflect either the skills their ancient male predecessors developed, or high risk to reward ratio. Many males love to play competitive games online that model ancient hunting and warrior skillsets, like first-person shooters and fighting games. Men also dominate high risk professions at least to the same extent that females dominate nurturing ones. Among other things, they work in mines, on oil rigs, or as firemen and soldiers - all professions that women generally want nothing to do with by choice, unless it's watered down for them in some way.

This explains a great deal, but it's the male fascination with things that explains even more. Males often spend a great deal of time with interests totally unrelated to interaction with people. They construct items or pull them apart to learn how they work, generating an interest in science, construction and engineering. There's an obsession with denying this today, and it's causing terrible consequences to the psyche of men and boys. Males are expected to give way to females at every turn because masculinity is considered toxic and oppressive. What if this behaviour is just part of who we are? There's certainly a dark side to male nature. But as long as we're raised by loving parents who have the support of family and social networks, males always grow up well rounded and psychologically healthy. Equally, however, there's a dark side to female nature that's not nearly acknowledged enough in this day and age.

We're now building up a better picture of what's wrong with the world we live in today, and why a term like men's rights might emerge. Feminists ultimately argue that all the problems women face come down to male oppression - what they call patriarchy. Patriarchy comes from the Greek word patriarkhia, where fathers and male elders govern society. Feminists use patriarchy theory to claim that men acquired this power by preventing women from progressing past customs and traditions related to child-rearing and home life. Not only is it self-evident that these customs emerged from biology, where men received greater risk to reward for much more dangerous work, but the modern workplace clearly demonstrates that men and women both prefer professions that tap into their sex based instincts. There's nothing wrong with this, and the very notion that men and women must by identical, otherwise it's oppression, is just plain nonsense. As long as females have the same opportunities as males, that's what counts, which takes us back to what I said at the beginning of this chapter about equality of opportunity, as opposed to equality of outcome.

The Pay Gap

One of the most persistent feminist myths is the pay gap, which completely epitomises why feminism has become so divisive. Feminists claim that women earn x amount less than their male co-workers, and this can be anything from 20-30% per unit of currency (£, $, €, etc.). The fact is that this is a persistent lie, lie being the most charitable word to use for a claim that's been refuted so many times over decades. The crux of this lie is that women earn less money than men because they're deliberately underpaid, since they're prevented them from getting pay rises and promotions. Feminists further suggest that this is part of systemic oppression of women that prevents them from achieving equal status to males. The problem with this claim is that it's just not true in any theoretical or practical sense. Yes many workplaces have historically been very masculine places given that men generally worked there. But it's just as absurd to look down on this as it would be to go into an environment with lots of women, only to complain that it's too female.

When there's an objective male and female nature, even with some outliers and blending in the middle, why on earth would we expect anything other than environmental settings that are inherently male or female? What's more, women aren't paid less because they're being oppressed. Rather, they're paid less because the work they choose to do is lower paid. For example, being a teacher is not generally a profession that pays well compared to others (although it certainly has better holiday pay and pension benefits to make up for it). Men tend to gravitate towards those professions that reflect very high skill and knowledge, which most people aren't capable of doing. This makes demand for this work very high, and very well paid as a result. We're talking about professions like engineering, architecture, or theoretical physics – the most time consuming and difficult areas to train in. Not only are women generally not interested in those professions, but males tend to be the highest IQ individuals in society, which makes them more capable of these professions.

Is this a question of nature or nurture, given that most women don't express interest in these professions, no matter how hard people push for them to get involved? It's probably partly a question of enjoying what naturally comes easier to us, though people are more likely to get bored of activities that aren't very challenging. One must also bear in mind that male intelligence is more evenly distributed from high to low, while female intelligence is more likely to cluster around the average for the population.[6] This means that while there are more male geniuses, there are also more males of lower than average intelligence.

This pattern of males occupying the top and the bottom is reflected right across society. While you will find that men dominate the highest skilled or paid work, you'll equally find that they do most of the unskilled work that women don't choose to do because it's not as prestigious or desirable. This includes unskilled work like bin/trash collection, street cleaners, etc, and blue collar jobs like car mechanic, plumber or electrician. That being said, you will find a lot of women working in retail and hairdressing because (surprise, surprise) this appeals to their sensibilities. Again, there's nothing wrong with that, but in such a volatile climate, anything that challenges the notion that men and women are the same will be treated as offensive.

The moral is that there is no patriarchy in the feminist sense. There were indeed patriarchal societies than emerged out of innate biological tendencies within males and females - be it preferential or practical. Due to these roles, men became leaders because they took greater risks and led from the front, unlike modern politicians. Was this perfect? No! But the impending necessity of survival led to customs that evolved over centuries of successful strategies, and to compare this to a modern day sense of equality is deeply flawed. Such equality of outcome is impossible, and any attempt at this will lead to the othering of a particular group, to prevent a hypothesis from collapsing under the weight of reality. Women choose certain jobs, even though they pay less than high skilled work that requires physical and mental abilities more commonly found in men. There is no so-called 'toxic masculinity' other than that associated with the demonisation of men by feminist theories, based on half-truths and outright lies.

When faced with so much misrepresentation, one must ask why anyone would go to such lengths. At this point in the book, the answer should be starting to become more apparent. When natural behaviour is framed as bad, people will have an excuse to intervene. Feminists are fundamentally socialist in their outlook, so it's really no surprise that their complaints are used to justify socialist intervention into every aspect of our social and economic life. As I said in chapter 1, this comes to down to forms of control, and everything about feminism attempts to legitimise this strategy. After all, if men can't stop oppressing women, then authoritarianism can be promoted as the solution.

Chapter 6: Destruction of the Family

Society falls apart when biological fathers and mothers can't raise children as couples.

As well as explaining in chapter 1 that feminism is a form of economic and reproductive control, I also set out how controlling the family has always been the goal of totalitarians. This is easy to prove historically and philosophically, whether it's Nazi Germany, Stalinist Soviet Union, or Plato's Republic. The reason for this is not hard to see; if you're able to influence the development of children, you can then imprint on their personalities at such an early age that this will be virtually impossible to alter later on in life. It was Aristotle that once said, "Give me a child until he is 7 and I will show you the man," further demonstrating this point. In this chapter I want to go into greater depth about how this affects the modern family, as well as how laws and customs are transformed so much that family becomes too dysfunctional to operate in a healthy manner.

During the most nihilistic times of my life I still knew I wanted to be a father. As soon as my oldest daughter was born, I'm not ashamed to admit that I was so emotionally overwhelmed that I couldn't help but cry. Although it's clichéd to add that I never cry, this is the truth, even after I discovered that my father passed away, including when I attended his funeral. There are various psychological reasons that crying doesn't come naturally to me, but in this instance the experience of seeing my very own child for the first time consumed me with emotion. This didn't happen when my second daughter was born – not because I love her any less, but because it's less of a shock to the system to see your child for the first time when you've already experienced this with one of your older children.

The feeling of seeing your child for the first time and realising that they're a part of you is quite remarkable. It's not uncommon for famous musicians to say this as the greatest thing they've experienced, which is quite something when you imagine what it feels like to be cheered on by thousands of fans in a concert. Bonding to your child is a biological process where your body is flooded with hormones. It was previously thought that only mothers went through this, such as mothers receiving oxytocin when they're pregnant, or prolactin when they breast feed. But evidence now shows that men go through a similar bonding process with their children.[1][2] We hear a lot about post-natal depression these days, but the inability to bond with your child isn't normal when you consider that nature helps this along. Thus people that struggle to bond with their children should do some serious soul searching, preferably with a good therapist.

That being said, we're deliberately being conditioned not to bond with our children, and with each passing year this begins at an ever younger age. The result is twofold; either you won't want children at all, or you'll be so self-absorbed that you'll be incapable of prioritising the needs of your children above your own. It's important to bear in mind that it was much harder to parent in history. The struggle to survive meant that large families were common, and with large families comes less attention and resources for each individual child. Often children had to work from a young age, to help the family survive. Why did parents have so many children, you might ask? For starters, contraception is a modern luxury. So it was easy for sex to lead to more children, especially among the poorly educated that had no idea about ovulation cycles. Secondly, larger families were the historical version of a pension. There was no welfare system to provide for you when you retired. Your family would do that for you. And yes, it would usually be the responsibility of women to take care of elders because men would work.

Obviously children from wealthier homes have always had a much better quality of life, and only in recent centuries has the middle-class grown so substantially. With the emergence of the middle-class came increase to quality of life for the masses, including the working class, who gained amenities and luxuries that previously only royalty and the upper class could acquire, like indoor plumbing and regularly eating meat. Nonetheless, having more children is a natural strategy for poorer people because when the chances of survival are lower, it makes more sense to have more offspring. Today these natural survival strategies have been perverted on a number of levels, not least because the welfare state encourages people to have more children just to receive more support from the government, be it a council house or enough benefits to never have to work. Plus, when you can do some cash in hand work here and there which the tax man can't easily trace, you'll actually have a relatively high standard of life. The very idea that someone would live like this is anathema to a normal person with a sense of pride and achievement. But when everyone around you acts the same way, it's like crabs in a bucket that drag you down whenever your try to become something more. Some call this a poverty trap because people are stuck in their own self-made prison when they refuse to aspire to become something more when, at least in the short-term, this would lead to a more uncomfortable existence. Equally, blaming the state of modern parenting purely on the lower economic end of society, or the 'welfare class', is not completely accurate. Something else is going on here that isn't purely about financial incentives.

Casual sex

I remember when I first found out that people have casual sex, as in sex with people they're not in a relationship with or don't know well, if at all. I was 14 years-old when a family member was bragging about his sexual exploits. The next day I went to school and told my friends what I'd discovered, and I'm not sure any of us were aware that sex could be that carefree. With each passing decade in the second half of the 20th century, casual sex became increasingly normalised via popular culture. Growing up, I recall seeing soaps on TV where every episode would have at least one scene involving sex. Often this revolved around some scandalous affair between two people, although in the 80s era of dramas like Dynasty or Dallas, it was much more subtle than what appeared later. One thing popular culture did do in this decade was normalise divorce and adultery. Previously this came with stigma attached, and when I was a child it was relatively rare in many communities. By the 90s, however, divorce had risen substantially since the 50s.[3][4] But it wasn't just divorce that was becoming normalised as a result of this transformation in society. Children out of wedlock became more commonplace, obviously meaning that meant that sex outside of marriage was much more acceptable, too.

Let's put this into perspective; the 60s free love era was just the start of the erosion of sexual restraint, but most people were still pretty conservative at the time. Each decade led to more sexual taboos being broken down, but in the latter part of the 20th century this was predominantly an increased acceptance of divorce, sex outside of marriage, adultery, and casual sex (homosexuality also on the rise). Data from the United States Center for Disease Control bears this out,[5] with a significant rise in children being born outside of marriage, sex outside of marriage also increasing sharply since the 1940s, and a comparison to other countries showing similar trends. Data from a 2002 survey showed that 75% of people had sex outside of marriage by 20 years old.[6] These trends are easy to verify by merely frequenting clubs and bars at some point in your life. There's no shortage of people going home with one another in one-night stands, which Americans refer to as hook-up culture. It's important to understand why this is happening so often in this day and age. Admittedly, these trends have started to alter since I used to go to bars and clubs, because millennials are having less sex than prior generations.[7][8] To comprehend the change, however, we need to realise what came before.

The prevailing attitude I came across in my teens to early twenties was that if you settled down before having several sexual partners, you were less likely to have a relationship that lasts. What's amazing about this is that the complete opposite is actually true, and various studies prove this.[9][10] Being short, skinny and suffering with acne, I didn't exactly have much confidence around the opposite sex when I hit puberty. I didn't kiss a girl until I was 16, and I was honestly ashamed of this for many years. Looking back, this was no big deal, but I was too naïve to see this at the time, plus pressure to conform made this really difficult to see. What's more, in my day you'd only have to turn on Saturday afternoon television to see Pamela Anderson running down a beach with a bikini on, creating a constant reminder of sex. Despite all this, I fell for the first real girlfriend I had when I was 18, thus behaving like a naïve fool. I met her when I went to a nightclub one evening, and at first I tried to maintain the attitude that it was just a fling that could give me some experience with the opposite sex – just as friends and others led me to believe. But it wasn't long before my naivety resulted in me falling for her, and I had no idea how to deal with this whatsoever.

I then ended up spending lots of my hard earned money on her because she didn't have a job, because I wanted to convince her to see me more often. Within 3 months she was bored of me, and by that time I'd lost my casual attitude to our relationship because I was smitten. It took me months to get over her when she ended it. I'm not going to sit here and say that she was a beauty queen. I don't even describe my feelings for her as love in the true sense – more like infatuation that you get in the early stages before love. It's extremely hard to keep an emotional rollercoaster like this in check, and this is one of many reasons why match-making between parents was more common in the past. I'm not against people choosing who they settle down with, but this is easier said than done when you look at the rise in divorce across the Western world since the 1960s.[11] It's easy to get caught up in the early stages of lust and attraction, especially when you're young.

One might be tempted to say that allowing young people to make mistakes is part of the process of finding happiness. The problem is that there are some mistakes you might never recover from, like pregnancy. Obviously being a parent isn't a mistake in itself, but if you end up becoming a parent with the wrong person, the consequences are far-reaching for all involved, including the child. Furthermore, the more short-term or casual sex partners you have, the more it hardens you inside. In my case, a few months after the relationship with my first girlfriend ended, I had a series of flings that lasted no more than 3 months. Having learnt a very painful lesson, I didn't allow myself to get too emotionally involved. But then I met someone around a year later, when I was 19. I then allowed myself to get emotionally attached to a girl once again (she did have the same name as my first girlfriend – so maybe it was subconscious). After a record 4 and-a-half month relationship, she returned from a week long holiday and ended it. I was thus blindsided for a second time, and given that this was the longest relationship I'd had, this hit me even harder. When I finally emerged from this months later, I was much tougher, but also much colder.

In all honesty, if one of my first girlfriends I fell for had committed to me, I may well have settled down. But by the time I'd felt prolonged heartache on two occasions, my attitude changed towards commitment. Before this took place, a series of experiences in my childhood and early teens meant I lacked self-confidence, as I've mentioned previously. I set out to rebuild my self-esteem when I turned 16, but this is easier said than done in a culture centred on narcissism and hedonism, plus getting knock backs from females further hardens you. Due to my experiences, I therefore became another selfish participant in the bar and club scene, especially when social alienation is far more likely in a culture based so much around drinking and casual sex. If I'd known what I know today I would have rejected this for something healthier, but it's not easy to do this when you're too young to know any better.

Through a process of trial and error, I gradually became rather good at cold approaching women. The techniques I developed are not unlike what some call 'pick-up artistry' or 'game theory' today. I was never involved with this community in any way, but given that human attraction is so predictable, it's no surprise that men can independently develop similar strategies. Much of my ambitions were driven by the fact that friends, family and culture perpetuated the idea that 'notches on a bedpost' matter, and by the time I was 20, movies like American Pie glorified hook-up culture as well. Conversely, movies like American Beauty presented family life as miserable and repressive.

Thankfully in my case, I met the woman that would end up being my wife when I was in my early 20s. Unfortunately, however, a lot of damage had already been done, so I had to deprogramme myself from the culture around me. I grew accustomed to relying on attention from the opposite sex to build my self-esteem, and it took some time to see that this was a shallow existence that didn't compare to the love of one good woman. You can map out the problems that come from a very sexually open society, and how it can lead to an inability to commit. The stats regarding an increased likelihood of divorce are therefore not so hard to believe. In my case, I met someone early enough that made it worth striving to change, but it was difficult to do this when your sense of self-worth is so wrapped up in female attention. The story ended well for me because my desire to be a father and husband were stronger than hedonism. Others aren't so fortunate, and so end up psychologically incapable of being happily married.

Attachment issues

When casual sex is normalised, it leads to attachment issues. The reason this happens is because the excitement of a new relationship or sexual encounter can be addictive, thus preventing you from moving onto later stages of attraction and attachment that develops into love. What this means is that people can't commit to one person when they crave something new and exciting. The idea of settling down with one person then seems dull and boring. But the best kept secret in this culture is that having a family gives life purpose that mellows us as we get older. Otherwise we run the risk of becoming self-destructively self-absorbed in short-term pleasure-seeking that is not only harmful to ourselves, but to others. Consider alcohol, staying up late, gambling, or even recreational drugs. In moderation, perhaps all four can have a marginally harmful effect. Certainly in the case of the first three, you can engage in these activities within moderation without doing any harm. But if you can't control your urges these things become addictive, and if you substitute meaningful experiences in your life, particularly being a parent, husband or wife, then you'll quickly find that your life is so empty that you care very little about anything other than yourself.

Imagine a world full of people like this. Wouldn't it be akin to what we have today, with everyone running around shopping, partying, entertaining themselves, and caring very little about the world we leave behind for children? Huge national debts are one result, as is the decline of stable family life. We built ourselves a world so comfortable and pleasurable that it's very hard to see beyond that, especially for the world we leave behind. The baby boomers were the start of this decline, but what we've experienced since the 90s takes this to a whole new level.

There are other consequences as well, because as much as it's psychologically harmful for men to have many sexual partners, it's even more harmful for women. Setting aside risks of sexually transmitted diseases or infections that can be mitigated with condoms, psychological effects are another major factor with casual sex. For women, however, this is more profound, and studies prove it.[12] When we're living in a time when men and women are not considered different, this can be hard to accept. But our instincts are a product of our biology, and this applies to male and female anatomy. When survival pressure is high, it's beneficial – even necessary – for polygamy to take place. Polygamy is defined as males that have lots of sexual partners at the same time. The advantage is it raises the population more rapidly in smaller populations. It's less ideal for child-rearing, however, because each child is competing for resources and time from a father that has lots of children. Hence, monogamy not only works better in larger societies, it's also better for parenting. Egalitarians will protest that this is sexism that objectifies female sexuality, and that polyamory (women with lots of male partners) is only rare due to patriarchy. Biologically this makes no sense, though, since women have to wait 9 months after getting pregnant, meaning that the same advantage of faster population growth with polygamy isn't possible. Therefore, all you get are the parental disadvantages of polygamy, but none of the advantages.

Nature clearly factors this in by making women more psychologically sensitive to sex with multiple partners. Meanwhile in the case of men, they do experience some psychological issues related to pair-bonding, but from a man's perspective, if polygamy sometimes helps population growth, it can be beneficial not to express much attention to particular children that he fathers, if he has a lot. That way, all his children have a similar chance of his investment. The mother also benefits from this arrangement by getting male support in a difficult environment, which includes her children, despite having to compete with the attention of other mothers that have children with the same man under polygamy. So it's not too difficult to understand why women are more affected than men when they have multiple sexual partners, especially when there really is no biological advantage to females being sexually promiscuous, whatsoever.

Stable monogamy

Obviously polygamy is less than ideal, and this is why monogamy is more stable. First you need to have enough people in the population to make this more feasible, at which point smaller monogamous families are much more ideal. Bonding is easier and more intimate when families are smaller, while half-brothers/sisters only make things more complicated. The same can be said for step families because these involve divided loyalties for parents. Combine this with greater disadvantages for women being promiscuous, and we can really see why monogamy is preferable. Many men won't risk life, limb and effort to raise children that aren't their own because there is no biological advantage to raising another man's child. Altruism is noble up to a point. But if you aren't prepared to invest in your own future lineage, this becomes pathological. Therefore women are very much geared towards encouraging men to make them the centre of their attention, and by extension this applies to any children she has with a man.

No matter how much biased research is carried out by feminist sympathisers, common sense shows that there's no positive biological trade-off for women being promiscuous. All it does is increase fatherlessness, where the social impact is profound. When adults are incapable of bonding with one another in long-term relationships, the state can step in as the surrogate parent. In this scenario, adults are too psychologically damaged to bond and have children with one person in a monogamous relationship, or too selfish to care about the consequences of divorce on children. All they really care about is their own advancement via a career, or their own hedonistic exploits. Once again we see how those with aspirations for a Plato style Republic would want to sow such chaos, for it allows them to step in and socially engineer children from the youngest age, just as Aristotle said about a child at 7.

Making impulsive sexual decisions certainly doesn't help with combatting this chaos, which is why we've gone too far into the realm of choosing who you settle down with. Choosing who we marry is one thing, but without some kind of better wisdom from the older generation, young people will make the kind of mistakes that they can never recover from, like having children with the wrong person. This is overwhelmingly the saddest consequence of a feminist society, and this is what I will be exploring in the next chapter.

Chapter 7: Broken Family Life and Single Motherhood

When faced with the overwhelming evidence for the harm caused by breakdown of the family, only a delusional or heartless person would ever support a continuation of policies that further this in society.

In this chapter, I will examine the impact that a rise in broken family life and the ensuing single motherhood has had on society. We've looked at how my journey made me realise that feminism wasn't what I thought it was, and certainly not what we're told it is by mainstream society. It started with my realisation that feminism was a form of economic and social control designed to benefit the power elites of the world. I then discovered that this lie is perpetuated by the myth of patriarchy, and how it's completely disingenuous to suggest that men deliberately kept women down, rather than adapted to biological roles that made survival more likely. This wasn't perfect, but to call this systemic oppression is at best hyperbole, and at worst downright deceptive. In the previous chapter, I addressed how social engineering has led to the destruction of the family, by making men and women too psychologically damaged to take on the role of parenting. Achieving this was done through the normalisation of casual sex, and though this is damaging to both sexes, women are the worst affected.

In tandem with this sexual push, I've explained how women have been culturally shamed for not entering the workforce. They've have been made to feel inadequate if they stay at home to raise their children, as though a woman is freer working for a boss than being a housewife and mother. True freedom of choice isn't centred on employment or 'career'. It's one thing if you make money doing something you love, but there's more to life than unadulterated self-interest. If you're not even prepared to put the needs of your own children above your own, you'll quickly find that life becomes shallow and unfulfilling. Evidence for this can be found in the way that, after decades of feminist indoctrination, women are less happy than they were in the 1970s.[1] This is one of many examples of the consequences of feminism teaching women that their own needs should always come first, not least with personal success.

Speaking as a stay-at-home dad, I can attest to the rewarding nature of a hands-on approach to raising your children on a daily basis, rather than going to work and coming home too late to spend quality time with them. It's easy to get so caught up in a job that you miss those special moments as your children grow up. At least when more mothers were home full-time, the father knew that the children were being taken care of by her. We're conditioned to believe that a mother can be replaced by a child minder of one kind or another, but the love of a parent is the backbone of a healthy childhood, and cannot be substituted with someone paid to do a job, especially when this person has numerous children to take care of at the same time. Numerous studies have demonstrated how pre-school children sent to day care are more likely to develop behavioural problems,[2][3][4] especially if it's more than a few hours per week.

As you can imagine, counter-studies attempt to disprove this (like anything else that runs counter to the left-wing narrative), but you only need to look around to see how child behaviour has been declining for decades, although this is much harder to notice when you're too young to know any different. Popular culture also denigrates past family life as archaic and repressive, making it even more difficult to realise how much better family life was when both parents didn't work full-time, and didn't pedestalise a 'career'. Some of us have livelihoods, but the idea that our value as human beings is shaped by a job is blatantly preposterous. Many noble endeavours involve making no money at all, and that certainly includes parenting.

Given how unhappy many women are in this feminist culture, a fundamental difference exists between men and women – men are happier when they have a passion, and women are happier when their nesting instincts are being met. As such, I have a confession to make about being a stay-at-home dad (to once again clarify, this is a title I loosely use considering I've made money working from home, ever since my first daughter was born) – as much as I love being around my children, being male, I can't feel completely content unless I have a passion other than my family. This very book is testament to this because, in the years I've been home taking care of my children, I filled much of my spare time researching and learning about subjects I now cover about in videos, articles and books, therefore acquiring the opportunity to fulfil my passion for philosophical thinking. So as much as I wouldn't change spending a lot of time raising my children, a man often doesn't feel content unless he has hobbies and interests that exist outside of family life.

Women are different in this sense because they have a strong nurturing instinct to stay close to the nest at all times. This is the most obvious reason why women are unhappier, despite decades of feminist propaganda. I'm certainly not saying that men don't have the parenting instinct, too. But this manifests as a desire to provide for the family, and make the world around the nest much safer and comfortable for women and children. All around us we can see the evidence for what happens when those instincts are tampered with. Broken family life a significant example of that, and so are single mother homes, which are fundamentally disastrous.

The murder of James Bulger

I'd like to give a very sobering example of what society has become since divorce and family courts gutted family life, leaving it without strong fathers, instead dominated by a strong sense of female entitlement. In 1993, over 20 years since the second wave of feminism campaigned to eradicate the role of women as housewives and stay-at-home mothers, a two year-old boy by the name of James Bulger was brutally tortured and murdered by two ten year-old boys by the names of Jon Venables and Robert Thompson.[5] Although I've been aware of the severely damaging effects of broken homes on society for some time, it was much more recent that I looked further into what happened when this murder took place. What I uncovered made it crystal clear just how far Britain has fallen without family life at its core. I believe something died in British society when that murder took place, because the way James Bulger was treated could never happen in a healthy setting.

The two boys responsible for the murder spent the day shoplifting at a shopping centre in Liverpool, England. Not only did they throw stolen items down escalators, but they tried to entice another boy to go with them, thankfully found by his mother before it was too late. Tragically, James Bulger wasn't so lucky, drawn away from his mother while she at a butcher's shop. Shoppers saw the boys with James Bulger, but no one did anything - apparently there's nothing strange about seeing two 10 year-old boys walking around with a 2 year-old. By 3:42pm, CCTV caught the boys leaving the shopping centre with James Bulger. By 4:15pm the mother had already notified shopping centre security to no avail, so a report was filed with the local police station.

What happened next is testament to how insular and antisocial British society has become. Despite repeatedly seeing Jon Venables and Robert Thompson walking through the streets with James Bulger, no one did anything. Perhaps this could be dismissed if the boy looked content, but he was not only seen in distress, but had visible injuries - one woman seeing James Bulger lying on the ground at the side of a canal *after* being dropped on his head. From here, he still followed his abductors, who put a hood over him to cover his injuries. However, the injuries could still be seen by passers-by, with one person seeing a tear on the poor boy's cheek. Throughout the day they then wandered down some of Liverpool's busiest streets. Witnesses claimed he was crying out for his mother, while others said he was laughing. A boy dropped on his head wouldn't be laughing about anything, and anyone that can't tell the difference between laughing and crying suffers from a serious lack of empathy. If you're still not convinced that this is the case, one person saw Thompson kick James Bulger in the ribs, with a woman closing her curtains after she saw Thompson punching Bulger in the ribs.

One woman did notice the injuries and approached the abductors, satisfied when she was told that they found him at the bottom of a hill, subsequently telling them to take him to a police station. Though she was concerned, another woman told her that she saw James laughing, so she didn't take the matter further. One of these women later called the police when she saw the news about the missing boy, regretting her prior decision. But it was too little, too late, and it doesn't get any better from here. Another woman did actually say she would take the boy to the police station herself, but when she asked another woman nearby to look after he daughter, she refused because (shockingly!) her dog didn't like children. So much could be said about this in relation to humans being just as important as animals, but that's another issue entirely.

Two shopkeepers, along with two older boys that knew them, also allowed Thompson and Venables to continue on their way, in spite of suspicions. The abductors then took the little 2 year-old James Bulger to a deserted railway to brutally torture and murder him. I won't go into the details of what they did because a) it's unnecessary, and b) if you want to know you can look it up because it's too graphic for what I'd like to put in this book. What I will say is that when the police found Bulger he was so mutilated that they couldn't tell which injury killed him. Ask yourself what makes a society become so apathetic that even the suffering of a 2 year-old is ignored until it's too late? It's all well and good reacting after the fact out of feelings guilt and horror. But I believe this tragedy demonstrated a fundamental transformation in the psyche of British society for the worse. Since this took place in the early 90s, it certainly correlates with a downturn into very antisocial and dysfunctional trends in not only family life, but British society as a whole.

The indifference shown by the mothers of Venables and Bulger was another very telling aspect of this tragedy. The mother of Jon Venables shocked the police by constantly repairing her make-up in the interview room with her son, while Thompson's mother was an overweight drinker that scarcely attended the trial of her son, spending most of her time at bars, rather than home raising her 7 children. The parents of Thompson and Venables were both separated, during a time when broken homes were becoming a major social concern. In the 90's, conservative minded people were constantly warning about the decline of the family, as the left dismissed and defended this growing dysfunctionality at every turn. You can see this in the way that The Guardian newspaper pushed back against questions about the home lives of Venables and Thompson.[6] The Left constantly defend irresponsible, deviant and criminal behaviour - doing everything they can to invert the victim narrative.

After the trial of Venables and Thompson, the judge stated that, "In my judgement, the home background, upbringing, family circumstances, parental behaviour and relationships were needed in the public domain so that informed and worthwhile debate can take place for the public good in the case of grave crimes by young children." All these concerns have fallen on deaf ears for the Left, however, which is why the decline continues year after year, decade after decade, as socially conservative people continue to lose any influence over society.

Although much more can be said about the tragic murder and torture of poor little James Bulger, I'll conclude this harrowing section by saying that each boy served a mere 8 years for their crimes, with Venables returning to prison from 2010 to 2013 for possession of downloaded images depicting sexual abuse upon male toddlers, and again in 2017 for possession of a manual giving instructions on how to sexually abuse children. Thompson did not return to prison after he was released, but is now believed to be gay. I will say nothing about this revelation because it's not part of what I cover in this book.

Single mother homes

This terrible account can help provide perspective about the impact of broken homes in society. We could certainly call this murder an extreme case, but be under no illusion that the general impact of broken family life is dire across the board. Single mother homes are testament to that, and the experiment in social living that began in the 60s has been nothing short of a disaster. In the 60s, baby boomers began to reject the values of their parents, and wanted to create a communal society where the state was the centre of life. Instead of organic institutions like the family and social clubs, they wanted to replace these with unelected bureaucracies that directed from above. The first thing to go was traditional family. I'm no fan of the term 'tradition' because it's very simplistic to define organic culture in this fashion. It also allows opponents to associate this process with being old-fashioned. While we must certainly be mindful of values that no longer serve their purpose, we should be careful not to throw out the baby with the dirty bathwater, which is exactly what 60s radicals did. These people wanted to tear down every single tradition that existed. Over time you can forget why traditions were established in the first place. At the same time, we shouldn't dismiss the possibility that there are psychotic personalities against basically any order at all. What makes someone this rebellious is another topic, but as you can imagine, childhood experiences play a major role.

As a result of the utopian and rebellious thinking of the 60s, we're now faced with the consequences of jettisoning former traditions like the family, which kept society stable and strong. Bear in mind that one rotten apple spoils the whole barrel over time, and for this reason it's taken some time for the attack on family life to turn into a genuine social crisis. Any sincere and rational person would be open to turning the clock back, if changes they made or support were provably harmful, but not once in the decades of left-wing progressive politics has the left done anything other than deny that their policies have been terribly harmful.

Detrimental effects

This harm has manifested in a great deal of detrimental effects on society. Along with the harmful effects of casual sex and early year childcare that I've already addressed, the increase in single mother homes has had a severe effect on the social fabric. According to a 2002 paper by The Institute for the Study of Civil Society (CIVITAS),[7] single mother homes have led to an array of negative outcomes too numerous to fully address, though some key issues quoted from this paper include:

1. **Poverty:** Single parent mothers twice as likely as two-parent families to live in poverty at any one time (69% of lone mothers are in the bottom 40% of household income versus 34% of couples with children. Children living in lone-parent households twice as likely to be in the bottom 40% of household income

distribution, compared with children living in two-parent households (75% versus 40%). A major longitudinal study of 1,400 American families found that 20%–25% of children of divorce showed lasting signs of depression, impulsivity (risk-taking), irresponsibility, or antisocial behaviour compared with 10% of children in intact two-parent families.

2. **Psychological problems:** At the age of 33, divorced and never-married mothers were 2.5 times more likely than married mothers to experience high levels of psychological distress. Even after accounting for financial hardship, prior psychological distress, and other demographic factors, lone mothers were still 1.4 times more likely to have psychological distress. Among children aged five to fifteen years in Great Britain, those from lone-parent families were twice as likely to have a mental health problem as those from intact two-parent families (16% versus 8%).
3. **Physical health issues:** Results from the British General Household Survey showed that, even after controlling for demographic and socio-economic circumstances, lone mothers still had significantly poorer health than partnered mothers for four out of five health variables.
4. **Difficulties with social interaction:** Young people in lone-parent families were 30% more likely than those in two-parent families to report that their parents rarely or never knew where they were. After controlling for other demographic factors, lone parents were 2.25 times more likely to report their child's behaviour was upsetting to them, and 30% more likely to report significant arguments with their children.
5. **Trouble in school:** Children from lone-parent families were more likely to score poorly on tests of reading, mathematics, and thinking skills. After controlling for other demographic factors, children from lone-parent households were 3.3 times more likely to report problems with their academic work, and 50% more likely to report difficulties with teachers.
6. **Risks of abuse:** According to data from the National Society for the Prevention of Cruelty to Children (NSPCC), young people were five times more likely to have experienced physical abuse and emotional maltreatment if they grew up in a lone-parent family, when compared with children in two-birth-parent

families. Analysis of 35 cases of fatal abuse, which were the subject of public inquiries between 1968 and 1987, showed a risk for children living with their mother and an unrelated man which was over 70 times higher than it would have been for a child with two married biological parents.

7. **Sexual health:** According to the National Survey of Sexual Attitudes and Lifestyles, children from lone-parent households were more likely to have had intercourse before the age of 16 when compared with children from two-natural-parent households. Boys were 1.8 times as likely (42.3% versus 23%) and girls were 1.5 times as likely (36.5% versus 23.6%). After controlling for socio-economic status, level of communication with parents, educational levels and age at menarche for girls, the comparative odds of underage sex actually increased to 2.29 for boys and 1.65 for girls.
8. **Criminality:** Children aged 11 to 16 years were 25% more likely to have offended in the last year, if they lived in lone-parent families. Young men from lone-parent families were 1.6 times as likely to be persistent offenders as those from two-natural-parent families. In focus group discussions, young people in prisons spoke frequently about disruption in their family lives and about their fathers' absence.

Considering these quotes are only a fraction of what the report showed, it's not hard to see that broken family life is a very serious social epidemic. By far the saddest thing is how the Left continues to defend its social policies that led to this outcome. If nothing else, this proves we're dealing with a sociopathic ideology that shows no regard for whoever is caught in the crossfire. All the more infuriating is the pretence that the Left care about human suffering, when the evidence proves that this is merely a front for gaining power, through rebellion against normality.

What I haven't done in this chapter is talk about the way the role of fathers has been marginalised. That is the topic of the next chapter, but as I conclude this one, we should not be surprised that a society of broken homes creates children like Jon Venables and Robert Thompson, not to mention victims like little James Bulger, who suffered in ways that no human being should ever have to, let alone a 2 year-old.

Chapter 8: Marginalising Fathers through Family Law

Family law has become the embodiment of social engineering and financial exploitation of fathers.

If anyone asks why it would be in the interests of a sociopathic ruling class to usurp the role of parents in society, they're either woefully naïve, or too dishonest to admit this would be desirable to those wicked enough to try. There's no shortage of people that are far too trusting of authority, refusing to believe that malevolence would ever be clandestine. For the small percentage that *are* genuinely psychotic in nature, caring nothing for anything but personal advancement and profit, this undue trust is highly advantageous. They want nothing more than to increase the number of people with pious adherence to authority, whenever a false air of compassion and concern is expressed. Wise people know, however, that the wicked hide their true nature from the public, but if you learn the signs and tells, it's much easier to see this coming.

Thus it's obvious why anyone would want to implement a Plato style republic that I mentioned in chapter 1. We've seen the tragic consequences of this in the last chapter, which hammered home the impact of children being raised by single mothers. Before people try to blame this on men (as is usually the case in a feminist culture), there's another tragic tale within this unfolding tragedy related to fathers – the silent victims of broken family life. Men aren't generally respected if they can't behave stoically during hard times, and fight through to the other side. Certainly there's a time and a place for such masculine qualities, but there's also a time when the suffering of men should be recognised, lest we not only become heartless, but aid in wrongdoing.

We've already seen that single mother homes are more numerous today, often due to a rise in divorce since the 1960s. It was at the end of this decade that no-fault divorce[1] began to grow rapidly across the first world, bolstered by the utopian demands of baby boomers that wanted a more carefree way of life that wasn't based around family. Women in particular were sold the idea that personal gain was much more important than being a good mother and wife. Conversely, both men and women started to partake in more casual sex, leading to the growth of hook-up (or pick-up) culture that was covered in chapter 6. It wasn't long before the flip-side of this carefree living began to hit home – literally!

The 1960s sexual revolution was sold on the premise that everyone would be so much happier when they were liberated from the past. When men complained about their wives not being housewives or stay-at-home mothers, they were mocked and ridiculed in the media for being oafish cavemen that wanted to chain women to the kitchen sink. If feminism was a sincere and grassroots movement it would not have been pushed by corporate and political interests that wanted more workers to pay taxes and/or drive down wages. Instead, families would have been encouraged to strike a better work-life balance, where men could work less and women could work more if they chose to. In instances where women do want to work more, family life should not suffer. No such approach was taken because feminism is an artificial movement pushed by corporate interests that wanted to dilute wages, and political groups that want to socially engineer society.

Much more can be said about this, not least that marginalising fathers is a significant part of this agenda. The relaxing of divorce laws since the 60s caused a spike in broken homes shortly after, and although it did level off or lower over time, this never returned to previously lower rates. Fathers are the invisible casualty of this breakdown, but it must be said that awareness of this problem has been gaining momentum since I began talking about it in 2010. The name given to this problem is parental alienation, something that doesn't affect mothers to anywhere near the same degree.

Divorce laws overwhelmingly prejudice fathers, who are far more likely to lose contact with their children after divorce. Statistics vary in this regard, be it 1 in 5,[2] 1 in 3,[3] and other similar rates. In the United States, 1 in 3 children lived without a father according to 2010 census data, with the number of two parent households falling to 48.4% in the same year.[4] Given that fathers are much more likely to lose access to their children after separation, the fact that a quarter of children in the UK were being raised in single mother households in data released in 2014 (the fourth highest compared to EU countries) should be of great concern.[5] Statistics vary from year to year and country to country, but all paint a very bleak picture of fathers being alienated by women, socially conditioned to be selfish and heartless enough to conspire to keep children away from them. I appreciate that there are instances where this might be necessary when fathers are genuinely abusive or neglectful, but when millions of fathers are systematically kept away from their children by a structure of prejudice, the only word that can truly sum this up is evil.

A substantial reason that mothers are able to get away with this is that they're legally treated as the primary carers of children, receiving automatic custody in the vast majority of instances. This is known as the *tender years doctrine*, introduced in the late 19th century as Christian family values were beginning to be undermined. Although it's suggested that this attitude is starting to improve, changes continue to further erode the automatic rights of fathers.

In chapter 1, I mentioned the programme I saw on Channel 4 about father's being denied access to their children. Surprisingly, it did a very fair job of representing the way fathers are treated by the family court system and the estranged mothers of their children. Previously I had no idea fathers were treated this way, but when I watched this programme I was so shocked and upset that I couldn't watch another episode. Around this time, father's rights activists were gaining a lot of attention in the media, one example being the well known group, Fathers 4 Justice. Many presented these activists as a joke – people that dressed up in superhero suits and climbed onto rooftops.[6] It was around this time that I read the misandric Kathy Lette article that I also mentioned in chapter 1, which led to my gradual realisation that all the things I was told about feminism were based on myths and lies.

This was the beginning of my descent into a rabbit hole that revealed the reality of the world we lived in. Being more naïve when I started making videos, I thought that people would change their minds just as I had, when they learnt the facts. Nothing could be further from the truth! Instead, I met a wall of resistance and vitriol that only got worse as I became more educated. I've already explained that I was more left-wing when I started my YouTube channel. As this changed, opposition to my discoveries became downright vicious. Many of the excuses and dismissals I received from this section of the internet revolved around excusing the actions of women, something reinforced by mainstream society. The fact that divorce resulted in single mother homes was blamed on deadbeat dads that abandoned their families out of choice. No one honest would deny this happens, but an overwhelming number of fathers are prevented from seeing their children after separation from the mother.

Family law

To demonstrate how this happened, we need to look at family laws passed by the state. The UK 1989 Children Act abolished the automatic role of a father if he isn't married to the mother,[7] his parental rights dependent on the testimony of a child's mother or a court judgement. Fathers are, however, still left with parental responsibilities that require them to support their children, and yet possess no corresponding right to be a part of their lives. The natural role of the father was thus abolished by the state, as rights became subject to the whim of authority, as we find under tyranny. Typical legalese was used to hide this transformation, by putting the onus on 'welfare of the child' that almost always bodes favourably for the mother.

What we have here is merely an excuse for authoritarians to use the state to control reproduction in society – exactly as Plato set out thousands of years ago. Furthermore, we must understand that evil people always suggest that they care so much about the welfare of others, but as soon as the evidence shows the harm they're doing, they'll dismiss or bury it wherever possible. This should make anyone with a semblance of compassion furious, because these monsters are playing god with people's lives. All the while, they don't have any true regard for welfare at all, cynically exploiting this for their own gain. We've seen the product of this deception in the last chapter, with an examination of broken homes. Through this destruction of family life, the state is usurping the role of the father, and it's being done by pretending that the best interests of the child are of paramount importance in legal proceedings. Clearly the evidence proves that this is false when people insist that this dysfunctional system of family law should not only remain in place, but continue to transform into one where a parent's role is subject to state decree.

With this undermining of fatherhood in mind, David Cameron's 2011 speech on Father's Day should appal any decent human being. Special days throughout the year are often used to push radical politics, and on this occasion David Cameron made a speech while he was Prime Minister, shaming fathers in a way that would never be done to mothers.[8] In this speech, he stated, "It's high time runaway dads were stigmatised, and the full force of shame was heaped upon them. They should be looked at like drink-drivers, people who are beyond the pale." The trouble with this picture is that it's not even half the story. Not only are fathers regularly prevented from seeing their children by vindictive mothers and a corrupt family court system, but it completely ignores the emotional and financial lengths fathers must go through to fight this system. Not only do most fathers *want* to see their children after separation, but they spend a fortune in court to gain the ability to do so.

Worse still, many mothers will ignore court orders and make up false accusations that prevent fathers from seeing their children. Not only do these accusations take a while to resolve, but mothers will continuously make up new accusations, thus preventing the father from ever seeing his children. Meanwhile, in the UK the father is expected to pay 15-25% of his net income to the mother in child support, which even doesn't guarantee him a legal right to see his children.[9] This ties directly into family laws I've already addressed, where fathers only have a responsibility to take care of their children, but no right to be a part of their lives.

Years ago, accounts of fathers losing access to their children were less common. As time has passed, this has become so commonplace that it's hard not to know a father directly affected by this terrible injustice. Generational decline bears this out - the baby boomers were relatively unaffected, making it easier to dismiss the alienation of fathers as a fringe problem. Likewise, generation x were still affected to a smaller degree, therefore allowing people to ignore and dismiss this problem as an unfortunate by-product of women's liberation. But now people are beginning to take notice because the millennial generation have far less experience living with their fathers. In my family alone, this problem has grown exponentially within a single generation, whereas in the previous generation it was not only rarer, but less severe. Yes divorce occurred, but it was more likely to lead to an amicable resolution for the father.

Another factor that's significantly increased the recognition of this problem is grandparents affected by their son losing access to his children. A growth in stepfamilies also means that women can be affected when their partner is dealing with parental issues from a previous relationship. At first glance, it might seem reasonable that a father pays money to support his children upon separation. However, the mother has no obligation to document how this money is spent, and what further compounds the lack of accountability for the mother is that, legally, the father is usually required by the court to allow the mother to live in the family home until the children leave full-time education at 16 to 18.[10] If the mother is reasonable, much of this can be avoided, but if it can't, the father had better make sure he's earning a good salary because not only will he lose up to 25% of his net income, but it will be harder for him to borrow money for a second home that he can actually live in.

Impoverished fathers

Fathers are essentially impoverished by family law because responsibilities go way beyond expectations of a father that isn't separated from the mother. A father that isn't separated from the mother isn't legally required to fund the education of his child after the age of 16, but this *is* often a requirement if he separates from the mother. He isn't legally required to have his 16 year-old child live under his roof at the age of 16, although upon separation from the mother he could be financially responsible until his child leaves full-time education at up to 18 years-old, or well into a college and university education up to 21 years-old. Don't get me wrong, it's not morally acceptable that a parent should expect their children to leave their homes as soon as they're 16 to 18, but this is beside the point. The expectations are way beyond his *legal* requirements in this regard. What's more, does the state always tell parents how much money they should be spending on their children, scrutinising their income in this intrusive manner? Certainly not, and this should be considered a gross violation of an individual's rights. The fact is that net figures from the UK's Child Support Agency (CSA), like 15% towards one child, 20% for two, and 25% for three, are so arbitrary that they're clearly just a financial shakedown of fathers by the state.

Since the state has no money in practice, it must find ways to take money from people in society to fund its programmes. As such, to become surrogate father and husband, the state must coerce separated fathers out of their income, redistributing this to the mother via government bureaucracies like the Child Support Agency in the UK. This creates a form of bribery that conditions women into supporting big government programmes. The father then suffers with unjust rulings regarding his financial responsibilities, which no one would dare demand of poorer families. Why? Because common sense alone demonstrates that basic subsistence is relatively inexpensive in a first world country, meaning that you cannot justify such high financial demands on father. If you doubt this, here are some examples:

John is a UK resident who earns a decent full-time salary of £50,000 per year before deductions, for the tax year of 2018-19. This is well above the 2018 average, according to the Office for National Statistics (ONS).[11] Having separated from his wife, he's required to pay 20% of his net income towards their two children because she doesn't work. Based on tax rules in the same annual period,[12] after his £11,500 tax free allowance is deducted, he pays 20% income tax on £34500, which is £6900. His tax increases to 40% for earnings that are £34500 above his tax free allowance, subtracting a further £1460. He then pays an additional 12% national insurance of £4555. Finally, he has to pay another 2% national insurance on £3616, subtracting another £72.[13] The total amount of income tax and national insurance adds up to £12987, making his net income £37000 – respectable, though John is now required to pay a further 20% of his net income in child support, subtracting yet another £7400, and leaving him with £29600. You can certainly get by on this figure, but we must consider that this is a pretty good salary by UK standards, even with these deductions. To really see how painful this is, we need to look at a more humble salary.

James earns a salary of £30,000 per year working full-time, which is about average in the UK for 2018, and is required to pay 25% of his net salary to his unemployed ex-wife, as per the Child Support Agency's requirements based on three children. Once again based on deductions for the tax year of 2018-2019, James pays 20% income tax on £18,150, amounting to £3630. He then pays 12% national insurance on £21576, subtracting a further £2589 from his salary. He therefore has £6219 subtracted from his gross salary, leaving him with £23781. He then has to deduct 25% child support, a further £5945, leaving him with merely £17836. Good luck getting another mortgage, paying the legal costs if your ex-wife doesn't adhere to a father's visitation rights, let alone clearing your name of false allegations made against you, because on that salary, you'll never be able to afford it, and vindictive wives know it!

Shared parenting

As you can see, even with an average income, the situation grows bleak, only worsening as your income lessens. The silver lining (if you can call it that) is that you pay a flat fee of £5 per week if you earn between £5-100 per week. You also pay nothing at all if you earn less than £5 per week, but at these levels you have no employment to speak of, and are probably living on welfare. Despite having less pressure from the CSA, that doesn't mean you'll be able to see your children, let alone meet the requirements of a spare bedroom for each of your children to stay with you overnight. Are you required to have a bedroom for each of your children under other circumstances? No. Is the mother of the children required to stick to this? No.

There will be instances where the father becomes the primary carer, but these are rare exceptions when the mother is blatantly negligent or wishes to sever ties with her children, and if the father isn't married to the mother upon separation, this is not an automatic arrangement. What makes matters so much worse is that the family law system is clearly designed to be adversarial. When people separate, it's often on bad terms because it causes heightened emotions. Amicable separations do happen, but usually it takes time for emotions to settle down, allowing people to interact calmly with one another. When children are involved in separation, you can't simply walk away and never see each other again, either, causing yet more complications.

The trouble is that the adversarial nature of the family law system incentivises mothers to limit access of the children to the father, as payments from the father could be reduced. The mother gets a reduction of one seventh of weekly payments, per day that the child stays with the father overnight. However, once custody is equally shared between the parents, you halve weekly payments and reduce them by another £7 per child. Although this is a significant reduction, even with shared parenting the mother still gets some child support from the father. The entire system still favours the mother as primary (resident) parent, so there is a long way to go before shared parenting is not only automatic, but for the father to have equal parental rights.

I'd like to pose following the question; are the requirements for child support that I've outlined a realistic estimation of how much it costs to raise a child? Despite all the speculation about how much it costs, you can raise a child perfectly well without adhering to consumerist pressure. In fact, too much focus on material possessions destroys a child's appreciation for the simple things in life. I also reiterate that you would never make high financial demands on poorer families, because people realise that there's a big difference between essential requirements like food, shelter and basic clothing, or luxury items like designer wear or expensive gadgets. Do John and James in my examples therefore need to give £7400 and £5945 respectively to the mother of their children, wherein the mothers have no obligation to justify how they spend it? Far too many mothers are using their legal advantage to coerce men that they once had a relationship with, and political entities enable this system because it aligns with a social engineering agenda to make the state a surrogate father.

To conclude this chapter, there's a cold place in hell for the solicitors, lawyers and judges involved in this system, who fleece fathers for personal gain. This is nothing short of a legalised racket that requires monstrous degrees of heartlessness to take advantage of. To change this system will require fighting against the special interest groups that want this to continue. To top it off, the legal costs that fathers have to pay, just to have virtually worthless contact orders to see their children is an utter disgrace.

Chapter 9: No Justice for Men

When masculinity is demonised, justice for men will disappear.

By the summer of 2011 it was abundantly clear to me that feminism was not a sincere ideology, and did not present the truth in a remotely accurate or honest way. Warren Farrell's book, The Myth of Male Power, certainly hammered this home when I read it, but truth be told, this only confirmed what I already realised by then. By now I'd become closely connected with men's rights activists and advocates online, via a small and upcoming men's movement that was gaining momentum. As I've already said, I never actively called myself an 'MRA', but my videos online attracted the attention of this community, who took me in as one of their own. I had no issue with this, but I was conscious of the fact that my philosophical journey was not restricted to purely men's rights.

A website called A Voice For Men was the hub of this closely knit community speaking out against feminist propaganda, as well as raising awareness of mistreatment towards men and boys. This community and movement was attracting both positive and negative attention, the former from a growing number of supporters and content creators speaking out online, the latter via feminists and leftists angry about the backlash against feminist ideology. I've already covered many of the injustices against men, focusing predominantly on family law. As bad as this is, it only scratches the surface. Once you starting travelling down the rabbit hole of truth, you soon discover out how deep it goes. As a result, I increasingly began to notice the sheer injustice against men within the wider legal system of society.

Pivotal to this injustice is the lack of accountability for women making false accusations. Feminists demand that the word of a woman should be sufficient to prosecute men in all cases of violence, abuse, and harassment, eradicating essential legal protections such as the presumption of innocence and burden of proof. Other legal protections like the right to face your accuser and trial by jury are equally attacked through the feminist demand that a woman should always be believed, irrespective of evidence. This is carried out via the suggestion that cross-examining women who make accusations against men are forced to relive the trauma of their negative experiences. Naturally, it would be very difficult for a woman to face her attacker or abuser in a legal proceeding, but this doesn't discount the trauma of a man's professional and personal reputation being brought to tatters by a woman's false accusation, potentially losing access to his children due to child protection concerns, or being unable to work in certain jobs.

The first thing apologists will do when such concerns are broached is fall back on the scripted appeals to emotion and consequences akin to those just mentioned, which seek to prioritise the concerns of women above all else. One must understand that these appeals are merely rhetorical devices designed to shame and confuse people into silence, thus making them insincere at best, and downright dishonest at worst. This is something I struggled to come to terms with earlier in my journey, but the more you're attacked for making fair and logical observations, the more you realise that the people making these arguments are lashing out angrily at the world, sparing no thought for anything that contradicts their ideological framework. The other significant accusation is, of course, sexism, as though believing that a man having a right to a fair trial means you're prejudiced against women.

Types of court cases

Courts are broken down into two key types of court cases; civil and criminal. The burden of proof for a civil case is significantly lower than a criminal one, causing a great deal of problems when a woman makes a false accusation against a man. In a criminal case, there must be no reasonable doubt that the accused committed a crime, whereas a civil case only needs a greater than fifty percent possibility that the accused is guilty - otherwise known as the preponderance of evidence or balance of probabilities.[1] The trouble is that the family court system technically takes place in a civil court, meaning that accusations against the father are based on civil rather than criminal standards of proof. The man may not go to jail for child abuse allegations taken to a civil court, but lower standards of proof are required to deny him access to his children. Gone is the necessity for no reasonable doubt to be met, replaced with preponderance of evidence that creates many problems for an accused father, especially considering the way modern family law adheres to the so-called 'child's best interests', where the court prevents the father from seeing his children upon the slightest accusation from the mother. In cases of questionable and false accusations, children can be coached by mothers to say certain things to social services or child protection agencies, which itself is a form of parental alienation that poisons a child against the father.

What makes matters worse is that family courts are often held in secret, where people involved are not allowed to speak publicly and journalists cannot report anything. Therefore, any public remarks about a case can lead to parents being prosecuted. Yet again it's the 'child's best interests' that are used to justify this, as well as other euphemisms like child protection. None of this is sincere, however, and only serves to hide the injustice of the family court system from the public. Steps are being made to change these gaping flaws in family law, but progress is slow,[2] especially with shared parenting. There are a growing number of cases where mothers making false accusations are prosecuted or lose custody to the father,[3][4] but the law still makes it far too easy for mothers to get away with this most of the time.

The cost of a family lawyer or solicitor also cannot be overlooked, although fees vary so dramatically that it's difficult to provide an average - unsurprising when special interests don't want to encourage demands for reform, plus the legal industry profits greatly from this extortion. It costs well in excess of £100/$100 per hour for a family solicitor or lawyer, plus extra costs for legal letters, and further expenses on top. Legal bills can thus be in the thousands, even if you strip costs to a bare minimum, forcing you to choose between financial poverty, or losing access to your children. The thought of making such a choice chills me to the bone, particularly when you consider the aggressive way that the state pursues fathers for child support, whether or not they're allowed to see their children. Also bear in mind that the figures I've provided are very conservative, and can reach five to six number fees in a prolonged legal dispute. The notion that the state can stand between a parent and their child, in all but proven examples of objectively definable abuse, should terrify and appal any decent human being, and it's this sort of interference in the life of the individual that we find in repressive societies. The only reason people don't notice and oppose this interference more is all the distractions in modern society that make us too self-absorbed to care about anything that doesn't directly affect us individually.

False rape accusations

Another sobering example of miscarriage of justice for men is false rape accusations. When feminism began to catch on in the 19th century, more moderate feminists were concerned with civic issues like universal suffrage and property ownership for women. Radical feminists pushed additional concerns like so-called rape culture, increasingly inflating and exaggerating rape in the most deceptive manner imaginable. A foundational template for this became the 1987 Mary Koss study published and commissioned by Ms., a magazine co-founded by Gloria Steinam. The study is called The Scope of Rape: Incidence and Prevalence of Sexual Aggression and Victimization in a National Sample of Higher Education Students, involving 6159 males and females enrolled in 32 United States higher education institutions, aged 14 onwards.

Feminists were disillusioned with the fact that plainly asking women if they'd been raped did not yield the kind of inflated results they were looking for. Koss, who at the time was public health professor at the University of Arizona, came up with 'creative' ways to increase this to 25% via her aforementioned study,[5][6] which featured the first large scale survey of its kind. This was achieved by classifying certain experiences as rape, unbeknownst to those being asked, meaning that 42% of those classified as rape victims went on to have sex with their alleged assailants. Although it's conceivable that this could happen, a further 73% of those classified as rape victims said they hadn't been raped. When faced with this, feminists and their cohorts protest that women are too intimidated to report their crimes, but this is hardly an issue in an anonymous survey.

Mary Koss, and others that followed in her footsteps, mimicked these ambiguous criteria for rape that were highly subjective. For example, terms like "date rape", "hidden rape", "unacknowledged rape", "acquaintance rape", and "campus rape" were subsequently coined by feminists,[7] allowing for an experience to be interpreted as rape, whether or not the female consented. This clearly explains why so many of the women questioned by Koss in her initial survey did not consider themselves rape victims.

A 2000 campus rape study by the US Department of Justice further confirms these ambiguous criteria. 65% of those classified as "completed rape", and 75% of those under "attempted rape", did not think their experience was serious enough to report. Furthermore, they did not believe their experience resulted in emotional or physical injuries. As we can see, feminists muddy the definition of rape, allowing women to withdraw consent after the fact. Contradictorily, feminism is promoted as a sexually liberal movement, and yet here we see that it leads to an attitude that makes it impossible for a man to prove consensual intercourse has taken place. The effect this has had on state policy cannot be overstated. For example, in 2012, the FBI redefined rape as[8]:

The penetration, no matter how slight, of the vagina or anus with any body part or object, or oral penetration by a sex organ of another person, without the consent of the victim.

Ostensibly, this was sold on the premise that penile penetration of a vagina is no longer the only definition of rape, therefore making it "more inclusive". Thus, penetrating a man anally can now be considered rape, something that does indeed take place in prison populations in particular. However, if we note that this new definition states that penetration can be considered rape, "no matter how slight," given the way feminists have already attempted to make rape completely open to interpretation, this makes their job a lot easier.

Some people will struggle to accept that feminists would be this underhanded, but the facts speak for themselves. No one goes to such extremes to inflate rape statistics unless they have an ideological axe to grind, and feminists certainly fit that description. Since the 70s, feminists have used sham activism to lobby the government for increasingly unjust laws that allow the prosecution of men for consensual sex. In the US, it was the Take Back the Night foundation. For the UK it was Reclaim the Night, similar organisations popping up across the western world. These are top-down funded organisations, designed to push a social engineering agenda that makes women see men as their enemies. Paid activists march in the streets with their professionally designed signs, claiming that society must make it safer for women to go out at night. Instances of rape do of course happen, but if you say that women need to be mindful of their behaviour in public by reflecting on the quantity they drink and how provocatively they dress, particularly when frequenting unfamiliar or more crime ridden neighbourhoods, and you'll be accused of victim shaming.

I obviously have zero tolerance for rape as a crime, especially as a father of two daughters. But nonetheless, I will tell my daughters that they need to avoid putting themselves in situations where they can be taken advantage of by predators. Feminists don't care about common sense like this, however. They just want to drive a wedge between men and women, so it feeds their psychological dysfunctionality and propels their political agenda.

When we actually drill down into rape statistics, this further outlines the dishonesty at play.[9] For one, when charges of rape are dropped, or a not guilty verdict is reached, it begs the question of whether a woman lied. This might seem like a risky precedent for genuine victims of rape, but we must take into account the way that men have their lives destroyed by false allegations, especially if we factor in the treatment of men in prison, who were convicted of a sex crime. Numerous studies have sought to investigate the prevalence of false rape reports, but this is conservatively placed at 2-10% in the aggregate. Philip N.S. Rumney compiled data from a selection of sources for a 2006 paper that appeared in the Cambridge Law Journal. Among these findings, he stated that a 2005 study by Kelly et al recorded 67 out of 2643 accusations of rape as false allegations, with a further 22% recorded as "no crime". This means that around 581 accusations of rape did not result in a conclusive outcome, therefore open to the possibility of being false accusations.

Rumney also referenced a 2003 study by Lea et al, stating that 11% (42) of 379 rapes crimes were false reports, as well as a joint data from Her Majesty's Crime Prosecution Service Inspectorate (HMCPSI) and Her Majesty's Inspectorate of Constabulary (HMIC), which stated that 11.8% were false reports. Note that left-wing academics have tried to dismiss the credibility of Rumney's data. Not only should we bear in mind that some of this data comes directly from government sources, but we've already seen the way that feminists dismiss anything that doesn't align with their own ideology. The full list of Rumney's findings is as follows:

Source	**Number**	**False reporting rate (%)**
Theilade and Thomsen (1986)	1 out of 56 4 out of 39	1.5% (minimum) 10% (maximum)
New York Rape Squad (1974)	n/a	2%
Hursch and Selkin (1974)	10 out of 545	2%
Kelly *et al.* (2005)	67 out of 2,643	3% ("possible" and "probable" false allegations) 22% (recorded by police as "no-crime")
Geis (1978)	n/a	3–31% (estimates given by police surgeons)

Smith (1989)	17 out of 447	3.8%
U.S. Department of Justice (1997)	n/a	8%
Clark and Lewis (1977)	12 out of 116	10.3%
Harris and Grace (1999)	53 out of 483 123 out of 483	10.9% ("false/malicious" claims) 25% (recorded by police as "no-crime")
Lea *et al.* (2003)	42 out of 379	11%
HMCPSI/HMIC (2002)	164 out of 1,379	11.8%
McCahill *et al.* (1979)	218 out of 1,198	18.2%
Philadelphia police study (1968)	74 out of 370	20%
Chambers and Millar (1983)	44 out of 196	22.4%
Grace *et al.* (1992)	80 out of 335	24%
Jordan (2004)	68 out of 164 62 out of 164	41% ("false" claims) 38% (viewed by police as "possibly true/possibly false")
Kanin (1994)	45 out of 109	41%
Gregory and Lees (1996)	49 out of 109	45%

Maclean (1979)	16 out of 34	47%
Stewart (1981)	16 out of 18	90%

Many other sources have demonstrated the prevalence of false reporting of rape, such as a 2005 study by the UK Home Office concluding that police classified 8% of reports to be false. A 2009 study by Burman, Lovett & Kelly studied data from several countries in Europe, including Austria, Belgium, England, France, Germany, Greece, Hungary, Ireland, Portugal, Scotland, Sweden, and Wales. Between 4-9% of reports were false, but they noted that suspected cases of false rape allegations were "hidden in the 'no evidence of sexual assault' category". And if this isn't recent enough for you, 2018, figures in England and Wales show that up to one third of rape investigations are dropped,[10] once more posing the possibility of false reports amidst feminist concerns about the way rapes are classified. We've seen the way feminists would *like* rapes to be classified, and it's falls very short of anything reliable or fair.

All this demonstrates that we should always consider that whenever a conviction isn't reached, a false accusation is a very real possibility, and we should be especially mindful of the fact that feminists want the word of a woman to be sufficient to convict a man of rape in a court of law.

Domestic violence

The final area I will cover in this chapter is domestic violence. This is another problem that can shatter a man's life if not dealt with objectively and impartially, and we're a long way off anything of the sort. The main premise that feminists demand is men being the primary aggressors in abusive relationships. They then lobby the state to automatically take the side of women, as a reaction to their hyperbole. Precisely the same mendacity is found with rape statistics, and the implications of this on men are equally far-reaching. Feminists claim that as many as 1 in 4,[11] or even 1 in 3 women have experienced domestic violence, and promote these statistic via major anti-domestic violence organisations like the National Coalition Against Domestic Violence in the United States.[12]

Just like rape, the feminist definition of domestic violence is so subjective that virtually any male and female interaction can be put in this category, the Duluth model[13] being one prominent example. In this case, a wheel is used to demonstrate how violence and abuse are broken up into eight categories driven by power and control from men in patriarchal society. Recall how I already put the myth of patriarchy to rest in chapter 5, and we can see how this theory allows feminists to acquire power through victimology. Here is an example of this 'Duluth wheel' (also known as the power and control wheel):

One such category in this wheel is "using isolation," described as "controlling what she does, who she sees and talks to, what she reads, where she goes, limiting her outside involvement, using jealousy to justify outside actions." It should immediately be apparent why this broad definition is problematic. Whenever you're in a relationship, it's normal to want to know where your partner is, who their friends are, what they do, and so on. A monogamous sexual relationship is a deeply interpersonal arrangement that involves more intimacy than any other relationship in society. Referring to the person you're in a monogamous relationship with as your 'other half' is testament to how close-knit this can be, so why, then, are feminists making it far too easy to classify this as a form of violence and abuse?

Another category in this wheel I will bring attention to is "using male privilege", where "treating her like a servant, making all the big decisions, acting like 'the master of the castle', being the one to define men's and women's roles" are highlighted. In other words, if, as a man, you feel the need to have a strong influence on the dynamic of your relationship with a woman, this can be spun as abuse by feminists and dishonest women, with a broad term like "male privilege" that's an extension of deeply flawed patriarchal theory. "Using economic abuse" is also considered abusive when "preventing her from getting or keeping a job, making her ask for money, giving her an allowance, taking her money, and not letting her know about or have access to family income" take place. Imagine, then, that you're in a relationship with a woman that spends money so frivolously that she gets your household into debt. It would be easy for feminists to twist this into some sort of abuse if you establish a budget that she needs to learn to keep to, otherwise you risk losing the family home. In fact, financial budgeting is a common sense approach to life, and yet feminists can spin this as a form of abuse if you expect this in a relationship, even though finances are generally shared between couples on the condition that both parties are financially responsible.

Many other glaring problems could be pointed out with the Duluth model, but this doesn't stop it being the most commonly used "batter prevention programme" in the United States, despite a growing amount of evidence that abuse in relationships is similarly split between men and women.[14][15] Instead, men are automatically being treated as primary aggressors in cases of domestic violence and abuse, requiring them to leave the house and sometimes face mandatory arrest[16][17] in many parts of the United States.

As I close this chapter, I hope it's now much clearer that feminism is truly a twisted ideology. Why it's so twisted is something I'll be uncovering in the chapters that follow.

Chapter 10: The Cultural Marxist Connection

Cultural Marxism is the bedrock of the modern left.

By now it should be obvious that the Left are fundamentally deceitful, either to themselves or to others. What they say and do is at odds when their policies are so incredibly destructive. We can talk all day long about what the Left are supposed to, or once, represented, but if we're honest or observant enough we'll realise that this is irrelevant. The Left are never going to admit their shortcomings because their ideology is based on doing whatever it takes to realise their goals, and to achieve this, they exploit the resentment of those that struggle in life. Sometimes people genuinely have problems that should be taken into consideration, but the solutions of the Left always make things much worse for society, ostensibly for the benefit of a small minority who are eventually thrown under the bus with everyone else.

There's one term that strings this entire strategy together – *cultural Marxism*. Once you understand this ideology, the values of the modern Left make substantially more sense. In 2011, about 8 months after I started making videos on YouTube, I started to notice people using the term cultural Marxism to describe not only feminism, but the wider identity of the Left. Being a naturally inquisitive person, this intrigued me for several reasons. I was still pretty sympathetic to left-wing ideology at that time, but I was beginning to notice cracks in this side of politics, and that something monolithic was driving feminism. When I then started digging into cultural Marxism, what I found pieced this all together.

Wikipedia has certainly gone downhill over the years, making it necessary to question what you read on this site. Back in 2011 there was a cultural Marxism entry that was very helpful, but would eventually be removed due to the site's systematic purging of left-wing 'heresy'. Cultural Marxism can fundamentally be described as a form of academic critique called *critical theory,*[1] underpinning every aspect of modern leftist thought. When I say 'modern' I mean the last 100 (certainly last 50) years, and this timeline is quite detailed when dissected in depth.

Marx's failed prediction

The starting point for this timeline is just after World War I, when Russia was the only country that experienced a communist revolution in 1917. This was not what Karl Marx, the founder of Marxism, predicted. Neither did his close associate and co-author, Friedrich Engels, do any better. According to Marx's theory of historical materialism,[2] societies were supposed to transition to socialism via a working class revolution, once the *bourgeoisie* were overthrown. Rather than the popular Marxist slogan of "workers of the world unite", it was only Tsarist Russia (a country that hadn't even fully transitioned from feudalism to capitalism) that experienced a socialist revolution. Communist intellectuals were baffled that more working class people around Europe didn't come together for a *proletariat* revolution, overthrowing their governments in the same fashion as Russians had.

Marx believed that society goes through 6 stages. He described Stage 1 as primitive communism; a hunter-gatherer society with no money, private property, state or social class. Stage 2 was then described as a slave society, or antique mode of production. Here slavery was the driving force of an economy, where a large percentage of people were forced into servitude. Ancient civilisations were based on this system, marking the early formation of states, money, private property, and class structure in society. Stage 3 is feudalism, where an entrenched nobility and serfdom is formed, while simple commodity production shapes around agricultural goods, mining, and other commodities. Stage 4 is a capitalist society, where mass production would lead to the formation of a 'bourgeois' middle-class that grew wealthy from commodity trading and exploitation of the 'working class' proletarian. As opposed to the closed guild system of a feudal society, capitalist society is driven by markets that are opened up to competition. Marx believed this would culminate in late stage capitalism, where the working class would revolt against ever more bourgeois monopolies and economic recessions. The result would be a socialist society that would gradually centralise the means of production and collectivise property ownership. Once this was fully realised, the state would wither away in a cultural revolution that would end money, family and religion.

We see now why Communists were baffled with the outcome of World War I. They believed the working class would realise their best interests by rising up against the bourgeoisie, just as Marx predicted, but many Communists began to think that Marx was wrong in some respects (actually, he was wrong in many respects). They wondered why the working class were so loyal to their rulers if they had such a difficult plight. The answer, they concluded, was cultural hegemony,[3] and only by destroying this could communism prevail. Before we address what that entails, allow me to dispel some myths in this regard.

Marxism has always centred on culture. Although it presents itself as an economic theory, this is merely a by-product of an ideology based on cultural revolution. Anyone that's read chapter 2 of The Communist Manifesto should be aware of this. Marx and Engels state in this manifesto, which they co-wrote, that the nation, family and religion must be eradicated for a communist utopia to come about. With regards to the nation, it says "The working men have no country. We cannot take from them what they have not got. Since the proletariat must first of all acquire political supremacy, must rise to be the leading class of the nation, must constitute itself the nation, it is so far, itself national, though not in the bourgeois sense of the word." For religion the manifesto states, "But Communism abolishes eternal truths, it abolishes all religion, and all morality, instead of constituting them on a new basis; it therefore acts in contradiction to all past historical experience." Family is addressed in the following; "The bourgeois family will vanish as a matter of course when its complement vanishes, and both will vanish with the vanishing of capital."

This is merely a snapshot of the cultural nature of Marxism, clearly found within The Communist Manifesto, and proving beyond a shadow of a doubt that Marxists have been at war with the nation, family and religion since the very inception of their ideology. Let us not, then, doubt that Marxism has always been focused on culture, irrespective of how this adapted over time. Another key element to consider is that there has always been a split within communist circles, meaning that there is no one faction that holds the monopoly on this ideology. Revolutionary Marxists believed that the working class would rise up through their own accord, overthrowing their masters with sheer weight of numbers, despite the fact that Russia still hadn't experienced the industrial revolution that would transition from capitalism to socialism, as Marx claimed. In Russia, these Marxists became known as Bolsheviks, Vladimir Lenin being their infamous leader. Also in Russia, another faction called the Mensheviks, led by another infamous communist named Leon Trotsky, believed that communism would be implemented through gradual transformation of Russian society from feudalism to capitalism, followed by a later communist revolution, much like Marx believed. Prior to the Russian revolution, these two factions fought one another for dominance, and it was the Bolsheviks that won. Once the Russian revolution took place, however, Lenin and Trotsky set their differences aside for the benefit of their cause.

Another gradualist form of socialism comes from the Fabian Society,[4] a British socialist organisation founded in 1884. Its members advocate the gradual move towards a socialist society, achieving this without any violent revolution. This is embodied with the symbol of a wolf in sheep's clothing that represents the use of deception to dupe the masses into accepting reforms that radically change society, much like a wolf in sheep's clothing tricking its prey by taking on their appearance. Another symbol of the Fabians is a striking tortoise, with the motto "When I strike, I strike hard" written underneath it. Being a slow but powerful animal, this denotes the slow but effective strategy of Fabian socialism. The name Fabian socialism stems from the Roman general named Fabius Maximus, who wore down the superior forces of Carthage, under the renowned general Hannibal. He did this with persistent hit and run tactics, as opposed to facing the superior numbers of the enemy in open battle. This further represents the underhanded tactics of Fabian socialism that do not operate openly.

Gradualism is the predominant form Marxism takes today – the linchpin that unifies all aspects of the modern left, which some people refer to as cultural Marxism. One must understand that the Left have an infinite number of names to describe various ideological components that continuously shift and change, partly because this makes it harder to see that all these labels are the same thing, and partly because leftists abandon any label that becomes toxic - communism being a good example of a label no longer fashionable among the majority of people that support the left. To further muddy the waters, leftists accuse people of conspiracy theories if they highlight anything that exposes their subversive tactics. Referring to cultural Marxism is one instance where this will usually occur, and I myself have experienced this many times over the years. What's critical is the realisation that any label you use is not as important as the definition. In philosophy we call this an axiom – if you call a chair a dog, it still has the qualities of a chair, irrespective of the change of name. In this sense, anyone that refuses to accept that cultural Marxism exists is too disingenuous or ignorant to take seriously.

Antonio Gramsci, György Lukács and the Frankfurt School

Antonio Gramsci was one of the earliest post-World War I Marxist intellectuals to lay the foundation for cultural Marxism. He was pivotal in describing the loyalty of the working class to the bourgeoisie as cultural hegemony, and set out to explain how to destroy this from within a nation. A *strategic distinction* was made between a *war of position* and a *war of manoeuvre*, wherein the former involves the creation of a proletarian culture that's distinct from the bourgeoisie. Gramsci believed this would increase *class consciousness* in the workers, in contrast to *false consciousness* that kept them loyal to the bourgeoisie. *Class struggle* in society would subsequently increase, creating the necessary support for a revolutionary socialist *war of manoeuvre*. In 1926, Gramsci was imprisoned under Benito Mussolini's fascist regime.[5] During the years that followed, he wrote many notebooks that set out his theories. By 1967, the German student movement leader, Rudi Dutschke, took inspiration from Gramsci's theories when he formulated the phrase, the *long march through the institutions* - a prolonged process of taking over the institutions of society, until Marxists were the ones that had cultural hegemony.

Another Marxist who saw the value of expanding the cultural dominance of Marxism was György Lukács. In 1919, he was made Deputy People's Commissar for Education and Culture in the short-lived Béla Kun regime of the Hungarian Soviet Republic.[6] His goal was to eradicate Christianity from Hungarian society by undermining sexual morality. To this end he introduced compulsory sex education in schools, a strategy that's become very common under Marxism.

Arguably the biggest influence to the cultural expansion of post-World War I Marxism was the Frankfurt School.[7] Like Gramsci and Lukács, the Frankfurt School was made up of Marxist intellectuals who were determined to expand the cultural scope of Marxism. More like Gramsci than Lukács, however, the Frankfurt School were Marxist intellectuals frustrated with the lack of progress of Marxism after World War I. Increasingly a distinction was made between *classical Marxism* and neo-Marxism as a result, of which critical theory became a central pillar. What these intellectuals did was define a theory that criticised every aspect of western culture from a Marxist perspective, going much further than nation, religion and family under classical Marxism. The result was the deconstruction of anything and everything in society, subsequently constructing an all-encompassing Marxist framework.

Thinkers that formulated this theory were officially part of the Institute for Social Research. They became known as the Frankfurt School because they frequented Goethe University Frankfurt from 1918-1933. In light of their Jewish ethnicity, plus the Marxist clash with Nazi ideology, these intellectuals fled Germany, settling in Columbia University, New York City from 1935. It initially baffled me why mentioning the Frankfurt School would be met with accusations of anti-Semitism, but given the sheer number of Ashkenazi Jews involved in founding Marxist schools of thought, including Karl Marx himself, this is a convenient canard against the many valid criticisms of a totally destructive ideology.

Several prominent figures of cultural 'neo-Marxism' emerged from the Frankfurt School. These included Theodor Adorno, Max Horkheimer, Walter Benjamin, Erich Fromm, and arguably the most prominent of all, Herbert Marcuse. Theodor Adorno wrote The Authoritarian Personality[8] in 1950 - a breakdown of the nine criteria that make someone fascist. He called this the 'F scale' ('F' standing for fascist), and described fascism as a product of childhood experiences that shape conventionalism, authoritarian submission, authoritarian aggression, anti-intellectualism, anti-intraception, superstition and stereotypy, power and toughness, destructiveness and cynicism, projectivity, and exaggerated concerns over sex. Despite criticism of bias and poor methodology, Adorno's book was highly influential in American social sciences, a field that critical theory would utterly dominate in the years that followed.

A core text for critical theory itself became the 1944 book, Dialectic of Enlightenment,[9] jointly written by Max Horkheimer and Theodor Adorno. The book criticised the failures of the Age of Enlightenment that took place in Europe around the 18th century, blaming this on social dominance. Walter Benjamin was another major contributor to the Frankfurt School, creating another form of critique called literary theory (sometimes called literary criticism). By adapting aspects of critical theory, this criticises literature in the same Marxian manner that relates everything to class struggle. Erich Fromm is known for his theory of "freedom from," which he describes in his 1941 book, Escape From Freedom. The key position of his book is that if people grow to hate their freedom due to primary ties like family, nature, work, etc., they will become fascistic. He describes this thusly:

> *However, if the economic, social and political conditions... do not offer a basis for the realization of individuality in the sense just mentioned, while at the same time people have lost those ties which gave them security, this lag makes freedom an unbearable burden. It then becomes identical with doubt, with a kind of life which lacks meaning and direction. Powerful tendencies arise to escape from this kind of freedom into submission or some kind of relationship to man and the world which promises relief from uncertainty, even if it deprives the individual of his freedom.*[10]

This is an obvious adaptation of Marx's theory of alienation, where he argued that social classes emerging within industrialised societies alienate people from their humanity. Herbert Marcuse became prominent in the 1960s for several books that expanded on this theory of alienation, as well as the work of psychoanalyst Sigmund Freud. His work is arguably the most influential on the left since the 1960s, when the term 'New Left'[11] became in vogue. Marcuse is considered the father of this movement, demonstrating the scale of his influence. His 1955 book, Eros and Civilization,[12] contradicts Freud's view that humanity must contain the destructive nature of the ego to stop civilisation falling into chaos. Instead, Marcuse believed that humanity should fight against the repression of such instincts because this would be the catalyst for a better society. In his 1964 book, One-Dimensional Man,[13] Marcuse argues that advanced industrial society creates false needs that lead to social repression. His answer to this is the "great refusal" of methods of control. Shades of Gramsci's 'cultural hegemony' are deeply embedded in this critique, as are wider parallels between neo-Marxist, New Left or cultural Marxist ideology, which leftists insist are conspiracy theories, despite obvious commonalities.

Repressive tolerance

Off the back of the Marcuse's proposal for a great refusal, he co-wrote a book released the following year called A Critique of Pure Tolerance. One contribution to this book was an essay called Repressive Tolerance.[14] The modern Left are known for extreme intolerance towards anything that doesn't conform to their beliefs, and it's when we examine this essay that we see a major influence for this today. Marcuse argues in this essay that tolerance should never be given to those that don't align with the values of the left. He outlines this in the following passage:

> *Surely, no government can be expected to foster its own subversion, but in a democracy such a right is vested in the people (i.e. in the majority of the people). This means that the ways should not be blocked on which a subversive majority could develop, and if they are blocked by organized repression and indoctrination, their reopening may require apparently undemocratic means. They would include the withdrawal of toleration of speech and assembly from groups and movements which promote aggressive policies, armament, chauvinism, discrimination on the grounds of race and religion, or*

which oppose the extension of public services, social security, medical care, etc. Moreover, the restoration of freedom of thought may necessitate new and rigid restrictions on teachings and practices in the educational institutions which, by their very methods and concepts, serve to enclose the mind within the established universe of discourse and behavior--thereby precluding a priori a rational evaluation of the alternatives. And to the degree to which freedom of thought involves the struggle against inhumanity, restoration of such freedom would also imply intolerance toward scientific research in the interest of deadly 'deterrents', of abnormal human endurance under inhuman conditions, etc.

Marcuse uses the word subversion here – a very important term when it comes to understanding the insidious success of the Left. Subversion is the attempt to destroy, overthrow or undermine, though this is not a form of direct aggression. Rather, it relies on subtle techniques that destroy from within, like treason, sedition, and demoralising propaganda spread by self-serving collaborators and outright treachery I described earlier under gradualist socialism. In the passage, Marcuse is describing a form of cultural Marxist subversion colloquially known as *political correctness*. Once again the Left will fixate on words rather than meaning. Thus, if they can't get away with dismissing political correctness as a conspiracy theory, they'll deflect attention by calling Christian morality another form of political correctness, despite the fact that this isn't subversive. Christianity certainly defends moral standards within society, but it doesn't use clandestine tactics that feign intent, unlike cultural Marxism. As such, political correctness has become synonymous with the kind of repression Marcuse described in such a flagrant fashion in his essay.

The conclusion of left-wing orthodoxy that grew out of 1960s counter counterculture is that the Left is no longer constrained by economic class. In fact, economic class is barely even relevant anymore. In place of class, its sex, race, religion, sexuality, and a whole swath of categories that continuously expand. Put in these terms, it's a lot easier to see why feminism is so oppositional to family life, but it it would be myopic to think there's a limit to how much cultural Marxism subdivides. As Gramsci described, the aim is a Marxist culture that indoctrinates the masses, putting them at odds with established and traditional values that he classed as bourgeois. By constantly creating conflict, a critical mass will eventually lead to transformation of society, be it violent or gradual. This means leftists are constantly searching for new ways to create division, which can never be satiated. It's for this reason that sexuality keeps endlessly expanding into yet more forms of acceptance, no matter how far this goes, and why even conservation efforts in nature have been completely hijacked by the Left. Even cyclists are being put into opposition with drivers of cars, as the cultural Marxist agenda expands into green policies. While no single issue can truly epitomise this subversion, the history outlined in this chapter at least helps us understand why the Left is so hell bent on pushing policies that wreak havoc in society.

Chapter 11: Crimes of Communism

The worst crimes against humanity have been committed by those who believe anything is possible.

At the halfway point of this book, I'm hoping that it's very clear how much soul-searching I did to move away from left-wing ideology. This didn't happen overnight – far from it, and it certainly wasn't reactionary. If anything, it was my move towards left-wing ideology in the prior years of my life that was reactionary, which is actually very telling when we drill down into how this form of politics began. People suggest that fascism is a reactionary movement, but a more accurate interpretation is that it's a reaction to a reactionary movement called communism. As time went on, leftist ideology didn't match up to experiences I had in the real world, leading to me questioning the dominant cultural narrative we live in. Thanks to the internet, this type of questioning has become a tsunami that's all but unstoppable without totalitarian repression that always accompanies utopian left-wing ideologies.

Lest I assume people know what ideology or reactionary means, I'll define these terms before proceeding. An ideology is a set of beliefs that make up a social, economic and religious system. The more ideological a system, the more it demands control until it totally consumes every part of our lives – hence why some ideologies are *totalitarian*. The difference between ideological versus other forms of belief is compulsion. In other words, if you're compelled by a group to respect a system of rules going beyond *natural rights* described in chapter 4, this invariably becomes ideological.

Reactionary (or person who is *a reactionary*) describes the process of politically reacting to another ideology. Some will suggest reactionaries only have traditional and conservative beliefs, but this is just one way that communists try to label anyone that isn't a communist as a reactionary Nazi. It's not hard to see why this is intellectually dishonest, although one cannot fail to notice the growing range of views labelled as Nazi in this day and age. Make no mistake, this is no accident, and provides an inkling into why communist ideology is so utterly evil. I don't use the word evil lightly, nor should we ever, but communism is the root of all evil in the 20th century, at least on the surface. Yes, Nazi, or 'fascist' ideologies were a reaction to communism, but if it wasn't for communism, they would never have gained traction without a similar ideology coming about.

Perhaps if I start with the death toll under communism, it will be easier to see why this ideology is so terrible, and why the reaction was another part of this. A special term known as *democide* defines the murder of people not during war, but by the state against its own citizens. Based on historical figures accumulated by Hawaii University,[1] communist regimes committed acts of democide on over 148 million people in the 20th century when we include China, the USSR, Vietnam Cambodia, Yugoslavia and North Korea - a shocking number for just one century. In no other time in history does anything come close to this scale of murder. You might be tempted to think some of this can be dismissed by the number of people alive relative to previous centuries, but these numbers are still unprecedented. With such a gargantuan figure in the back of our minds, we can begin to explain why human beings felt justified in committing such utter evil.

First, how were so many people murdered? The answer is famine, torture induced death, slave labour, unbelievably barbaric imprisonment, and execution. Accounts of life under communism have been notoriously hard to attain because totalitarian regimes constantly lie and misrepresent facts or statistics. However, whistle-blowers and dissidents have successfully provided an accurate picture of life under communism, albeit the full scale of brutality is extremely difficult when people simply disappear, the very record of their existence completely eradicated. Imagine, if you will, what it would be like to sleep in your bed at night, when suddenly government agents break into your home and drag you out of bed, carting you off to a facility for political dissidents. Here you're interrogated, tortured and imprisoned for years at a time, forced to endure arduous manual labour on trumped up charges that are impossible to disprove because there is no presumption of innocence. Instead, you must protest your innocence as you're put under intense pressure to confess to crimes you didn't commit, like being deprived of sleep in the day and interrogated at night. You must also implicate others of false crimes, who will subsequently go through exactly the same unimaginable experience as you.

Gulag Archipelago

Aleksandr Solzhenitsyn was perhaps the most prolific documenter of life in the Soviet Union, receiving numerous awards for his literature. His three volume text, Gulag Archipelago,[2] draws from Solzhenitsyn's own experiences, along with reports, interviews, statements, diaries and legal documentation. In one section, Solzhenitsyn describes Sukhanovo Prison,[3] a former monastery that interrogators would intimidate prisoners through the mere mention of being sent there. So terrible was this place that prisoners ended up mad or dead – no wonder it invoked such terror! Prisoners were regularly tortured, sleep deprived, and kept in unimaginably cruel solitary confinement that involved small, closet-like cells where you couldn't sit or move, while other rooms were freezing or excruciatingly hot. In Butyrki prison, cells were so overcrowded that Solzhenitsyn describes how for "weeks at a time there were three persons for each square yard of floor space," and that during 1948 in Vladimir Internal Prison, "thirty people had to stand in a cell ten feet by ten feet in size," such close proximity that "naked bodies were pressed against one another, and they got eczema from one another's sweat. They sat like that for weeks at a time, and were given neither fresh air nor water — except for gruel and tea in the morning."

In Kirov transit prison, Solzhenitsyn describes how inmates "kept their knapsacks in their hands or on their knees because there was nowhere to put them down," and "there were so many bedbugs that they went right on biting in the daytime, and they dive-bombed straight from the ceiling." Solzhenitsyn describes acts of torture by interrogators, like that of Yelena Strutinskaya being "forced to remain seated on a stool in the corridor for six days in such a way that she did not lean against anything, did not sleep, did not fall off, and did not get up from it." He states that "prisoners would have their skulls squeezed within iron rings; that a human being would be lowered into an acid bath; that they would be trussed up naked to be bitten by ants and bedbugs; that a ramrod heated over a primus stove would be thrust up their anal canal (the "secret brand"); that a man's genitals would be slowly crushed beneath the toe of a jackboot; and that, in the luckiest possible circumstances, prisoners would be tortured by being kept from sleeping for a week, by thirst, and by being beaten to a bloody pulp."

Labour camps were equally harsh and brutal, known as gulags. People were worked to death in freezing conditions, under slave labour that only involved basic tools for complex construction projects like the White Sea–Baltic Canal built between 1931 to 1933.[4] It's estimated that the mortality rate for those working on the canal was about 8.7%, although many others became sick and disabled. In spite of the gruelling work often carried out by political dissidents, the canal was too small for larger ships, and was thus a typical failure of communist central planning.

I trust this picture is bleak enough to give some insight into why communism is such a terrible ideology, and yet we hear next to nothing about this. It isn't taught in schools, and ignored in the media. Academics brush this aside for a primary focus on fascism as the greatest evil of the 20th century (unsurprising when you consider the long march through the institutions by Marxists). If you ask most people about Holodomor,[5] they have no idea that this was the starvation of a minimum of 6 million Ukrainians by the Soviet Union, between 1932 to 1933. Some blame this on collectivisation of farming seen in other communist regimes like China during the great leap forward,[6] taking place from 1958 to 1962. This caused the starvation of at least 18 million people, with upper estimates being around 30 million. Communists have a knack for giving grand names like this to so-called 5 year plans. They also have a way of denying reality when this goes wrong, either by covering up their own failures, or blaming them on fascists, capitalists, counter-revolutionaries – anyone but themselves. They then argue that they should try all over again because we didn't get it right the first time, thanks to human greed. Thus communists are prone to saying "it wasn't real socialism," as though next time their impossible ideas will be the real thing (it never is).

The other explanation is that the mass starvations are quite deliberate, even if incompetence does play a part. Leon Trotsky is noted for saying, "In a country where the sole employer is the State, opposition means death by slow starvation. The old principle: who does not work shall not eat, has been replaced by a new one: who does not obey shall not eat." Karl Marx himself stated in the New York Daily Tribune on 22nd March 1853,[7] that "The classes and the races, too weak to master the new conditions of life, must give way." Friedrich Engels stated in Neue Rheinische Zeitung No. 194, 13th January 1849 that "All the other large and small nationalities and peoples are destined to perish before long in the revolutionary world storm. For that reason they are now counter-revolutionary."[8] I could keep giving historical evidence and quotes indicating the sheer inhumanity of communism, but we should stop and ask ourselves how so many people have been fooled into thinking that Marx really cared about the masses. The answer is a utopian idea so enticing that people desperately cling to it, spearheaded by one Karl Marx.

Karl Marx

Karl Marx[9] was born on the 5th May 1818, in the Prussian town of Trier (now a city in Germany), and lived a lavish childhood due to his wealthy family background. As the third of nine children, he became the oldest son when his brother Moritz died in 1819. His family were Ashkenazi Jews that converted to Christianity, but after Marx left school he turned away from this faith in a dramatic fashion. Having been given a private education, Marx wanted to study literature and philosophy when he was 17. However, his father wanted him to study law, so this is what he enrolled in at the University of Bonn. Having managed to escape military duty at 18 by claiming he had a weak chest, he became a sort of proto-student layabout and rebel. As well as joining the Poet's Club, a group of political radicals that were monitored by the police, he served as the co-president of the Trier Tavern Club drinking society. Marx soon became embroiled in disputes, one of which resulted in a duel. When his grades began to decline he was transferred to the University of Berlin by his father. Not long after he met his future wife, Jenny von Westphalen, whom he married in 1843, 7 years after she broke off her engagement to a young aristocrat to pursue a relationship with Marx.

Once he enrolled at the University of Berlin, Marx joined the Young Hegelians in 1837, expanding his interest in literature and philosophy. It was during this time that he was exposed to ever more radical thinkers such as Bruno Bauer and Ludwig Feuerbach, both atheists and strong critics of Christianity. Marx received his PhD from the University of Jena in April 1841, after submitting a controversial thesis arguing that theology must yield to the superior wisdom of philosophy. Along with his friend, Bruno Bauer, Marx caused scandal by getting drunk, laughing in church and galloping through the streets on a donkey. He then moved to Cologne in 1942, which is where he got involved in the radical newspaper, Rheinische Zeitung, and started developing his early socialist views. The paper soon attracted the attention of the government, so he moved to Paris in 1843. Here he wrote for other radical newspapers, and further expanded his ideas and theories by writing Introduction to a Contribution to the Critique of Hegel's Philosophy of Right, and On the Jewish Question.

Marx then met Friedrich Engels in 1844, the friend and associate that played a significant role in the rest of his life. They co-wrote and released The Communist Manifesto in 1848, when Marx was living in Brussels after being expelled from France. As time went by, Marx relied on the financial support of Engels, a wealthy owner of factories in England and Germany. His father also financially supported him when he was a student in Berlin, with a huge monthly allowance of 700 thalers a year (only 5% of the population earned more than 300 thalers). Yet Marx had little time for his family, lusting after inheritances upon their deaths. As his uncle was dying in agony, he wrote, "If the dog dies, I would be out of mischief." Engels replied, "I congratulate you for the sickness of the hinderer of an inheritance, and I hope that the catastrophe will happen now." When this uncle died on the 8th March 1855, Marx wrote, "A very happy event. Yesterday we were told about the death of the ninety-year-old uncle of my wife. My wife will receive some one hundred Lst; even more if the old dog has not left a pate of his money to the lady who administered his house." Perhaps you may be inclined to think this is merely an insensitive reaction towards the death of a relative he wasn't close with. However, he was not on speaking terms with his mother, and when she died in December 1863, he wrote, "Two hours ago a telegram arrived to say that my mother is dead. Fate needed to take one member of the family. I already had one foot in the grave. Under the circumstances I am needed more than the old woman. I have to go to Trier about their inheritance."[10]

Marx squandered the generous income he was provided by others making failed stock market investments, and living an idle, irresponsible existence. Yet he's widely considered a great economist, and supposedly underwent an intensive study of political philosophy from October 1843 until January 1845, as he lived in Paris. He's also believed to have spent a large portion of his father's inheritance to arm Belgian workers planning a revolutionary uprising. The claim is disputed, but the Belgian Ministry of Justice arrested and accused him of this crime in the same year that he released The Communist Manifesto, to which he subsequently fled back to France. Later that year he went to Cologne, Germany, hoping to start another uprising, issuing a handbill entitled the Demands of the Communist Party in Germany, and financing the daily newspaper, Neue Rheinische Zeitung, through more of his father's inheritance. Several attempts to prosecute Marx failed during this time, though his political efforts were eventually suppressed by the 16th May, 1849, so he fled once again to France before ending up in London by 1850 because he was unable to return to Germany or Belgium.

Marx treated conventional employment as something beneath him, at the expense of his family's wellbeing. Despite the financial support of Engels, the health of his family declined rapidly after moving to London, to the point where his 3 room flat in one of the worst sections of the city was described as a "pig-sty" by a visitor[11]. Whether it was a chair with a missing leg or a tattered and torn sofa, the house was dirty, dusty, messy, and had no good furniture. Due to conditions of poverty, hunger and filth, four of the seven children Marx had with his wife died young. He also had an eighth illegitimate child with a maid named Helene Demuth, whom his wife could afford to hire after she received an inheritance. It was claimed by Marx that the child belonged to Engels, and the boy was placed in a working class foster home shortly after his birth in 1851[12]. Rather than concerning himself with supporting his family and children (including his illegitimate son), or being financially responsible, Marx chose a life of pseudonyms for himself, and those around him, to avoid arrest, living hand to mouth as he depended on the handouts of others – a reflection of the entitlement prevalent in the ideology he concocted.

Dictatorship of the proletariat

Central to Marx's theories was the *dictatorship of the proletariat*, where the working class would take power through violent revolution, when society transitioned from capitalism to socialism during the grand timeline of his historical materialism theory. He also said that "Democracy is the road to socialism," indicating that he wasn't averse to nudging society in the direction outlined in his writing, hence his numerous revolutionary activities throughout his life. In the prior chapter I touched on the fact that Marx argued that every economic decline would be worse than the last, thus pushing us closer towards late stage capitalism. In this setting the workers would be increasingly incapable of profiting from their labour, and as such, the interests of the workers would not align with the owners of the means of production - the bourgeoisie, the class that rose out of the industrial revolution when society came out of feudalism due to capitalism. Essentially, the bourgeoisie were the foundation of today's middle-class - hugely resented by the aristocracy because the growing social mobility of the middle class became a challenge to their power. Feudalism was a rigid caste system with little to no potential to move upwards in society, not unless a king or queen bestowed you with a title or you could take power by force.

One must understand that an effective charlatan takes elements of truth and twists them to their advantage. Thus Marx describing capitalism and the bourgeoisie as a class that grew out of feudalism is not inaccurate. The con lies in Marx's simplistic notions about the means of production, and his so-called *theory of alienation* that he described as workers being unable to directly profit from their labour, particularly in factories during the industrial revolution that took place from the 18th century. Marx's solution was for the workers to acquire direct access to the means of production, cutting out the middle man in economic life. Marx, however, failed to factor in the immense risk that comes with owning a business. Although workers lose their income when they lose their jobs, business owners are directly liable to suppliers and borrowers in the event of financial ruin, as well as suffering loss of income that befalls workers. Employees therefore suffer less risk – a calculated choice we all take when deciding whether we'd rather be in charge, or go home every night without having to worry about your business going under. The boss doesn't necessarily get the steady pay cheque of his employees, either. Some months the boss may make no profit at all, or less profit than the workers. But the potential reward for running a business could become very lucrative, making the risks worthwhile.

A well known quote from Marx that summarises his utopian worldview is "From each according to his ability, to each according to his needs." This epitomises Marx's breeding of resentment towards success, and his naïve belief that needs could actually trump ability because communism would lead to a huge surplus in productivity. Rather than merit being the basis for economic prosperity, generating greater economic opportunities like growth in employment and availability of goods for the masses, Marx thought it would be better that workers seized the means of production and ran the factor as a collective – the dictatorship of the proletariat. In this setting, humanity would supposedly realise Marx's utopia, but as we've seen in this chapter, nothing could be further from the truth.

So much more can be said about where Marx went wrong in his theories, and how this is a reflection of his idle and resentful nature he exhibited in his life. The leftist mind is prone to rationalising deep-seated selfishness with shallow displays of virtue, such as arguing for more taxation and government bureaucracy for the greater good (helping the poor, creating a social safety net, etc.), when, in actual fact, they're direct beneficiaries of the policies they demand. Consider the nurse, teacher, doctor or council worker that benefits from a very generous state pension that's way above average, as people in the private sector pay ever more debilitating taxes to fund their comfortable retirement. They simply don't care to consider how they're destroying the ability for people to make a living which doesn't revolve around crushing government expenses that kill the private life of the citizen, both economically and socially, and that their demands for more government, more taxation, more benefits, more public services, etc., will be the death of society in the end.

In the Soviet Union, government bureaucracies provided the best employment, although becoming a bureaucrat was nigh on impossible unless you knew someone that could pull strings inside the corridors of power. Favours called 'blat'[13] were regularly required for such employment, with the entirety of society run in a similar manner. We see this pattern again and again as socialism increases in a given country. Access to scarce resources becomes equally prone to this kind of nepotism, as the private sector is choked so tightly that no one can realise a destiny that isn't controlled by the state. If food and medical shortages don't kill you in this system, the slave labour might, but is it so surprising that this is what the road to communism amounts to when Marx spent his whole life breeding animosity towards success, as he sat on his backside and expected others to provide for him? I think not!

Chapter 12: Stateless Utopia

A stateless society is a utopian pipedream.

Once you start to realise that the state is undeniably the biggest cause of death other than natural forces like disease, earthquakes or extreme weather events, only a fool wouldn't conclude that government should be significantly curtailed. Prior to the 20th century, it's estimated that around 600 million people were murdered by the state since the dawn of civilisation.[1] We should bear in mind that it's estimated that the human population didn't pass 1 billion until somewhere around the late 18th to mid-19th century,[2] which certainly puts the scale of this brutality into perspective. Approximately a further 262 million people were subsequently murdered by the state in the 20th century alone[3] – close to half the number for the entire history of civilisation! Despite these figures, to suggest that the 'state' is responsible for this terrifying inhumanity is very much a misnomer because the state is merely an abstract concept that represents groups of people. It's therefore people operating through the state that do the murdering, not the state, which doesn't actually exist in the material sense.

That being said, state power has become like a religious cult in the modern secular age. People treat it like a deity that needs to save them from their strife. Like a saviour figure, the state is constantly what people turn to when they have a problem to solve, thus conditioning the masses to accept extremely invasive government intrusion into their lives. People have grown so accustomed to this state dependency that the very notion of independence is too inconceivable to imagine, and far more terrifying than sobering statistics about democide. When security is valued more than freedom, personal responsibility is sidelined. Benjamin Franklin, one of the founding fathers of the United States, is often quoted for saying "Those who would give up essential liberty, to purchase a little temporary safety, deserve neither liberty nor safety." Never a truer word was spoken, but it's easy to get so enamoured with freedom that you end up believing no government is necessary at all – a philosophy otherwise known as anarchy. In this sense, anarchy is the complete opposite of those totally dependent on the state. The question is; what role should the state play in our lives, if any at all?

With this question in mind, I began to flirt with anarchy around 2012, after decidedly moving away from socialism within the first year of my

YouTube channel. As outlined in chapter 3, I realised that socialism is a toxic ideology that creates an entitled mob mentality. Exposure to libertarian philosophy was the final catalyst I needed to join the dots I'd already started to connect. As part of this process, I started to realise that not every problem is caused by a lack of government, which leftists insist on. Rather, excessive state interference in the life of the individual, such as high taxation and regulation, has unintended consequences that work in favour of those that covet power. I then started down the road of a stateless society after coming across Stefan Molyneux, a well known Canadian anarchist philosopher on YouTube. Like so many political terms, general agreement on anarchist philosophy is widely disputed, although it's widely described as a philosophy that entails no government. What form this takes, however, varies greatly. Technically, the definition of anarchy is no rulers, stemming from the Greek word 'an', which means 'without', and 'archon', which means 'ruler'. This does not necessarily mean 'no government', but for the purpose of this chapter we will go with this definition.

Anarcho-capitalism

Stefan Molyneux can be described as a *voluntaryist* or *anarcho-capitalist*. In other words, he advocates a stateless society where all interaction would be based on freedom of choice in a market economy. When no interference from government takes place, be it regulations or laws, people often call this a free market. It would be very easy to assume that this means no rules, but that would be false. Trade is obviously paramount in such an arrangement, with the aim of creating mutually beneficial interactions for all involved. It's for this reason that anarcho-capitalism is often called *voluntaryism*, because all interaction requires consent that's completely voluntary.

Murray Rothbard was one philosopher that took libertarianism to what some would call its full anarchist conclusion. What he concluded was that true freedom should result in voluntaryism, although this term was coined long before Rothbard came along, in the 19th century. Murray Rothbard was a key thinker of the Austrian School of Economics during the latter part of the 20th century. Many great economic thinkers emerged from this school of thought, Rothbard being a product of the moral dilemma that comes with realising that the state can only exist through force, because unless you consent to being governed, the government is forcing, or 'coercing' you to accept its authority. This brings us onto taxation. If we don't consent to taxation, is it theft? That question infuriates many people because the moral dilemma it creates is impossible to resolve if you believe that government has the authority to force us to obey. Anarcho-capitalists are prone to lumping everyone into the statist camp if they aren't anarchists. But they do have a very good point when it comes to taxation. If you don't believe it's automatically theft, when is taxation so high that it's no different? The answer you'll receive from hardcore statists is basically never, as long as you get goods, services and protection in return.

There's so much wrong with this conclusion that it's amazing it would be considered an argument. In chapter 3, I touched on the fact that slaves were fed and clothed. Slaves living in ancient Egypt, Greece and Rome, would receive regular food, shelter and medical treatment.[4] This makes sense when you consider that if slaves didn't have a basic level of care they would die, and since slaves were treated as property, owner's needed to preserve their investment. Some slaves were allowed to marry and have children, although children of slaves were the property of their owners as well, creating a perverse incentive to multiply the number of slaves. Slaves obviously weren't free, but they weren't necessarily worked to death, either. Consider now that many people think it's okay to tax and tax until most of the income someone receives is directly lost to taxation, along with indirect losses like sales or value added tax, let alone capital gains and local property taxes, to name a few other forms of taxation. At which point do we say that we pay too much to the government? Some people argue that they'd rather pay more tax if it means better government services, otherwise known as public services. However, these people are invariably thinking about themselves, not morality. How easy it is to lecture others about the virtues of taxation when they receive welfare, or have a job directly tied to taxation, while others make all their income in a private sector that pays for you!

It's therefore logical to conclude that unlimited and unrestrained taxation is just a form of modern slavery. Just because modern people live more comfortable lives than slaves in antiquity, it doesn't make the logical conclusion of taxation any different. The more the government takes from the citizen, the more akin to slavery it is, especially when we consider that slaves have always been given something for their work, if only to keep them alive. What's more, debt slaves were common in history – can't pay what you owe? Pay it off through slave labour! What happens when you can't pay your taxes? You'll be sent to jail. In fact, jail time for unpaid tax is usually the only form of jail time you'll serve for debts in the modern world.

By the time you end up with a system like communism, where you aren't directly paid anything at all, what autonomy do you have left that isn't on a par with a slave? This is what makes communism such an evil system – it promises so much, but in the end it delivers nothing more than dependence on the state, just like a slave dependant on their master. Sure communism makes all sorts of promises about being able to work as much as you like, and always being given what you need, but what about that little bit extra to enjoy ourselves? You can forget about that because communists can't deliver it. Instead they demonise materialism as bourgeois and exploitative, while the ruling class enjoy luxuries that the common folk could never dream of.

Many people reframe the legend of Robin Hood as a hero that fought against the rich to give to the poor, but this is wildly inaccurate. Robin Hood fought against unjust taxation that left the people destitute. I'm certainly not arguing that taxation in the Western nations has fallen to this level, but try starting your own business and you'll soon see that it's taxation that's by far the biggest obstacle to success. Recall in chapter 2 that I talked about my own experiences starting a clothing stall in the indoor market of my home city of Cardiff. My business was going to turn a half decent profit in the first year, but coupled with extortionate rent that I was actually paying to the council, plus the eerie signs of an economic downturn, I decided to 'shut up shop'. Furthermore, there comes a point when you're paying so much tax that it really isn't worth the time to run a business. Overheads are a killer in business, and taxation is often the biggest one, even after rent. In my case I was paying rent to the government that was so high that I discovered it was 3 to 4 times more than high street premises. It certainly taught me that turnover is vanity and profit is sanity, as they say in business.

Those that insist taxation isn't theft usually make appeals to the democratic mandate of government. But without limits, possibly enshrined within a constitution, tyranny is inevitable. Anarcho-capitalists will argue that a constitution is just a piece of paper, and therefore does nothing to restrain megalomaniacs constantly chipping away at limits to power. This certainly happened with the US constitution, where it's argued that the 16th amendment that allowed the introduction of tax powers wasn't properly ratified.[5] Whether or not you believe this, it should not be possible to constantly amend a constitution until you're left with nothing but a legalistic mess of subjective interpretation, where government can twist everything in its favour.

The core moral argument for most anarcho-capitalist and voluntaryist philosophy is the *non-aggression principle*, typically shortened to the NAP. It states that the initiation of force is illegitimate because, unless someone consents, you cannot force an individual to do anything. Hence, government has no way to govern those that do not consent, which is why government is compared to having a gun in the room by Stefan Molyneux[6] and others. Imagine you're in a room with someone holding a gun, as you're trying to negotiate something. Are you certain that person won't use the gun to force you to do what they want, if you disagree with them? The answer is no.

The non-aggression principle is not without its flaws – a child's consent cannot always be accepted because they're too young to face responsibility for their actions, meaning that another moral layer called personal responsibility is necessary. But it does help us challenge the view that the initiation of force is legitimate, a position that's sadly endemic to the times we live in. That being said, consent is *not* the true basis for a logically consistent moral code. One obvious reason is that parents need to force their children to do things. If they didn't, their children would partake in destructive behaviour like eating too much chocolate, spending too much time playing video games, and failing to develop an appreciation for the deferment of gratification. Denial of this is why promoters of the NAP are prone to utopian beliefs about human nature, where children are only naughty because they learnt it elsewhere. This delves into the nature/nurture argument that I won't get into here, but if you've ever been around children, it should be obvious that this is far too simplistic.

Anarcho-Communism

The previous two chapters of this book covered communism, though I've yet to explain that communism is often considered a form of anarchism, at least in theory. In the last chapter I covered some of the disagreements between revolutionary versus gradualist Marxists. One must bear these disagreements in mind when it's stated that Marxism is supposed to lead to anarchy, especially after many communists deviated from the original theory when put into practice. For example, Vladimir Lenin implemented the New Economic Policy in 1922,[7] after the turmoil of the Soviet economy contributed to anti-Bolshevik rebellion. These alterations became known as Marxist-Leninism, although many Soviets still hoped that Marx's anarchist goal would manifest in the not too distant future.

Faithful advocates of a stateless communist society are sometimes referred to as *anarcho-communists*, but just as Karl Marx is not the only communist, nor is he the only anarcho-communist. Peter Kropotkin in particular had a major influence on left-wing anarchism, as did Pierre-Joseph Proudhon, who argued that it isn't taxation that's theft, but property. Karl Marx himself believed that as society progressed through 6 stages of historical development, the final stage would be communism. Following the progression of primitive communism, ancient modes of (largely slave based) production, feudalism, and capitalism, socialism would become the intermediary stage before communism itself. Pivotal to this development is the dictatorship of the proletariat[8] I addressed in the last chapter. The very name gives us a hint as to why communism is such a totalitarian ideology, predicated on the notion that the masses are the ones in control, therefore making any dictatorship morally justifiable. As I've also explained in prior chapters, this is not what happens in practice because communism requires heavy centralisation of every aspect of society, making tyranny not only inevitable, but unimaginably brutal. The masses are sold this pipedream on the basis that they'll never have to go without, as per Marx's adage, "From each according to his ability, to each according to his needs." Central planners administer everything in society from the top-down, even though communism is supposed to be egalitarian. Nothing could be further from the truth in practice because the people at the top control all the guns, so no one can stop them abusing their power. The masses become sitting ducks in this setting, forcing them to adhere to everything the central planners say, or else!

Setting this aside, socialist central planning is supposed to be the catalyst for the abolition of social classes, money and the state,[9] not to mention religion and other competing ideologies or philosophies. Gradually the state is supposed to become superfluous because somehow human nature will not abuse so much centralisation. Instead people will allow their better nature to flourish, and once class traitors are eradicated, society will become so peaceful that love for fellow man will prosper, bar a few exceptions that rehabilitation can fix. When any distinction between humanity is erased, only then do communists believe their utopia will be fully realised. With so many idealistic expectations, is it any wonder that communism is such a disaster in practice? Just in case you thought this system wasn't idealistic enough, workers can choose any job they want in this paradise. Gone is the need for specialisation that comes with more advanced society, where people need many hours of study, training and experience to become adept at a job. Rather, Marx argues that capitalist society makes workers less productive, since they lose the ability to affect their own lives when they're cut off from decision making and the means of production. He called this sense of helplessness the theory of alienation.[10] As he puts it in The German Ideology, co-written with Friedrich Engels and released in 1846:

> *For as soon as the distribution of labour comes into being, each man has a particular, exclusive sphere of activity, which is forced upon him and from which he cannot escape. He is a hunter, a fisherman, a herdsman, or a critical critic, and must remain so if he does not want to lose his means of livelihood; while in communist society, where nobody has one exclusive sphere of activity but each can become accomplished in any branch he wishes, society regulates the general production and thus makes it possible for me to do one thing today and another tomorrow, to hunt in the morning, fish in the afternoon, rear cattle in the evening, criticise after dinner, just as I have a mind, without ever becoming hunter, fisherman, herdsman or critic. This fixation of social activity, this consolidation of what we ourselves produce into an objective power above us, growing out of our control, thwarting our expectations, bringing to naught our calculations, is one of the chief factors in historical development up till now.*[11]

The labour theory of value and commodity fetishism

One might be wondering how any of this is possible in the mind of Karl Marx. The answer lies in his explanation of economic value. Marx believed that this is not based on supply and demand outlined in chapter 3. Instead, value is based on labour, thus meaning that the amount of work put into a product dictates its worth. Even on the face of it, this is absurd. If I spend 10 hours crafting something out of wood, does that mean it will be more valuable than if I spent half the time on this endeavour? Considering my lack of skill as a carpenter or joiner, you wouldn't think so. Equally, the more skilled you are in this area, the less time it would take you because you become more efficient. So clearly labour is not the driving force of value at all, at least not exclusively. Nonetheless, this is a very popular position to take in the left-wing anarchist and Marxist camp, encapsulated by the labour theory of value.[12]

Value is obviously somewhat subjective. Our needs and desires vary so greatly that it would be impossible to generalise at all times, though we do have essential requirements that Marx would call 'needs'. We *need* food, water, shelter and clothing, but acquiring these things requires tools that make it easier to gain access to resources or do certain tasks. Then we have luxury goods that we can live without, but nonetheless make life more enjoyable and raise morale, especially during more difficult times. At the very least we can break down value into three categories: necessities, tools and luxuries. Sometimes these categories cross over, like luxury clothing. But this doesn't make the categories less valid. Marxism not only disregards luxury goods, but demonises this as an exploitative element of bourgeois society.

Whatever the case, value is not driven by pure labour alone. Some goods are rarer than others because they're harder to attain, like precious metals and stones. What this suggests is that some goods have intrinsic value that goes beyond labour. It's all too easy to dismiss this, just as Marx does when he talks about commodity fetishism,[13] where he suggests we irrationally associate value with certain goods. But this is a mistake. While gold and diamonds are highly coveted luxury items that people use in jewellery or furniture, they're still very useful for industrial equipment and tools. In chapter 2 I explained that gold is one of the most durable metals in the world, though it's also a very good conductor. Hence gold is used for a huge variety of industrial processes and electronic components. Gold can be shaped into a variety of uses because it's so malleable, and its rarity makes it more expensive than most other metals. Thus it's a good store of value. It's for this reason that gold has historically been considered money. By the same token, diamonds are so hard that they can cut through any mineral, but are very hard to come by.

Value is not therefore restricted to labour. In some instance you could even argue that labour has nothing to do with value because no matter how long you spend on a certain task, it could have no value to others. You might spend hours painting a picture, but no one likes it enough to give you money for it. All value is therefore based on the worth of the product in the eyes of the consumer, along with rarity and desirability, contrasted with time as a very valuable commodity in our lives. Once you add all these factors up, we should always consider our competence in a certain task before attempting to profit from this in the marketplace. Sometimes persistence can lead to a development of skills over time, but labour alone is a virtually meaningless metric.

What I hope I've made abundantly clear as we close this chapter is that communism is a failure because it relies too heavily on wishful thinking, not least a stateless utopia. Although it's certainly fair to say that anarcho-capitalism is also utopian, at least it makes more economic sense.

Chapter 13: Militant Atheism

Atheism has been turned into an anti-theist movement driven by angst.

Atheism is supposed to be an absence of belief in God or gods - a sort of descriptive explanation for existence that requires scientific evidence for truth. When you drill down further, however, atheism imposes a prescriptive view of the world, and leaves us with a spiritual vacuum that's consistently filled with subjective morality. This has fostered the rise of nihilism, moral relativism, postmodernism, and other ideologies that stem from purely empirical thinking. All this is connected to internal angst brought on by experiences in our lives. In this chapter I'll provide a personal account of my own transition to atheism, and how this led me to the realisation that atheism is overwhelmingly political in nature.

My history with religion is turbulent. I was born and raised Greek orthodox Christian, baptised into this faith when I was a baby. As a child, I was a strong believer in God, and felt profoundly attached to Christianity. Until around 14 years-old, I was an altar boy at my local orthodox church, and enjoyed contributing to the service. My parents weren't ones for deep conversations, which frustrated me because, as you can probably tell, I have a yearning to answer philosophical questions. I can't really remember a time when I wasn't like this; ever since I was capable of philosophical analysis, I remember taking great enjoyment in questioning things. I soon grew to realise that this isn't a quality that people appreciate, however. Most people don't spend their time questioning anything spiritually or philosophically. They'd rather have others tell them what to think because they tell themselves they're too busy. In actuality, they're too lazy or preoccupied to ask deeper questions. Whatever critical thinking remains is then crushed by peer group pressure.

One of the fondest memories of my paternal grandfather was when he told me about Heaven when I was about 6 or 7. This is my first recollection of having this described to me. My grandfather and I would spend hours having deep conversations, and this is one of my first memories of my passion for philosophy. The discussions that my grandfather and I had weren't sophisticated, but they helped me flex my young analytical mind and develop my Christian faith. Yet despite regular church attendance, and going to an Anglican Church school, by 16 years of age I slowly but surely started to move away from Christianity. The reasons for this are several: for one, I endured a lot of bullying until I was 14, and this shook my faith because God didn't answer my prayers. From about 6 to 10 years old, teachers took an intense disliking to me because I found school incredibly boring, plus it was easier to blame me for the bullying I went through. This is a quietly acknowledged problem where teachers worry more about their performance and the school's reputation than the wellbeing of children. We're a long way off fixing this, even today, because teachers and politicians don't want parents to demand reform, especially if state schooling loses public support as a result. Today bullying is generally framed as minority prejudice like racism[1] and sexuality.[2] Whenever I see racism framed in this fashion it makes me angry because I was a short and skinny Greek kid that endured bullying for years. Yet bullying is now being politically weaponised at the expense of children that still suffer in silence because they aren't part of a special victim class. A vivid early memory of mine is being told to go back to my own country - no one would have dared say anything like that to the black children that attended my school. This just goes to show that the powers that be don't give a damn about anything if it doesn't suit their political narrative.

What's more, when I tried to stand up for myself, I often only made things worse. In primary (elementary) school, the teachers took the side of bullies, using my reaction to justify their bias. As I got older, I'd try to associate with more popular kids, and behave in the same mean-spirited way as other pupils, but I hated the way this made me feel, and it only got me into more trouble with teachers. To top it off, I had bad acne when I was 13, which became another excuse to be singled out, leading to one of the darkest times of my youth. I would pray for God to make these struggles come to an end. When it felt like these prayers weren't answered this had a profound effect on my attitude to religion later in my life. The fact that I went to a church school certainly didn't help in this regard – Christianity didn't exactly improve the way fellow students and teachers treated me, which became another contradiction that drew me away from my childhood faith as I grew older.

Thanks to medication, and the weight training and karate I mentioned in the introduction, I began to overcome this social alienation. While things did get start to get better, the psychological effects of bullying stayed with me for years, which would affect my faith as my life progressed. It didn't help that teachers wrote me off academically by the time I was around 8, which led to classmate mockery. This left a lasting impression on my interest in academic study, but I now realise that one size fits all state schooling just didn't work for me. I didn't like learning by repetition, and even logical subjects like maths seemed pointless and meaningless when regimentally prescribed. I'm not a genius, but I certainly didn't become the failure that teachers expected. I'm a natural autodidact and critical thinker who just didn't respond to large classroom sizes, because they can't accommodate someone that has my kind of learning style.

I struggled to scratch my philosophical itch until my early twenties, when the internet emerged as a great resource for self-directed learning. I'd bring up questions to friends in school, and at other times in my youth, but all too often this was met with ridicule – so once again I learnt to downplay this side of my nature. I didn't develop an appreciation for reading until later in life because I associated this with the tedious education I had growing up. Besides, reading is a very time consuming and sedentary way to absorb information, hence the reason I supplement this with audio I can listen to when I'm doing other things like exercising at the gym or walking outside. It's also hard to know which books to read without a teacher directing you, which is yet another reason that the state education system is so stifling for personalised study. Today, self-directed online research is opening up a whole world of learning, and this helps establish a reading list far more efficiently than a library ever did. Libraries may be a good way to catalogue books, but very inefficient to browse, especially if you have no idea where to start. This is one reason why teachers in schools and lecturers in universities had a de facto monopoly on knowledge for so long.

Christianity undermined

At 16 I left school and went to college. I didn't really have a clue what I was going to do with my life, but it was during this time that I started learning guitar. The difference this made to my self-esteem was tremendous. Although I did attain a few GCSEs (high school qualifications in the UK), it was playing guitar that really taught me self-directed learning, and the satisfaction of personal achievement. I went on to do a higher national diploma in music in the mid to late 90s, but throughout my late teens I became increasingly exposed to people that undermined Christianity through mockery and derision. It wasn't particularly unusual for more devout Christians to be called 'bible bashers' when I was in high school - quite strange considering I went to a church school. To my shame, I remember succumbing to this form of mockery on more than one occasion, in an attempt to fit.

By the mid to late 90s mockery of Christianity was on the rise, and no longer being in a Christian school made it much more embarrassing to be associated with this faith. I remember that going to church, or having attended a Christian school, being met with mockery amongst my college friends. In one case, I recall it being described as weird. It felt like Christianity was being systematically undermined throughout the 90s, subtly enough to be undetectable to all but the most vigilant and dedicated Christian. I didn't really notice this at the time because the only thing I truly cared about was playing guitar and figuring out how to get female attention. I felt as though I had to find myself, and since God didn't appear to make life any easier for me in my youth, I slowly but surely distanced myself from my Christian upbringing.

Sunday shopping was introduced to the UK in 1994 - a major turning point for Britain's radical transformation into a secular society. By my early twenties I veered towards agnosticism – someone that wasn't really sure if God exists. My Christian upbringing wasn't robust enough to fight off more aggressive and intellectual criticisms that often centred on the Catholic Church, or the necessity for liberal reform in the Anglican Church. Strangely, the very year that England introduced Sunday shopping saw the first female priest[3] – another sign that Christianity was slowly but surely being undermined in British society.

As my early twenties continued, I began to search for a substitute for the Christian values I was raised in. Much of this came from popular culture and the media, which didn't lead to a balanced picture that I could use to form my own conclusions. It was Michael Moore and the BBC that became my most trusted sources, along with The Guardian newspaper. The internet was still growing as an information source, although it did allow me to pique my curiosity with searches for topics like 'Satanism'. I thus learnt of The Satanic Bible by Anton Szandor LaVey, and out of sheer curiosity I eventually purchased and read this book in an attempt to learn about such an unusual belief system. What I discovered was a lot of deeply selfish beliefs about humans being no better than animals - often no better than those that walk on all fours, and romantic notions of being your own god - free to live your life in any way you want. Despite claims that Satanism was unfairly maligned, the book was very open about morality being completely subjective. A whole chapter of the book is called "On the Choice of Human Sacrifice," and the book's author was very good at reframing such acts as personal choice or justifiable punishment.

Although I wasn't convinced that Satanism was the path for me, it was another contributing factor to feeling as though I should put my own needs first. Other than being surrounded by so many people that acted like this, the broader pendulum of secular society was pushing heavily in this direction. At the same time, sacrifice for the less fortunate has become the justification for cradle to grave state support – a so-called nanny state that provides a safety net for the less fortunate. In the United Kingdom, the National Health Service is particularly idolised in this regard. What this creates is a blatant contradiction within secular societies – on one hand human beings should put their own needs before anything else. On the other, human beings should be prepared to make great personal sacrifices for the greater good. By my mid-twenties I was immersed in this contradiction, where own personal happiness came first (if only for personal preservation against so many like-minded people), while also believing that high taxes were necessary to fund welfare and the NHS, and that government intervention in the economy was a necessary protection against corporate exploitation. My philosophical mind would not be able to sustain this contradiction between selfishness and selflessness indefinitely, and it was once I began to explore information online that I came across points of view that I'd never been exposed to before. Only then could I truly make an informed decision about where I stood. Yes, this came later on in my very early 30s, but so many experiences in my 20s led to this.

New atheism

Once I reached my late 20s in 2007, the internet was growing into a very interesting place. Not only were sites like Wikipedia becoming a fantastic way of cataloguing more information than you could ever dream of accessing without endless hours searching through bookshelves and countless pages of books, but YouTube was really starting to become a major phenomenon. Around this time, so-called new atheism became a massive online movement, resulting in a culture war with Bush era evangelical Christians. Quite honestly, I was in a place of my life where I'd just had enough of Christianity, drawing me towards new atheist YouTubers like ZOMGitsCriss, Peach, TheAmazingAtheist and ThunderFOOT. My Christian upbringing just didn't have the wherewithal to sustain the philosophical attacks of atheists, which weren't the most sophisticated, but without a strong understanding of both scripture and logical argumentation, Christians were being annihilated in a sea of mockery and strawman arguments. I thus became convinced that new atheists gave me the philosophical answers I was looking for, during a time when Christianity just didn't make any logical sense to me anymore.

The reason for the weakness in my faith was not purely down to past adverse experiences. Like Catholicism, the orthodox Christianity I was raised in focuses heavily on tradition. While traditions can be very good at preserving identity, they quickly crumble if they're the only basis for belief. If you don't even understand the philosophical basis for what you stand for, you'll have no way to defend your values from criticism. Some will weather criticism through pure faith, where the thought of living without your beliefs creates a crisis you'd rather not face. The most effective way to fight against criticism is certainly not to carelessly disregard traditions, however. Rather, the answer is a strong a strong philosophical understanding of your beliefs, so any criticisms are neutralised through reason. There are some traditions that should be jettisoned because they serve no basis other than to preserve corrupt institutions and practices. Other traditions make society safer and more prosperous for many generations to come, which necessitates some unchanging stability.

As a result of the gradual chipping away at Christianity in the western world, many Christians weren't prepared for the cultural attack that came from the new atheism[4] of the mid to late 2000s. Four pivotal intellectual figures in this movement became known as the four horsemen of the apocalypse. They were Sam Harris, Christopher Hitchens, Daniel Dennett, and of course Richard Dawkins – a huge influence on my step from agnosticism to atheism. Some people were already primed to embrace new atheism due to personal experiences that drew them away from their faith, and the angst of my youth is certainly an example of this. Many atheists talk about how terrible their Christian upbringing was, and how their faith was arbitrarily imposed on them. Others are victims of past abuse that hasn't been resolved psychologically, making them averse to any kind of authority whatsoever. What this leads to is a scorched earth mentality where people don't care who they hurt, as long as they can get what they want. Isn't this no better than Satanism? That is certainly a question worth asking, although I didn't make this connection until much later on in my journey, stemming beyond this book.

At first atheism seemed rational, and allowed me to replace religious unity with something else. While atheism is defined as an absence of religious belief, in practice atheists are very religious in their thinking. No they don't believe in God, but by the time I'd been making videos for about a year and-a-half, I could no longer ignore the fact that, overwhelmingly, atheists are zealously left-wing. If atheism was purely about absence of belief in a deity, singular or plural, then why is this pattern so consistent? Each and every atheist I've mentioned is left-wing politically, some more than others, but this would suggest that there's something else going on. I did come across atheists who were anarcho-capitalist, like Stefan Molyneux, or Objectivists like Ayn Rand, but compared to leftists, this was a small minority.

Anti-theism

I would later realise that it wasn't actually atheism that new atheists truly advocated, but virulent anti-theism, or *militant atheism*, where the world would be a much better place once religion became a thing of the past. I initially bought into this idea, but once I started realising how destructive left-wing ideology is, it soon became apparent that abolishing religion didn't make the world a better place at all. Communist countries of the 20th century were classified as state atheism, and yet these countries murdered more people in one century than any other. There's no doubt that a lot of suffering has occurred in the name of religion, but secular societies made bloodshed worse than ever. Was it therefore fair to blame all the problems of humanity on religious belief? Did religion really hold humanity back through superstition and tradition that prevented progress? In some ways, yes, but you'd have to blind not to notice that secular societies have their own unyielding beliefs - dogmas that cannot be questioned, and if you do, you'll pay a very heavy price – loss of friends, employment, even jail time.

Perhaps these claims seem hyperbolic. But it was important to use this chapter to lay the groundwork for what follows. I know what it feels like to grow up in an environment that makes you so sick of religion that you rebel against any kind of notion of God. I know what it's like to have your critical thinking beaten down so much that you feel resentful towards any structured education. I know what it's like to be alienated so much that you want to bring down any kind of authority in a fit of rebellious rage. I overcame that for one reason and one reason only; I have a relentless determination to question everything I come across. No I couldn't satisfy that itch when I was much younger, but as soon as I could, I broke though the conditioning all around me, whether it was social engineering of secularism, or indeed the experiences that made me feel bitter inside. Yes it took time, and yes I needed to go on a long journey to do it. But one thing it taught me was that religion is not necessarily a bad thing, and all religion is not necessarily about belief in God. Religion replaces material proof with faith. Sometimes this is a good thing when it teaches us that humans have moral limits, but faith can also lead to the justification of evil.

Equally, some people have so much faith in human institutions and laws that they treat them like deities. This is why secular societies or atheists can become fanatically dogmatic, even when God is removed from society, thanks to the widely held view in secular societies that morality is subjective. It's this claim of subjectivity that we must grasp if we're to understand why secular societies have failed on so many levels, which is what I'll be exploring in the chapter that follows.

Chapter 14: Immoral Relativism

Abandonment of Christianity is not a justification for immorality.

Atheists are generally very sympathetic to subjective interpretations of morality, where human beings get to decide what's right or wrong. Equally, they're much more likely to be politically left-wing. My experiences as an atheist confirmed this, as I was exposed to the commentary and writings of other atheists I came across. A major reason for this is communist propaganda. Chapter 2 of The Communist Manifesto states in no uncertain terms that:

> *There are, besides, eternal truths, such as Freedom, Justice, etc., that are common to all states of society. But Communism abolishes eternal truths, it abolishes all religion, and all morality, instead of constituting them on a new basis; it therefore acts in contradiction to all past historical experience.*[1]

Not only does this passage unequivocally explain that the goal of communism is to abolish religion, it states that communism abolishes morality and "eternal truths", which is basically another way to describe values that exist outside of subjective opinion and experience – sometimes referred to as *objective truth*. It's clear, then, that the popularity of communism since its inception has played no small part in making left-wing ideology extremely relative – relative being another word that philosophers use for subjective.

When I began to realise how morally relativistic atheists are, I was taken aback given that many of the arguments Christians use against atheists revolve around the inhumanity of atheist regimes and movements in history, to which atheists dismiss with counter claims about Hitler's alleged Christianity or how religion is responsible for so much suffering in the world, like the Crusades and Inquisition. As I explained in the previous chapter, while religion can loosely be blamed for suffering at different times and places, nothing compares to the death toll of secular and atheist political movements in the 20th century – such brutality in one century has never been recorded before, least of all in such an inhumane fashion.

What's surprising is how quickly people dismiss strongly defined morality as soon as God is taken out of the equation. This poses the question of how you can possibly define what's right and wrong without a divine entity that sets out moral laws and punishes wrongdoing. Technically it isn't logically necessary to define morality through God, although it must be admitted that the task becomes much easier. The danger of religion being the sole basis for morality is that people are only being decent because they fear punishment from a deity. Conversely, behaving decently as an atheist is extremely difficult when you think you can get away with something that's immoral. A religious person generally believes they'll suffer the consequences of their actions when they die (even if this involves something akin to being reincarnated into a lesser form), and it certainly takes a lot of moral fibre to avoid temptation when you don't believe in divine retribution.

My exposure to atheism progressively made me realise that morality required objective standards. By 2008 I'd decided I was comfortable calling myself an atheist, but by 2012 I made it clear in a video called Militant Atheism that I wasn't interested in the anti-theistic approach to non-belief in God found in the new atheist movement. As someone attracted to the philosophy of natural rights, particularly as outlined by John Locke, I began to realise that this is the best description for how morality should work. At first it was difficult to explain how this works because I felt as though the best way to approach it was appealing to the natural empathy found in the animal kingdom. The more brutal the environment, the less likely it is that this empathy would exist, but there is absolutely no denying that life has a propensity towards kindness and compassion under certain conditions. Birds pair bond for life and nurture their young until they're old enough to leave the nest. Wolves are as loyal to their pack members as any human family unit. You could counter this with examples like lions killing cubs of a rival male as soon as they replace him in the pride, or the general dog eat dog world of predators and prey, but there's an undeniable empathy found in nature as well.

Such empathy is what makes it possible to define objective standards of morality. It would be absurd to suggest that the near universal repulsion towards murder, rape and theft among human societies is somehow learnt, because it's so prevalent among different cultures. It's certainly arguable that being raised in a harsh and difficult environment makes us less empathetic, but this doesn't mean that we shouldn't aspire towards respect for one another. How this could work is one thing, but many people completely reject any attempt to do this pragmatically, or indeed consistently, and what we've learnt since the surge in secular or atheistic philosophy, is that human beings are prone to moral relativism without religion.

Existential crisis of the Enlightenment

18th century Europe saw the beginning of an era that became known as the Enlightenment. Reason became the bedrock of this movement, where tradition, superstition and religion were supposed to make way for a new dawn of science and secularism. Gradually belief in God whittled away, as Christianity lost influence in European countries and colonies. The American Revolution separated the church and state, the French Revolution erased Christianity from society, and in the 20th century the Russian Revolution led to state atheism being the official position of the USSR, in accompaniment with many subsequent communist regimes that were equally hostile to religion. Developments in science caused many people to doubt the existence of God, and ever more intellectual debates further contributed to the decline of religion. Did this, however, lead to the enlightenment that many hoped for? Western society paid a heavy price for the erosion of Christianity, even though organised religion, particularly the Catholic Church, contributed to repression in certain times and places. Key to understanding this conundrum is distinguishing belief in God from organised religion.

The Catholic Church wielded so much power in Europe during the Middle Ages that it was inevitable people would react against the corruption this caused. Christians themselves revolted against the Catholic Church during the reformation, alluding to concerns like the unscriptural nature of paying indulgences or preventing Christians from reading the Bible in their own language. Though many believed that the abandonment of Christianity would create a better world, a growing cultural emptiness came to the fore. Thus, as people grew to believe that only a material world exists, and there is no afterlife or God to confine morality, an existential crisis emerged.

A key figure of this crisis was the German philosopher, Friedrich Wilhelm Nietzsche, who is known for proclaiming that "God is dead" in his 1882 publication, The Gay Science. Section 125 of this book included the parable of the madman. Here Nietzsche writes:

> *God is dead. God remains dead. And we have killed him. How shall we comfort ourselves, the murderers of all murderers? What was holiest and mightiest of all that the world has yet owned has bled to*

death under our knives: who will wipe this blood off us? What water is there for us to clean ourselves? What festivals of atonement, what sacred games shall we have to invent? Is not the greatness of this deed too great for us? Must we ourselves not become gods simply to appear worthy of it?[2]

Nietzsche is not proclaiming that he himself believed in God, or indeed that there is a God that can literally be killed, if such a thing were possible. Rather, he highlights that as belief in God disappeared, it coincided with the destruction of Christianity, and the God represented by this religion. Just as apparent in the passage is that Nietzsche was filled with a sense of apprehension entwined with excitement about what will become of humanity without belief in God.

Nietzsche's solution is the Übermensch,[3] a German word that can be translated into English as "Overman", "Superhuman", "Hyperman", "Hyperhuman" and other variations that can probably best be understood by the translation of "Superman". The latter conjures up an image of a superhero capable of inhuman physical feats, a description close to what Nietzsche envisaged. To the same extent, however, Neitzsche wasn't talking about a selfless superhero that would go to any lengths to protect the downtrodden, like the comic book character by the same name. The Übermensch represents the potential for those capable of evolving to the next level of humanity. To achieve this, humanity would need to go beyond conventional morality, especially what he called the '"slave morality" of Christianity:

The Jews—a people "born for slavery," as Tacitus and the whole ancient world say of them; "the chosen people among the nations," as they themselves say and believe—the Jews performed the miracle of the inversion of valuations, by means of which life on earth obtained a new and dangerous charm for a couple of millenniums. Their prophets fused into one the expressions "rich," "godless," "wicked," "violent," "sensual," and for the first time coined the word "world" as a term of reproach. In this inversion of valuations (in which is also included the use of the word "poor" as synonymous with "saint" and "friend") the significance of the Jewish people is to be found; it is with THEM that the SLAVE-INSURRECTION IN MORALS commences.[4]

What he meant by this was that Christianity was an offshoot of Jewish people learning to live with persecution, be it slavery in Egypt or being exiled at various times and places in history. Thus Nietzsche argued that Jewish morality was shaped by elevating the underdog, just as it states in Matthew 5:5 of the bible when it says "Blessed are the meek: for they shall inherit the earth." By the same token, Jews are the chosen people that have a special place in creation, despite the struggles of their history.

He outlined this perspective in another of his books called Beyond Good and Evil, 4 years after The Gay Science, where he described the polar opposite to slave morality as *master morality.* Whereas slave morality belonged to the weak and downtrodden that invented moral values that chastised those that persecuted others, master morality was for those strong enough to rule over others. This is defined by the conquerors of history – the Romans, Ottomans, Vikings, Mongols, and many other civilisations powerful enough to carve empires out of the world, at the expense of all they defeated.

The potential to become Übermensch was described by Nietzsche as the will to power – through pure will human beings could evolve beyond the limits of current humanity, and in the process serve as an example - a symbol - of what others can become. The word *Untermenschen* was used to describe deviant and inferior types in the Gay Science, while Übermensch was coined in a publication Nietzsche released a year later in 1883, called Thus Spoke Zarathustra.[5] There is some controversy regarding the will to power given that Nietzsche's beloved sister, Elisabeth, published a book in 1910 from the remnants of notes Nietzsche left behind after his death, literally titled The Will to Power.[6] However, when analysing Nietzsche's full body of work, it's clear that the will to power was certainly close to Nietzsche's philosophy as a whole. Much of the controversy revolves around the fact that the Nazis later appropriated his ideas for their propaganda, resulting in Nietzsche's admirers doing all they can to downplay the elitist tone of his work. Nietzsche's sister collaborated with this effort, hence the reason that the notes she compiled from his works are dismissed.

The counter-enlightenment

Nietzsche had a major influence on a particular intellectual movement that went against the founding principles of the Enlightenment. Various names have been given to this movement, from *counter-enlightenment* to *anti-enlightenment*, but names are far less important than intent. The chaos of the French Revolution that led to the rise of Napoleon, who humiliated Germany by successfully conquering much of its western territory, was a significant influence on reactionary German thinkers. Since the Enlightenment was driven by reason above tradition, particularly as it relates to monarchy and highborn aristocracy, new German thinkers began to attack the basis of this movement. This explains why Nietzsche was so besotted with the idea of an Übermensch, who was essentially a kind of post-enlightenment figure that preserved aristocracy. Numerous thinkers have built on what came before them, and in Nietzsche's case he was very inspired by Immanuel Kant and Arthur Schopenhauer.

Immanuel Kant[7] was a man deeply troubled by the way science increasingly encroached on any possibility of a world beyond the material. His reaction was a philosophy generically categorised as *German Idealism*. Kant's *transcendental* version of this philosophy was based on different forms that knowledge takes. Fundamentally, knowledge is broken up into rational or empirical, the former based on understanding that we already have about the world. Pure logic allows us to come to rational conclusions without any kind of further investigation, like all birds have wings, or all cars have wheels. Conversely, empirical knowledge requires further investigation, just as we see with scientific experimentation. Rational knowledge is *analytical* in nature, while empirical knowledge is sometimes referred to as *synthetic*. You can break this down further with *a priori* or *deductive* knowledge being an analytical form of understanding, and *a posteriori* or *inductive* knowledge being synthetic. All these terms are used in various times and places, but Kant broke the mould by coining *synthetic a priori* knowledge, which seems odd when there is usually only a distinction between logical and experiential knowledge.

Rational knowledge typically requires some sort of past experience of the world, even if taken indirectly from observations of others. You can make rational statements about the world without testing your theories empirically. Returning to the example of birds to demonstrate how this works, even if you've only ever seen a picture of a bird in a book, the conclusion that birds have wings is still drawn from human experience observing birds. Kant went further by using the synthetic a priori category to relate to concepts like mathematics that don't require any experiences of the world because they're purely logical concepts. He used this postulation as a stepping stone for his ultimate conclusion that we can only truly understand the *phenomenal realm* of reality based on experience, while the *noumenal realm* will always be unknowable because it's completely independent of experience. Thus while pure reason allows us to understand phenomena, the same cannot be said for noumena.

It's probably not hard to see what Kant did once we bypass his philosophical jargon; he was obviously very concerned about the cultural effects of the Enlightenment encroaching on religion, though Kant fell short of alleviating his concern. For one, mathematics is not independent of experience because quantities are a basic concept of material reality, thus meaning that mathematics is not evidence of some sort of unknowable noumenal realm. Whether there is indeed an area beyond the scope of pure reason is another matter, and it's certainly arguable that Kant was motivated by the noble intention of slowing down the atomisation of existence to such an extent that all we're reduced to is material matter. However, Kant opened the floodgates for the complete opposite; an even more vicious attack on the nature of knowledge, morphing into a form of relativism that attacks not only morality, but truth. This is called epistemological relativism, but be under no illusion that this is nothing new. As far back as Ancient Greece there were those who questioned that anything existed outside of our minds, known as *solipsism*.

It gets worse when we elaborate on Arthur Schopenhauer's own contribution to anti-enlightenment thinking. So pessimistic was his perspective on life that his writings are typically put under the philosophical category of *pessimism*. In an essay, he once wrote:

> *Human life must be some kind of mistake. The truth of this will be sufficiently obvious if we only remember that man is a compound of needs and necessities hard to satisfy; and that even when they are satisfied, all he obtains is a state of painlessness, where nothing remains to him but abandonment to boredom. This is direct proof that existence has no real value in itself; for what is boredom but the feeling of the emptiness of life? If life—the craving for which is the very essence of our being—were possessed of any positive intrinsic value, there would be no such thing as boredom at all: mere existence would satisfy us in itself, and we should want for nothing.*[8]

Schopenhauer is also considered an *antinatalist* because he believed that life was such an endless state of suffering that it's fruitless to bring children into the world. He demonstrated this deep sense of pessimism when he wrote:

If children were brought into the world by an act of pure reason alone, would the human race continue to exist? Would not a man rather have so much sympathy with the coming generation as to spare it the burden of existence, or at any rate not take it upon himself to impose that burden upon it in cold blood?[9]

These three thinkers; Kant, Schopenhauer and Nietzsche, embody the bleakness of a godless world that came out of the Enlightenment. Kant wanted to preserve God by making it impossible for science to encroach on religion, but opened the door to solipsism. Schopenhauer represents the despair of living with no purpose without God, and Nietzsche tried to turn that despair into a bold vision of man as God, instead reminding us that there's a monster within mankind that Nazis and Communists demonstrated in terrifying fashion.

Existentialism

Although Napoleon's emergence out of the French revolution fuelled reactionary thinkers behind German Idealism, anti-enlightenment momentum would pivot back to France during the nineteenth century with a movement known as *Existentialism*. Nietzsche was perhaps the first existentialist, a statement that some would contest. However, this applies because Nietzsche tried to provide an answer to the existential angst of godlessness - an existential crisis often called *nihilism*. Nihilists are prone to stating that there is no meaning in life – no objective morality or indeed any way to ascertain real truth. Schopenhauer argued for the pointlessness and boredom of existence by concluding that human will is what helps us overcome nihilism, if only for a brief period of time that itself becomes pointless. This he talked about this in his book, The World as Will and Representation.[10] Pure human will as a mechanism of actualisation is one obvious influence on Nietzsche, which he expanded on with his concept of the will to power.

Equally, the French existentialists expanded on German Idealism, as this reaction to the Enlightenment came full circle. Jean-Paul Sartre[11] was particularly instrumental in this regard. He argued for a total surrender to the self, where it would be considered *bad faith* to consciously attempt to deny who you are. What this meant for Sartre was to live without fear of shame, despair, anguish, or any emotions that suppress your inner nature.

Only then will we experience the kind of idealistic freedom that Sartre believed possible. In some sense this may seem liberating, but Sartre was actually very pessimistic about human nature. He basically sought to reconcile this through a pure surrender to the ego, where any kind of moral restraint was a form of psychological denial.

Upon closer examination of what Sartre was trying to convey with his convoluted writing style, he was obviously motivated by the desire to suppress the human conscience by cultivating a dominant ego. You could quite easily call this narcissism, but at the same time Sartre didn't believe individuals should be bound to one another through love, or indeed any other social convention that might result in bad faith. If we attempt to attach certain conditions to our relationships, Sartre argued that you turned an individual into an object, or what he called an 'in-itself'. Likewise, if we attempt to reciprocate these conditions, we do this to ourselves. Sartre's open relationship with fellow existentialist philosopher, Simone de Beauvoir, is testament to this way of thinking. In reality, Sartre was motivated more by his own desire to feed his sexual desires than he was for the feelings of others, but in Beauvoir he found a like-minded lover.

The most important takeaway from this chapter is that the Enlightenment created an existential crisis that could not be resolved philosophically. Not only were moral restraints completely broken down by the erosion of religion and tradition, creating chaos in the centuries that followed, but the very concept of truth itself was virulently attacked. In the next chapter, we will see how this destabilised the modern world.

Chapter 15: The Rise of Postmodernism

Postmodernism is the result of a dying society.

In the previous two chapters I explained how atheism spawned moral relativism. As well as this, it led to *epistemological relativism*, where truth itself is rendered completely subjective and unknowable. The reaction against this secular ideology sought to reimagine former aristocratic and monarchical traditions, like Nietzsche's will to power, and some, like Kant, wanted to preserve religion by making philosophical arguments against pure reason. The Enlightenment movement behind this reaction is sometimes referred to as *The Age of Reason*, owing to the fact that this era was centred on using reason to guide humanity into a new age. Alas, this was a fleeting success at best. What people soon began to realise is that a world without God is a world without restraint, as the worst atrocities of humanity came to pass under the tyrannical French Revolution, with communism emerging later. Secularism did not create a utopian age of reason at all, with the possible exception of the United States, which had far more respect for natural rights and religious freedom (the latter being enshrined in the first amendment of the 1789 United States Bill of Rights).

In this chapter I'm going to address the culmination of relativism – *postmodernism*. An utterly nonsensical ideology that its adherent refuse to consider a movement (since any law of identity or form is absolutely prohibited), it's foundationally an attack on any basis for objective truth. When I first covered postmodernism back in 2011, I didn't mention art. Not until 2017 did I eventually get round to this aspect of postmodernism because in the earlier stages of my YouTube channel I didn't speak about the arts and entertainment. I include it here because it's much easier to understand postmodernism if you put art alongside the philosophical underpinnings of this movement (and yes – it is a movement!). It was modernism, however, that laid the foundation for the rise of postmodernism.

By the 20th century, intellectual solipsism went from bad to worse. Erosion of Christianity created a vacuum that caused two world wars, but it didn't stop there. The late 19th century was when modernism began to take hold, affecting every aspect of society, sometimes for the better, all too often for the worse. When we look back through history, we see a consistent pattern in this regard – culture acts like a barometer in society, where endeavours like art, philosophy, music, and drama mould the politics of the age. It's for this reason that the late Andrew Breitbart once said that "politics is downstream from culture." What this implies is that culture will eventually translate into politics, hence the reason Marxism became fixated on culture after World War One – aka cultural Marxism covered in chapter 10. Equally, culture is a natural by-product of society, so to what extent politics shapes culture is an interesting question to ask. Thus culture is probably the strongest driving force of society, though we cannot underestimate the impact that economics has on its formation.

With this in mind, modernism[1] is considered a cultural reaction to industrialisation in the western world, also known as the *industrial revolution*. One consequence of this period was more people moving from the countryside into cities, as working the land was replaced with factory employment. Society then began to modernise when mass manufacturing drove down the costs of goods, through a process known as *economies of scale*. A simple description of this process is that when items are produced on a mass scale, this reduces costs for the consumer. Items become less unique due to generic parts and features, but a positive trade-off is that modern production techniques, with materials like plastic or metal, can compensate for the unique production of traditional craftsmen like carpenters and blacksmiths.

The industrial revolution was not all smooth sailing, however. In Great Britain, where the industrial revolution was pioneered in the 17th century with the modernisation of agricultural, followed by textile, industries, people endured harsh factory working conditions and unsanitary living caused by a rapid rise in urban living, because this was where most employment arose. Based on the key indicator of life expectancy,[2] this change brought little to no improvement for quality of life until around the middle of the 19th century, at which point average life expectancy rose rapidly from around 40 years old to the ripe old ages we see today. Some considerations must be taken into account in this regard; Marxist theory exaggerates the struggle for ordinary people during this time in history because it suits the narrative of cruel and wicked bourgeois factory owners oppressing the working class. As such, people should be conscious of life expectancy prior to the industrial revolution. In medieval Europe, the average life expectancy was around 30,[3] so 40 is certainly an improvement. In some quarters it's suggested that people were forced to leave the countryside when industrialisation reduced agricultural employment, but the idea that people were somehow better off working the land is not a reflection of historical reality, as feudal peasant life demonstrates.

Furthermore, evidence clearly shows that industrialisation was the turning point that drove society towards modernity, where people live longer and enjoy the kind of luxuries that even royalty didn't have hundreds of years ago.

Modern art

There was a price for this improvement, though. Culture became increasingly atomised in a secular and industrialised world. As society focused more on the individual, this stripped away any collective identity to such an extent that people were left feeling nihilistic, transferring to modernist culture. Art began to reflect this cultural transformation, too, although there were some interesting early developments that cannot be overlooked. Innovative techniques inspired a new form of art of French origin – Impressionism, Claude Monet[4] being a trendsetter of this movement, and indeed modernism as a whole. Rather than clear outlines found in previous art, Monet gave a dreamlike impression within his paintings by making an image appear out of focus, like squinting your eyes as you look ahead. And yet it was still possible to see what impression Monet was portraying, in a beautiful marriage between traditional technique and innovation. Monet's style was so unique that it's easily recognisable, whether it's the blotted outlines in Woman in a Garden, or the misty effect of Impression, Sunrise, though the continued erosion of form in his later paintings is evidence of the gradual destruction of artistic form as time went by.

Historically art built on prior technique that perpetuated new heights of realism. Renaissance era art was a milestone in this effort, reflecting a golden era of unparalleled realism and definition, whether it was Michael Angelo's Sistine Chapel ceiling or Raphael's remarkable clarity of form. All this began to change in the 19th century, amidst rapid cultural changes brought on by enlightenment thinking and industrialisation. Like oh-so many enlightenment movements, modernism incessantly rebelled against established norms, as the focus became purely relative and subjective interpretation. No longer were artists interested in developing form. Instead they conformed to the erosion of tradition, in a world moving away from God. If we consider the art of Pablo Picasso,[5] a dyed-in the-wool leftist, each year of his life coincided with further antagonism against structure. His art reflected a deep sense of melancholy, where faces stared aimlessly, as though longingly yearning to replace the emptiness in their lives. Edges in his paintings grew harsher as time passed, until they became little more than barely distinguishable abstract shapes.

Deconstruction is perhaps the most accurate term that describes this breakdown in form and identity. To construct obviously coincides with the building or creation of form. Thus deconstruction involves actively breaking form down until it's merely a sum of its parts, like cogs in a machine. For example, if you break a car apart, there's still the hint of a car, but unless the car is in one piece, it cannot operate as a car at all, let alone be called a car. Hence when taken to its logical conclusion, deconstruction represents a distinct lack of anything concrete and definable.

What we notice when we look closer at modernism is that both enlightenment and counter-enlightenment thinking contributed to deconstruction in their own way. It's certainly arguable that the likes of Nietzsche was completely opposed to Rousseau's vision of the world, but each side of the enlightenment paradigm still wanted to set the old aside and replace it with the new, making deconstruction a synthesis of these two worldviews. Initially counter-enlightenment culture was enmeshed with a movement known as Romanticism,[6] which sought to elevate the human spirit to new heights. In particular we can see this in Eugène Delacroix's famous 1830 painting, Liberty Leading the People, which romanticised the French revolution. But by the 20th century, modernism began to erode any kind of spirit of meaning and purpose in culture. Modernism had a sense of industrialisation about it, as though the artist was attempting to portray the mechanical atomisation of modern society. Early 20th century pieces like Picasso's 1910 Portrait of Daniel-Henry Kahnweiler is one such example, though there are numerous others, such as Jean Metzinger's En Canot. Both these pieces became part of a subgenre of modern art known as Cubism, an aesthetically ugly way to depict form by making it appear blocky and unnaturally proportioned. Guernica, Picasso's 1937 painting, is another example of this genre that highlights his leftist credentials, given that it was a protest piece against fascism.

Although Cubism marked a notable decline in the respect for artistic form, subjectivity was relentlessly pursued by many other modern artists. Fountain[7] by Marcel Duchamp is a key point where modernism began to morph into utter absurdity and degeneracy. A literal urinal with its orientation altered, R.Mutt written on its side, the piece was really nothing more than an attempt to open the floodgates for a total erasure of objective artistic standards. Completed and entered by Duchamp into an exhibition in 1917, held by the Society of Independent Artists, the original has now been lost. Nonetheless it served the purpose of further subverting a distinction between 'high' and 'low' art, in a desperate bid to preserve artistic beauty. Alas this failed, as Fountain paved the way for what would subsequently come to pass. I'm not going to dwell much more on art in this chapter because by the time we get to monstrosities like Tracy Emin's My Bed,[8] where rubbish is strewn around a bed (including condoms and underwear with menstrual blood) that the 'creator' remained in for several days during a depressive episode, it's obvious that objective standards of form in art have been completely erased. Perhaps Chris Ofili's 1996 piece, The Holy Virgin Mary,[9][10] epitomises just how far art has fallen since the Renaissance. Known for using elephant's dung in his work, this particular piece was surrounded by images from 'blaxploitation' movies. It also features close-ups of female genitalia cut from pornographic magazines, shaped into images akin to cherubim and seraphim. The Virgin Mary herself is depicted as black, further adding to the subversive nature of the piece. This person went on to win the Turner Prize two years later in 1998, with No Woman, No Cry.[11]

Enter postmodernism

The primary consequence of modernism is that it set the scene for the world we now live in. Consider what modernism started in relation to deconstructing form and identity in culture. This theme dominates today's culture, along with the destruction of any kind of artistic meaning. For the latter, an objective storyline that plays to traditional and successful tropes simply isn't allowed, as people perpetually criticise anything that doesn't reflect pessimism and rebellion against beauty. Meaning must now be interpreted by a description that's provided, or left entirely for subjective interpretation. If I showed you a picture of a landscape, you would immediately know what this portrays because it relates to what you know about the world. But when you're shown a postmodern painting of formless colours, you cannot interpret this in any objective way because it lacks clarity. Aristotle, the ancient Greek philosopher, set out why this is the case with his law of identity.[12] He posited that identity is in the subject itself. Therefore if we call a flower a car, it doesn't suddenly become a car. It's still a flower because it has certain qualities that go beyond language and interpretation. Aristotle used A is A to explain this basic axiom that we take for granted. Without it there would be no way to establish simple rules that we rely on to navigate the world. No matter what name or interpretation we make, there are certain objective qualities in the world that transcend what we 'think' or 'believe'.

Plato, Aristotle's teacher, did not think identity worked this way. He believed that the world we perceived through our senses is inaccurate. Instead, a perfect metaphysical realm embodies true form, and this requires special knowledge and understanding to attain.[13] This is a kind of mystical thinking that Plato is often attributed with, underpinning postmodernism, wherein there is no perceivable truth because our senses are flawed, and since our senses are flawed, so is our perception of reality. Once this is embraced, you're subsequently expected to accept a new way to traverse reality that fits a certain worldview. Before we arrive at this point, postmodernists deconstruct everything we know until all we're left with is hopelessness, at which point we turn to modern day mystics that tell us what to do and think, just like Plato's Philosopher Kings that I visited in chapter one. Plato argued that these benevolent dictators, owing to the fact they have the ability to transcend the limits of human perception, have the right to direct everything in our lives - for the benefit of society, of course! Wherever you find this kind of attack on truth, you're inevitably dealing with a form of cult brainwashing, and this only works once your sense of self is completely deconstructed - the true purpose of postmodern ideology!

The union of Marxism and postmodernism

Let's now revisit something I covered in chapter 10 that ties directly into this indoctrination – cultural Marxist critical theory. Recall that this centres on criticism of culture through a Marxist lens. We must grasp that we're no longer dealing with the classical or economic Marxism that Karl Marx developed. Postmodernism is really the marriage of neo-Marxian ideology with epistemological relativism. Some argue that Marx had a 'scientific' way of looking at society and economics that isn't compatible with epistemological relativism, but the outright failure of his theories demonstrates no empirical basis for this claim. It's worth pointing this out because classical Marxists will occasionally express opposition to postmodernism, but this doesn't change the fact that neo-Marxists have moved on from Marx's theories, morphing his ideas into the ideological hybrid we see today.

The transition from modern to postmodern culture is widely speculated to be around the mid to late 20th century, but when you consider Duchamp's Fountain, this obviously started much sooner, although people like Tracy Emin and Chris Ofili are really postmodern artists that reject any kind of label - precisely what postmodernism aims to achieve. That said, it wasn't until the 1980s and 90s that 'postmodern' became mainstream vernacular, and the 90s is certainly a time when postmodernism truly started penetrating more than the art scene. It's during this period that we can really start to see that critical theory is designed to spread festering pessimism that makes you hate the society you live in. What began with the deconstruction of form and identity with modernism was thus completed with the spread of postmodern pessimism.

Cultural Marxism therefore found a home in postmodernism, creating a union called *intersectionality*. Rather than disparate leftist movements that attack different aspects of the same foe, postmodernism brings them together in one giant hammer that constantly strikes against the pillars of society. The same can be said for literary theory that critical theory spawned, which further morphed into criticism of all aspects of culture, from movies and theatre, to novels and comics. What we see today is the Frankenstein's monster that was born from postmodernism, with a comic book that changes Thor to a female character who embodies feminist theory, movies like Fight Club that conform to Herbert Marcuse's one-dimensional man, or bands like Nirvana that spread utter pessimism and hatred of any disciplined form and structure in music.

Another important layer in understanding postmodernism is that the 20th century saw many philosophers like Jean-Paul Sartre move increasingly towards Marxist dialectic, contributing of the marriage of relativism and Marxism into postmodernism. In this case, Sartre moved away from the heavily egoistic individualism he espoused with his 1943 book, Being and Nothingness,[14] where the concept of 'bad faith' was first introduced, as covered in the last chapter. By 1960 he abandoned his purely egoistic stance and released Critique of Dialectical Reason, marrying Marxism with psychoanalysis by incorporating individual responsibility into class theory. This borrowed from the theories of the psychoanalyst, Sigmund Freud, much like critical theory as a whole.

Simone de Beauvoir,[15] Sartre's life partner that shared a polyamorous relationship with him, also moved in the same direction, initially considered an existentialist as well. She was central to the incorporation of feminist theory into postmodernism, becoming a catalyst for the postmodern attack on sexual dimorphism in human biology. Not only did this incorporate feminist theory, but wider gender ideology that spurred the formation of the gay movement in the 1970s and 80s. It was her 1949 book, The Second

Sex, which really saw further convergence in this regard, as feminism and the gay movement systematically came together under the umbrella of postmodernism.

Michel Foucalt[16] was another significant basis of the transition from modern to postmodern thought. Again I remind people that you'll struggle to find anyone that actively calls themselves a postmodernist, since this ideology vehemently opposes labels for all but the subject of criticism. It's not surprising, then, that Foucalt is known for post-structural theories that associate all aspects of identity to language and culture. Known as post-structuralism, this explains why so many leftists parrot claims about identity being a social construct, as though biology has no meaningful part to play in who we are, especially in relation to sex or race. Foucalt was also known for deconstructing society until all that's left are aspects of knowledge and power that marginalised groups must overcome. Consequently, Plato's Philosopher King has been adapted for the modern age, as individuals become nothing but cogs in a collective machine that are guided by political leaders. As we're quite literally brainwashed into rejecting all individuality, we turn into automatons of collective consciousness that chant slogans and hold placards at rallies. Any divergence from conformity is fiercely attacked, and any difference of opinion is met with merciless ostracisation.

To truly realise how absurd these modern 'philosopher kings' have made today's culture, we can turn to French postmodern feminist, Luce Iragaray, who made a statement about Einstein's $E=mc^2$ formula in her 1987 book, Parler n'est jamais neuter:

> *Is $E=mc^2$ a sexed equation? Perhaps it is. Let us make the hypothesis that it is insofar as it privileges the speed of light over other speeds that are vitally necessary to us. What seems to me to indicate the possible sexed nature of the equation is not directly its uses by nuclear weapons, rather it is having privileged what goes the fastest.*

The fact that Luce Iragaray even questioned the sexist nature of a completely objective mathematical equation should be a wake-up call for anyone still on the fence about the crippling influence of postmodern ideology. Postmodernism filters everything in our lives through the lens of Marxist class consciousness and relativism, leaving nowhere to turn without observing the debilitating effects of an ideological mind virus that's impossible to avoid. Instead of truth we get ideological brainwashing that deconstructs knowledge and perception, to the extent that we're no better than robots taking instructions from operators. Only by escaping this relativist programming can we escape their grip, and bring sanity to the world.

Chapter 16: Fascism is a Form of Socialism

Fascism and communism are two sides of the same coin.

Fascism has become the ubiquitous bogeyman of the Left. Even for the politically illiterate, they're still probably aware that fascism is a terrible ideology, and by extension, they believe that Nazism is the worst of all evils. Much of this is due to state education focusing heavily on the history of World War Two, and the role the Nazis had in its events, not least the Holocaust, but we've already looked at the horrendous death toll for Communism in the 20th century, which dwarfs all fascist regimes combined. Apologists will deny and downplay communist atrocities, albeit Nazism is an ideology that died in its infancy, having far less time to do as much damage as communism, if it ever would have reached such scales of inhumanity. Alas something happened in the 20th century that made communism a practically infallible ideology, while fascism was seen as the worst of all evils, even though people who typically believe this are generally moral relativists.

You cannot have your cake and eat it, however, so if morality is indeed relative, it's impossible to truly criticise fascism in any moral sense - far too rational a conclusion for the kind of people who fixate on fascism as basically the worst ideology in history. Moreover, there are some home truths about Nazism, and indeed fascism as the umbrella ideology, that people refuse to accept, but until they do, there really is no way to avoid making the same mistakes of the past. Communism and fascism are both left-wing ideologies, and though they differ in some areas, not to mention their conflicts in history, this doesn't change the fact that both of these ideologies were born out of socialism. Concluding this leads to cries of protest from both 'far left' and 'far right' proponents, who both feel that they're complete opposite to one another. Nothing could be further from the truth, and no, this is not merely something to do with horseshoe theory, where the far ends of a spectrum come together like a horseshoe. For the purpose of this chapter, I will not be tackling the political spectrum, however, because this is an entirely separate issue. Rather, I will stick to the similarities between communism and fascism, demonstrating how the biggest political con since World War Two was convincing the masses that these ideologies are opposites.

Socialism defined

Socialism has become so specific on one hand, and so ambiguous on the other, that it's impossible for its diehard adherents to accept any criticism of their ideology. Socialism is specific in the sense that, unless it's in line with communist theory, it will never be accepted by people generally considered far-left. As a consequence of this behaviour, socialism is so ambiguous that it's fallen a long way from the original definition set out in its earliest years. Fundamentally, socialism was originally coined to describe an attempt to socialise society into a collective endeavour. It's widely accepted that the etymology of socialism stems from the French word *socialisme*.[1] French philosophy and political economist, Pierre Leroux,[2] is believed to be the originator of the word, introduced in 1834 via his essay titled "Individualism and Socialism". Some credit Robert Owen as among the first to attempt to create a socialist society based on communes and cooperative ideals, in the 1800s. Nonetheless, Leroux still appears to be the earliest person to use this term.

Already we can see that socialism certainly isn't inherently defined by communism at all. The ideology is actually fundamentally based on group cooperation, as opposed to individual freedom. It may seem like a false dichotomy to distinguish between groups and individuals in such terms, but socialism is notorious for placing little to no consideration on individual rights. Socialism is equally notorious for shortcomings that make it impossible to imagine living without state intervention into every aspect of our lives, a problem recognised as far back as 1850, when French classical liberal philosopher, Frédéric Bastiat, wrote in his most famous work, The Law, that:

> *Socialism, like the ancient ideas from which it springs, confuses the distinction between government and society. As a result of this, every time we object to a thing being done by government, the socialists conclude that we object to its being done at all. We disapprove of state education. Then the socialists say that we are opposed to any education. We object to a state religion. Then the socialists say that we want no religion at all. We object to a state-enforced equality. Then they say that we are against equality. And so on, and so on. It is as if the socialists were to accuse us of not wanting persons to eat because we do not want the state to raise grain. I do not dispute their right to invent social combinations, to*

advertise them, to advocate them, and to try them upon themselves, at their own expense and risk. But I do dispute their right to impose these plans upon us by law – by force – and to compel us to pay for them with our taxes.

And so we see the key problem with those advocating socialism; a refusal to accept that anything can be done without collective effort, while at the same time refusing to see anything other than a very specific collective effort as socialism. Clearly this is contradictory, but more so, it's an intricate linguistic trick that makes it impossible for individuals to live outside of socialist ideology. This translates to never ending state intervention into our lives that's not only deeply intrusive, but extremely dangerous. The result is a dictatorship that gradually consumes society until it becomes all-encompassing, or *totalitarian*, a term for any ideology that places no limit to how far it encroaches on the life of the citizen.

Let us now return to communism and fascism. Both these ideologies are totalitarian given that they uphold no limit to how far they can impose on the life of the individual, or indeed group interaction. Whole swaths of laws are enacted for the supposed greater good of the collective, in a ploy akin to a slaver promising security in return for your freedom. Neither communism nor fascism is any different in this regard, portraying liberty as an arbitrary concept that has no basis in objective reality. Rather than the natural rights described in chapter 4, totalitarians will vehemently oppose this as somewhere between idealistic and irrational - even tyrannical.

We must appreciate that arguing with a totalitarian is like the doublethink set out in George Orwell's 1984 novel. In one scene in this book, Winston Smith is tortured by O'Brien in Room 101. Eventually this becomes so unbearable that Winston accepts that 2+2=5, his freedom of thought worn away until he accepts anything O'Brien says without any question. This was the ultimate goal of the totalitarian state in 1984, and although Orwell himself was a socialist, he based this novel on the Stalinist climate of the Soviet Union, where hellish conditions led to some of the greatest repression in human history.

All left-wing ideology stems from this doublethink set out by Orwell, where whatever you're told is really just the opposite in practice. On this basis, freedom described by the totalitarian is actually slavery, and Orwell encapsulated this contradiction in one of the three slogans of the totalitarian government in 1984 (called *the Party*); Freedom is Slavery, followed by Ignorance is Strength. You'd be amazed at the arguments totalitarians make to convince you that the loss of freedom actually makes you freer. For example, they'll describe too much choice as enslaving because it's too difficult to make the right decision. Therefore, better that an expert decide for you, and as you can imagine, this precedent extends to every facet of your life. It's difficult to understand why anyone would be this dishonest until you grasp that no tyrant in history has ever been forthright about their malevolence. When you realise this, it isn't difficult to believe that many a tyrant has even convinced themselves that they were right to be so dishonest, if only because they think morality and truth are subjective, and that the ends justify the means.

Thankfully, aside from fringe elements that still believe communism and fascism are feasible ideologies, most are prepared to accept that both ideologies are dangerous when socialism isn't put in the same category. It's for this reason that significant objection tends to arrive when fascism is defined as a form of socialism. The simple reason is that socialism is an idealistic theory that many are completely unprepared to denounce. Generally this is driven by what's occasionally called the politics of envy. Whether you're poorer or wealthier, human nature is prone to resenting others that are more successful. Poorer people can rail against those that are wealthier because it's a constant reminder of what they don't have. Meanwhile, wealthier people can end up loathing anyone more successful because they want to be the most prosperous. Socialism is the perfect vehicle for both states of mind, explaining why the poorest in society are attracted to socialism as a means to take from the haves, and why the richest in society will use laws that make it difficult for others to be as rich and powerful as they are.

What results is an intricate series of guilt trips to convince people that state coercion is morally justifiable. Generally you're told that people will suffer, even die, without state intervention, as the richest socialists manage to brush aside the hypocrisy of living a life far in excess to anything most people experience. Meanwhile, the poorest dismiss every aspect of their troubles as a consequence of greed, unable to fathom or accept that their own idleness causes their suffering. Even if they are unfortunate, the socialist state conditions poorer people to behave like wild animals used to being fed by humans, therefore making them incapable of feeding themselves, just as I described in chapter 3.

All the more complicated is the fact that people rarely call themselves socialists anymore. It's automatically assumed that the state has a natural role in the everyday life of the individual, however far this reaches. The very idea that this is the road to totalitarianism has systematically been eradicated through indoctrination. Thus when you're dealing with most people, they just can't imagine anything other than state intervention as a solution for any problem - a clear demonstration that the masses are so accustomed to socialism that they don't know any different. In fact, they tremble with fear at the possibility that people would be better off without the state in any part of their lives.

The Road to Serfdom

The Austrian economist, Friedrich Hayek,[3] was among the first to set out how the socialist state is the predecessor for totalitarianism via his 1944 book, The Road to Serfdom. He argued that state power erodes our liberties until we become serfs, allowing people in power to control the masses so completely that ideologies like communism and fascism take root. Today the modern state is larger than any time in history, bolstered by debt based currencies that facilitate massive credit expansion - part of the central banking system I described in chapter 2. This false economy is the backdrop for more taxation than any other time in history that's initially tolerable when times are good, but as the pyramid scheme of debt grows larger, the state takes ever more profit and creates more laws that suppress anyone that protests. In this climate of a state that has a monopoly on force, a ruling class slowly but surely pushes others aside, as meritocracy is replaced by ruthlessness and cunning. This pattern is so consistent because only the most megalomaniacal people lust after power, seeking to expand this wherever possible. Naturally the state is the most effective way to do this, but unfortunately most people are perfectly happy with their ordinary lives, usually leaving the worst of us to rise to the top.

It's therefore very easy to see why politics is renowned for skulduggery and dishonesty. Most people simply cannot cope with the stress of being around individuals constantly plotting their own advancement, as they lie, deceive, or destroy their opposition. And so we see that the world of modern politics is ripe for totalitarianism, with socialism being the catalyst for endless state expansion as two wings of the same bird fly in the same direction. On one hand you have the egalitarianism of communism, and on the other, the hierarchy of fascism. Both are nonetheless socialist, not only because they endorse unlimited interference into the life of the individual, but in a much clearer ideological sense that would be easy to see, were it not for the deliberate confusion. Though no one would argue that communism is socialist, the same cannot be said for fascism, since any association with socialism would harm the benevolent image of state intervention, landing a crippling blow for big government advocates.

For one, the socialist roots of fascism don't get more obvious than the etymological origin of the term Nazi.[4] Nazi and Nazism weren't generally used during World War II, least of all by the Nazis themselves. It had some minor use among southern Germans and those exiled abroad, but National Socialist, or *Nationalsozialist* in German, was always the preferred term. Further still, Nazi comes from *Nationalsozialistische Deutsche Arbeiterpartei* in German, abbreviated to NSDAP and translated into English as National Socialist German Workers' Party. The howls of protest this causes by communist sympathisers is precisely the reason that the masses are completely incapable of accepting, or indeed realising, that socialism is not only an extremely dangerous ideology that requires the kind of fetish for big government we see in the modern world, but that socialism itself is not exclusively communist.

If you bring up this etymological origin of Nazi to your average far-left apologist, however, you'll get familiar protests about National Socialism being nothing to do with real 'communist' socialism, where the means of production are communally owned, even though socialism itself existed long before communism came along, and this is far from the full extent of the proof that fascism is a form of socialism. Merely reading the 25-point program of the NSDAP[5] will provide further evidence of the socialist roots of Nazi ideology. Point 9 reads that "All citizens of the state shall be equal as regards rights and obligations." Yet we're told by communists that only their ideology stands for equality when the Nazi program certainly covers this in depth. The first 8 points continuously address the communal interests of Germans as a nation, from point 1, which reads, "We demand the union of all Germans to form the Greater Germany on the basis of the people's right to self-determination enjoyed by the nations," to point 4, stating, "None but members of the nation may be citizens of the state. None but those of German blood, whatever their creed may be. No Jew, therefore, may be a member of the nation."

You'll also hear that only communal ownership of property (also called nationalisation) can be described as economically socialist. Point 13 of the same plan reads, "We demand nationalisation of all businesses which have been up to the present formed into companies (trusts)." Point 14 then reads, "We demand that the profits from wholesale trade shall be shared out." These points alone firmly demonstrate the commitment to nationalisation of industries – a key component of communism. People then move onto welfare and public services as an important part of socialist ideology that National Socialism supposedly lacks, to which point 15 reads, "We demand an expansion on a large scale of old age welfare," most certainly fitting their definition in this respect. Point 20 reads, "The state is to be responsible for a fundamental reconstruction of our whole national education program, to enable every capable and industrious German to obtain higher education and subsequently introduction into leading positions," going on to say that, "We demand the education at the expense of the state of outstanding intellectually gifted children of poor parents without consideration of position or profession." So not only did the Nazis believe in welfare for the poorest in society, but the kind of education system we currently see in society, where the state closely controls and regulates how this operates.

The Fascist Manifesto

Rather than pointing out every single example that demonstrates the socialist credentials of this ideology, the crux is that National Socialists were motivated by the German race, rather than the proletariats of communism, but that is absolutely no basis for claiming that this makes National Socialism any less socialist. Those that lean towards communism will argue until they're blue in the face that this isn't the case, but that's precisely what you'd expect from those attempting to whitewash history by preventing people from realising that communism and fascism are two sides of the same coin.

To conclude this chapter I'll further demonstrate that communism is far from the only form of socialism by using another example of its socialist credentials - the 1919 Fascist Manifesto[6] of Benito Mussolini's Italian movement. The fundamental tenets that communists attribute to their ideology are equality, communal ownership and redistribution of profit. We've already seen that all these things can be attributed to Nazism *among the German people* (not the working class), but what about Italian fascism? The manifesto for this movement reads like a laundry list of socialism, starting immediately with the first 6 points centred on democracy. These include universal suffrage for all those of 18 years and older, proportional representation on a regional basis, voting rights for women, and the abolition of the senate, replaced by expert councils in various fields including industry, transport and public health.

7 to 13 focuses on social policy and labour, including an 8 hour work day, minimum wage, workers' representatives and unions, reorganisation of transport and railway sectors, along with revision of invalidity insurance and reduction of retirement from 65 to 55. 14 to 16 of the manifesto are military related, which aren't necessarily socialist policies, but 17 to 20 certainly are. These include a strong progressive tax policy (paying more tax the more you earn), seizure of religious property, plus the expropriation of other wealth. Some of the policies of the Fascist Manifesto are similar or identical to those found in the Communist Manifesto. For example, progressive taxation is the second plank of communism, as per chapter 2 of Marx and Engels' manifesto, whereas plank 6 states that communication and transport should be centralised, much like the Fascist Manifesto. More so, The 25 point program of the NSDAP shares similarities with the Communist Manifesto in many areas, including equal obligation to work found in point 10, also found in plank 8 of the Communist Manifesto.

Many of the policies in both the Fascist Manifesto and the 25 point program of the NSDAP don't seem out of place at all in modern politics, either, which tells us that the system we live in is not only fundamentally socialist, but verging closer to totalitarianism as governments continue to relentlessly expand – just as Hayek warned in The Road to Serfdom.

No, fascism isn't the total centralisation of communism where individual property rights don't exist at all, and state officials live lavishly as V.I.P's, but only a blind ideologue would deny the similarity. You'd also have to be blind not to see that communism and fascism are cut from the same cloth, and that cloth is totalitarianism. Hayek once said that "Fascism is the stage reached after communism has proved an illusion," which is exactly how the pattern plays out whenever socialism is in effect. Be in no doubt that both ideologies are extremely repressive, denying fundamental liberties like individual property rights, free speech and association, or personal responsibility. They do this by promising the earth –a utopia of man where paradise on earth can be achieved, though in truth, they lead to nothing but hell on earth. The bottom line is that too much state intervention is the road to totalitarianism that almost no one wants to acknowledge.

Chapter 17: Collectivism and Individualism

The left-right paradigm makes no sense when you put fascism on the far-right.

After reading the last chapter, it should now be much easier to break out of arguably the biggest lie of the last century – fascism is a right-wing ideology. Not only is this a categorically false myth that I will further refute in this chapter, it's actually a form of socialism, as I've already proven. Understand that there is so much proof for this that you could write an entire book on this subject alone. What this chapter will endeavour to explain is what a true left-right spectrum actually looks when we accept a more logical framework that doesn't place totalitarianism on both extremes of the political spectrum.

To start, I'll briefly explain how conventional political thought defines the left-right spectrum. On the centre-right you have capitalism (a loaded word used to describe free market economics) and conservativism (a word that has no real meaning without context). On the far-right you then have fascism and Nazism – allegedly the more extreme versions of right-wing ideology. By placing these ideologies on the far end of the right on a political spectrum, the logic supposedly goes that the more conservative or capitalist you become, the more fascist this makes you. Chapter 16 utterly refuted the idea that fascism has anything to do with capitalism, due to its fundamentally socialist nature. As for conservatism, context matters because the term really only denotes conservation. What exactly you're conserving depends immensely on the circumstances. In Communist China, conservatives were historically the hardcore communists that didn't want to open up their markets to commerce and private property rights, making conservatism so subjective that it's practically useless without significant clarification.

The centre-left of the political spectrum truly is a confusing mess occupied by liberalism. The further left you go, the closer to socialism this is, eventually reaching communism. Unpacking this is a philosophical minefield that readers will hopefully be able to understand, having come this far in the book. Liberalism is a philosophy of individual liberty that accompanies property rights and personal responsibility. It does not involve creating strong centralised government that systematically suppresses citizens and organic group structures like the family – all of which is prevalent under socialism. So why, then, is liberalism anywhere near socialism, let alone a step on the way to communism? The answer is that it should be as far away from these two ideologies as fascism is from capitalism.

Collectivism

Having already explained that communism and fascism are socialist and (ultimately) totalitarian, it should be easy to recognise another critical binding element for these ideologies – *collectivism*. Charlatans will invariably redefine terms because they profit from the confusion. When using a word like collectivism, do not therefore be misled into believing that this means you don't believe in cooperation between groups of people if you don't align with collectivism as an ideology. Collectivism is a very specific ideological requirement for absolute subordination of the individual to a group. Individuals therefore have no rights themselves and are required to subordinate their liberty to a collective, justified as cooperation for the good of everyone. At its core this is a totalitarian viewpoint that destroys any limits to what you can do to individuals, if it serves a greater good. Even those that would prescribe some moral limits under this system base this on arbitrary measures like democracy, as though a vote can make murder, theft or enslavement moral when a majority votes in favour of this in some shape or form.

This is the old idea of absolutism I described in chapter 4 - the very belief that led to monarchy and feudalism, along with other historical dictatorships of elite rulers that claimed to have a divine or natural right to rule, like the Caesars and Pharoahs of old. As the saying goes, there's nothing new under the sun, so don't expect totalitarian ideas to be original. The most you'll get is a new version of an old idea, which is exactly what communism and fascism amount to. Collectivism is a good way to describe these new ideologies because they're completely fixated on group identity, to the point that any individuality is completely eradicated.

In the post-enlightenment era, we discovered in chapter 15 that a counter-enlightenment took hold. Socialism was the result of that push, with communism and fascism emerging as the two competing ideologies of this totalitarian order. Their adherents endeavoured to create a new man for a post-enlightenment era, shaped entirely by collective identity. Communists called this the New Soviet Man[1] – the man of the future that transcended cultural, ethnic, and linguistic diversity. Fascists put ethnicity at the centre of their ideology, as they aspired towards the great rulers and champions of old, be it Romans like Julius Caesar, or Greeks like Alexander the Great. Nietzsche's Übermensch I outlined in chapter 14 became the template for the Nazi interpretation of a new fascist man. Much more hierarchical than communism, Nazis still sought to elevate the collective greatness of their people, in the hope that each generation would lead to the godlike vision of Nietzsche. Distinctions aside, communism and fascism were both collectivist ideologies that also had socialism and totalitarianism in common.

Followers of these ideologies openly acknowledged their similarities prior to World War II. In pre-Nazi Germany, Nazis and Communists were united in their hatred of liberals, squeezing them out of the political sphere before turning on each other to establish dominance. Gregor Strasser, a prominent Nazi official and politician, made several statements that exemplify this contempt for liberalism. In a 1926 pamphlet titled Thoughts about the Tasks of the Future Nazi Propaganda Minister, he said, "The spirit of our National Socialist idea has to overpower the spirit of liberalism and false democracy if there is to be a third Reich at all!" He was equally open about his belief that Nazism was a socialist ideology. He wrote in the same pamphlet that:

> *We are Socialists, enemies, mortal enemies of the present capitalist economic system with its exploitation of the economically weak, with its injustice in wages, with its immoral evaluation of individuals according to wealth and money instead of responsibility and achievement, and we are determined under all circumstances to abolish this system! And with my inclination to practical action it seems obvious to me that we have to put a better, more just, more moral system in its place, one which, as it were, has arms and legs and better arms and legs than the present one!*

Apologists exclaim that Gregor Strasser was murdered by Hitler during the night of the long knives in 1934, ending left-wing sympathies within the Nazi party. There is no evidence for this considering that the Nazis retained their big government socialist policies until the bitter end, and no attempt to redefine socialism can change that. However, Joseph Goebbels, the Nazi Propaganda Minister for Germany until the end of World War II, still retained these socialist sympathies, along with vitriol towards liberalism. He wrote in Michael: A German Destiny in Diary Form (his semi-autobiographical novel) that "Peoples do never govern themselves. That lunacy was concocted by liberalism." He said in the same book that "To be a socialist means to let the ego serve the neighbour, to sacrifice the self for the whole. In its deepest sense socialism equals service. The individual refrains and the commonwealth demands." In a speech in 1925, as quoted in the New York Times, he also said that "Lenin is the greatest man, second only to Hitler, and that the difference between Communism and the Hitler faith is very slight."

Leon Trotsky recognised this similarity between communism and fascism as well, pointing this out in chapter 11 of Revolution Betrayed, a 1936 book that he wrote after Stalin exiled him from the Soviet Union, where he said, "Stalinism and fascism, in spite of a deep difference in social foundations, are symmetrical phenomena. In many of their features they show a deadly similarity." Vladimir Lenin expressed a similar disdain for liberalism as Nazis when he stated in the 1913 publication of The Three Sources and Three Component Parts of Marxism, that "In one way or another, all official and liberal science defends wage-slavery, whereas Marxism has declared relentless war on that slavery. To expect science to be impartial in a wage-slave society is as foolishly naïve as to expect impartiality from manufacturers on the question of whether workers' wages ought not to be increased by decreasing the profits of capital."

There will be those that say these quotes do not demonstrate any kind of tangible alliance between these two ideologies, and that, in practice, they're oppositional. Objective history tells a different story.

The Nazi-Soviet Non-Aggression Pact

The Molotov–Ribbentrop Pact[2] is evidence that these ideologies have, in fact, allied with one another when convenient. On the 23rd August, 1939, just over one week before Britain and France declared war on Germany on the 1st September of the same year, and after the German invasion of Poland took place, Nazis and Soviets signed a non-aggression pact that carved out territories in Europe, as part of an agreement that would assure both sides did not interfere with one another's territorial expansion. Furthermore, a secret protocol within this pact meant that Romania, Poland, Lithuania, Latvia, Estonia and Finland were divided into German and Soviet spheres of control.

Anyone familiar with World War II history will be aware that this pact broke down when Hitler declared war on the Soviet Union in June 1941, with the Nazi invasion into Russia that followed was dubbed operation Barbarossa.[3] Why Hitler would risk a two-front war like this is a historically contentious issue. There are those that would argue Hitler's madness resulted in him turning on Stalin before Britain was defeated. This makes no strategic sense, especially when Hitler's forces were unstoppable until that point, having already conquered France, Belgium, Luxembourg and the Netherlands. Plus he had a non-aggression pact with Stalin that made this unnecessary and rash. However, compelling evidence suggests that Stalin was poised to betray Hitler, and historical events support this. For one, Stalin joined the Allied forces of Britain and France immediately after Hitler declared war on the Soviet Union. Anyone with a modicum of strategical common sense would consider this a stroke of military genius that put Hitler in an impossible strategic situation.

As Winston Churchill once paraphrased from George Santayana, those who fail to learn from history are doomed to repeat it. With this in mind, Hitler's subsequent military blunder was totally out of character, failing to account for history like Napoleon's past military mistakes. Getting drawn deeper into Russian territory was the beginning of the end for Hitler, just as it spelt catastrophe for Napoleon. Hitler's mistake is presented as a heroic struggle of the Soviet people, who saved Europe from fascism. The fact is, however, that this was a ruthless military calculation by Stalin, who used the environment and elements of Russia to his advantage, sacrificing Russian lives because he was so unconcerned with their suffering. Yes many Russians died fighting the Germans, but it drew Germans so deep into Russia that it would eventually be their undoing, as the extremely harsh Russian winter decimated Hitler's forces - picked off when retreated back to Eastern Europe. Like Napoleon before him, this led to a military disaster for Hitler's armies, relentlessly pursued all the way back to Germany. By the time the United States entered the war in December 1941, Germany was trapped in a war on all fronts, especially when the Italian's surrendered in the south of Europe in September 1943.

Thus everything that took place in World War II played right into Stalin's hands. Apologists and revisionists for communism will use the death of millions of Soviets in World War II to suggest otherwise, but the truth is that soldiers and citizens were forced to defend a regime that easily rivalled Nazis despotism. Soviet officials were known for their brutality, the NKVD working with commissars to prevent withdrawal of troops without military authorisation. Consequences for disobeying orders were extremely harsh, some soldiers sent to penal battalions called *shtrafbats,*[4] where the most dangerous fighting took place. The infamous "Not one step back!" order was in effect in those areas, along with summary executions for anyone that disobeyed. Among citizens, field expedient general courts were established to deal with military deserters, or people 'spreading rumours'. Others, like Soviet general Dimitry Pavlov,[5] were tried and executed for "military cowardice" and "criminal incompetence".

This aside, we should then look at what happened after World War II to see just how cunningly calculating Stalin was. Americans were convinced to leave Europe, allowing the Soviets to take control of an entire eastern front that they never rescinded until the collapse of the iron curtain in 1989. So rather than being the mortal enemy of Hitler, Stalin was merely far more devious. The pact he had with Hitler would never have held forever among megalomaniacs, but Stalin wasn't as exposed to his east as Hitler was to his, partly due to the sheer size of Russian territory.

To definitively prove that Hitler played right into Stalin's hands, we need only look at the fact that, by the end of World War II, Stalin controlled not only the territories outlined for the Soviets in the Molotov–Ribbentrop Pact, but those designated to the Nazis, with exceptions like Finland – a country constantly in danger of falling to the Soviets throughout the Cold War that followed. We can thus easily see that history doesn't paint an accurate picture at all when it suggests that Hitler actually betrayed Stalin. Nay; he was extremely exposed from the east, and needed his alliance with Stalin far more than Stalin needed one with him. Hitler, in fact, probably wouldn't have overstretched his forces were it not for the assurances he had from Stalin, a man that ended up manipulating both Allies and Axis forces in his favour. Looking at the evidence, it's therefore most likely that Hitler discovered how Stalin was planning to join the Allies, attacking him pre-emptively - almost certainly taking Stalin by surprise because he did not expect this to happen.

We can thus conclude that there was never anything more than self-interest and megalomania that separated communists and fascists in history, much like organised crime syndicates that work together when convenient, stabbing the another in the back when cooperation is no longer advantageous.

Individualism

Since collectivist ideologies place the group above the individual, it would be logical to state that the polar opposite would be the individual over the group. This is called individualism, and, like collectivism, is mischaracterised, this time by two groups of people. The first is collectivists themselves, who argue that individualism is the atomisation of people to such an extent that no groups exist. They then use this mischaracterisation to reject individualism. The second is those trying to legitimise their selfishness with a philosophical category called egoism. Having touched on *nihilism* in chapter 14, egoism isn't a big leap from there. Recall that nihilism is what happens in the absence of belief, leading to delusional thinking like relativism and postmodernism. Egoism is another form this takes, centring on the importance of the individual above all.

There are different kinds of egoism that can broadly be defined as the legitimisation of selfishness, the two most prevalent forms being rational or ethical egoism[6]. The rational kind asserts that the most logical choice is always acting in your own self-interest, thus maximising overall happiness. In accordance with this there is no such thing as true selflessness, since every act of generosity or kindness benefits the individual that chose to carry it out. Ayn Rand[7] is perhaps the most famous rational egoist, creating an entire philosophy called objectivism that's based on this philosophy. Conversely, ethical egoism is the complete denial of any kind of ethical position other than pure self-interest, meaning that morality is totally subjective. Friedrich Nietzsche, who I've already covered in this book, is probably the archetypal ethical egoist that typically presents his dearth of morality in a way that entices you into believing that something good can come of this, i.e., the Übermensch. While rational egoism at least attempts to establish some kind of moral limit, ethical egoism does no such thing. For all intents and purposes, it is the philosophy of psychopaths seeking to justify harm against others.

If there's one thing people need to realise it's that most modern political words have been redefined by those that opposed the developments of the enlightenment era. Therefore, collectivism and individualism cannot be the sole basis for how we define politics any more than communism, fascism and socialism are within the current false paradigm that most people adhere to. Although I have no particular attachment to individualism, I do think it's best to define this in the context of John Locke's philosophy that I touched on in chapter 4, which predates any of the latter corruptions by counter enlightenment thinkers I touched on in chapter 14. When we define individualism in this manner, it becomes a philosophy of unalienable natural rights that cannot be taken away by any entity, not even the state. By no means does this suggest that we cannot establish groups. It simply means that groups cannot enslave individuals to their will. What's more, we each have a right to free association, where we can *choose* which groups we associate with.

In a world where equality is absolute, this is completely unacceptable. Equality of outcome is the unconditional standard for everything in this setting, where quotas must be met for sex, sexuality, race, ethnicity, and numerous other forms of endlessly expanding identity based categories. We may not like the fact that the person down the street doesn't want to marry a person of a different race or ethnicity, and we may not like the fact that male only clubs exist, but changing this through imposed equality is totalitarianism. This is why freedom of association is so important, and why it should always fall on the individual to decide who they associate with. Of course laws should always seek to prevent harm against individuals of different identities, but we can still have this without a totalitarian government that forces individuals to violate personal belief and conscience.

Just as important as free association is free speech – an extremely important counterbalance to free association. We each have a right to say whatever we want, as long as it isn't incitement or defamation. Free association, however, allows the individual *not* to listen, or tell people to leave when they are on their private property. Collectivists will howl and complain about this because they believe people *must* coexist, but often the best coexistence is from a distance, with countries and private property that allow us to be good neighbours, as long as we don't break the most pivotal laws that all truly just morality stems from – opposition to theft, murder and fraud.

Equally important to individual rights is personal responsibility, where every right has a corresponding responsibility attached. For example, we don't have the right to force others to consent to sex, and we're responsible for any children born from our sexual experiences. This is why parents have a responsibility to take care of their children, but also have parental rights that cannot be violated in a truly free society. Alas, this common sense form of morality is a far cry from where we find ourselves today. Egoists and collectivists all rail against personal responsibility in their own way, wielding power to avoid personal responsibility wherever possible. This is why fathers have no true rights in the current system, by using the 'welfare of the child' as a precedent to deny their rights to be in the lives of their children, while at the same time making them responsible for taking care of them. Meanwhile, women have the right to abort their children before they're even born, or give them up for adoption if they'd prefer. It shouldn't be at all difficult to see how skewed this system is because all parental rights fall with the mother, while all true responsibilities fall with the father.

Collectivists don't believe in any individual rights that aren't totally subjective, while the more egoistic you are, the more likely you are to conclude that individuals can do whatever they want (as long as they don't get caught). Personal responsibility comes with similar problems within these two perspectives. Collectivists believe in imposed responsibility, irrespective of whether rights are attached, thus destroying the reward for good behaviour in society - just as we constantly see under socialism. The more egoistic you are, the more likely you are to deny that any responsibilities exist. All that matters is power, and using this to get what you want. Equally, collectivists believe the same thing, but hide behind the façade of equality and the greater good. At least rational egoists are honest enough to admit that their own self-interest comes first, although ethical egoists are more likely to lie about this because true psychopaths have very little regard for honesty.

My proposal to end the confusion of the political spectrum is that the 'Lockean' individualism I've described should sit on the furthest right, while the less inclined you are to believe individuals have unalienable rights, the further to the left you sit. The political spectrum will then be based on natural rights, not an arbitrary ideological belief system that has no regard for objective morality.

Chapter 18: Understanding Free Market Economics

Corporations are the result of socialism, not free market economics.

Of all the chapters in this book, this one will challenge the mainstream view of the world in ways that will be difficult for many to accept. I recall in my left-leaning days that corporations were of particular concern to me, as I saw the way they exploited the economy to their advantage, in ways I admittedly did not understand at the time. We're told that corporations are products of monopolies that occur in a free market, although this is far from accurate. I proved in chapter 16 that socialism is inherently totalitarian, so if you accept this, it shouldn't be hard to accept the next premise – all countries are socialist. When we return to the root definition of socialism I set out in the aforementioned chapter, socialism freed from the monopoly imposed by communists is an ideology that advocates group cooperation in an unlimited number of ways. If nothing else, this very straightforward original definition should help the most politically illiterate person see that there are no limits to what the government can do in the world today, whatever country you live in, meaning that every country is actually socialist. If the government decides to do something there are no true limits that can prevent this, and even constitutions will be changed to accommodate that outlook, undermining the point of a constitution in the first place.

Let us now ask what the alternative to this perspective is, before proceeding to whether or not corporations are the result of a free market economy. In Chapter 3 I gave an explanation of supply and demand which demonstrated why socialist economics don't work, proving that this ideology cannot replace price signals in a market economy. These signals provide the necessary information to meet the needs and desires of consumers, and without them, shortages will occur in some instances, and oversupply will occur in others. Some economists call this the local knowledge problem[1] because it manifests when people are incapable of seeing smaller details when they're preoccupied with bigger ones, like statistics. This creates a distinction between *micro* and *macro* economics, micro being the small scale local activity that cannot be effectively planned because human beings aren't pieces that can be moved around on a game board.

Conversely, macroeconomics suggests otherwise, with economic models that zoom out to the larger scale, as advocated by socialists of all varieties, including economic theorists like John Maynard Keynes (a socialist in the true definitional sense), whose entire economic model of *Keynesianism* stands in stark contrast to those arguing that central planning simply cannot work on a practical basis, and only creates decline in the long run. When asked about this long run, Keynes was known for saying "But this long run is a misleading guide to current affairs. In the long run we are all dead."[2] Apologists make excuses for this dismissal of economic reality, but the bottom line is that Keynes fudged the ebb and flow between economic supply and demand by coining a theory called *aggregate demand.*[3] As such, he believed you could end an economic decline by spending money, increasing debt and lowering taxes. However, later you would have to pay for this when the economy improved, hence Keynes' flippant response when questioned about the risks if his theory didn't pan out in the long run. Furthermore, 'aggregate' is another way of saying overall or total, highlighting Keynes' preoccupation with macroeconomics - something classical economists reject out of hand.

Classical economics

Adam Smith is considered by many to be the father of economics. Referring to Smith's work as *classical* economics has become necessary since the nineteenth century, when socialism began to capture the imagination of the ruling class that were disenfranchised by the move away from feudalism, along with intellectuals that wanted to replace monarchism with a new absolutist order. A split subsequently formed, where some wanted to continue down the road of more individual freedom, while others opposed this, as I explained in chapter 14 when I covered the rise of relativism. Adam Smith taught us that we don't need the state to interfere with our economic lives because this leads to unintended consequences beyond our control or understanding. Therefore it's better to allow the economy to operate without intervention, like an invisible hand. Adam Smith used this term once in his famous bible of economics called The Wealth of Nations, which epitomises his theory very well. The instance where he used this term states:

> *As every individual, therefore, endeavours as much as he can both to employ his capital in the support of domestic industry, and so to direct that industry that its produce may be of the greatest value, every individual necessarily labours to render the annual revenue of*

the society as great as he can. He generally, indeed, neither intends to promote the public interest, nor knows how much he is promoting it. By preferring the support of domestic to that of foreign industry, he intends only his own security; and by directing that industry in such a manner as its produce may be of the greatest value, he intends only his own gain, and he is in this, as in many other cases, led by an invisible hand to promote an end which was no part of his intention.[4]

He also uses the term on one occasion in his earlier book, The Theory of Moral Sentiments, when he wrote:

They are led by an invisible hand to share out life's necessities in just about the same way that they would have been shared out if the earth been divided into equal portions among all its inhabitants. And so without intending it, without knowing it, they advance the interests of the society, and provide means for the survival of the species.[5]

The crux of Smith's description in the prior passages is driven by self-interest, wherein individuals personally benefit from mediums of exchange. Imagine that you're a shopkeeper. To become successful in this endeavour, one must maintain a good reputation for providing goods to the public in exchange for money. Likewise, a customer that doesn't want to pay for goods will not be welcome in a shop. A mutually beneficial relationship therefore takes place, where customer and shopkeeper benefit from exchange of value. The customer receives a product that's more desirable than the money they possess, while the shopkeeper receives money that's more desirable than the products they sell. By placing one's self-interest above all, both customer and shopkeeper go away happy, actually advancing the interests of society by preserving and supporting this form of exchange, just as Adam Smith describes.

Self-interest is a crucial aspect of Adam Smith's economic theory, then, along with three other areas. Two of these are supply and demand, outlined in chapter 3 when I described the follies of socialism. One person supplies a product or service to the market, and based on demand, will adjust supply accordingly. This creates price signals that tell the supplier the best price to maximise profit - typically where socialists gets indignant. Profit is a sin for socialists, who see it as exploitative and parasitical. They fail to realise that a market economy may well result in some instances where people can't afford to pay for something they need, but it's still a far better alternative to any kind of central planning, as history shows us with the crimes of communism I covered in chapter 11. Recall that Marx said, "From each according to his ability, to each according to his needs," a utopian notion that fails to factor how central planning will inevitably fail to provide even the most basic needs of the masses, not to mention an ever encroaching totalitarian state. Despite this historical and practical reality, power is a temptation that few can resist, so people pepper their machinations with promises of equality, as socialism continuously reinvents itself over and over again because its proponents will never tell the truth about what it truly ends with.

The final aspect of Smith's theory is competition, and this is what keeps the self-interest of the supplier in check. When suppliers need to compete with other suppliers, it drives down prices and increases quality. After all, if your competitors do a better job than you, you can hardly expect to make much money. Why would a customer continue to frequent your establishment when another establishment does the same thing much better? That being said, competition isn't only driven by price, quality, service, etc. Sometimes factors like convenience play a role, as in the local convenience store or corner shop that doesn't require you to take a longer trip. It's important not to oversimplify economics, but it's easy to see why Adam Smith's four elements of supply, demand, competition and self-interest are foundational in this field.

Unregulated capitalism

Upon recognising that competition is necessary in a truly free market economy, socialists will complain about monopolies in unregulated capitalism. Monopoly is a familiar term that describes a lack of competition in an economy when one or a few large businesses control the market. Ironically, socialists typically insist on solving this problem by nationalising industries, as though this isn't a monopoly itself. Since communist socialists are hell bent on centralising every facet of society, they'll use the cover of injustice within a market economy to state that this would improve inequality, and yet the monopoly argument cannot hold water when communism itself is an ideology that requires total centralisation of all aspects of economic and social life. Once again I remind people that this creates less equality due to creeping totalitarianism and inefficiency.

As for the term capitalism, it must be stipulated somewhere in this book that the word was never used by Adam Smith or other early classical economists. Setting aside vague use here and there, the word was pushed by socialists like Pierre-Joseph Proudhon, as a pejorative that makes market economics appear ideological by associating it with an 'ism'. In a display of pure projection, it's socialism that's the true ideology, while market economics can hardly be considered ideological when this is a civilised form of mutually beneficial interaction that's taken place for millennia. Austrian School economist, Ludwig von Mises, pointed out this deceptive use of language by socialists in his 1922 book, Socialism: An Economic and Sociological Analysis, when he wrote:

> *The terms "Capitalism" and "Capitalistic Production" are political catchwords. They were invented by socialists, not to extend knowledge, but to carp, to criticize, to condemn. Today, they have only to be uttered to conjure up a picture of the relentless exploitation of wage-slaves by the pitiless rich. They are scarcely ever used save to imply a disease in the body-politic. From a scientific point of view, they are so obscure and ambiguous that they have no value whatever. Their users agree only in this, that they indicate the characteristics of the modern economic system. But wherein these characteristics consist is always a matter of dispute. Their use, therefore, is entirely pernicious, and the proposal to extrude them altogether from economic terminology, and to leave them to the matadors of popular agitation, deserves serious consideration.*[6]

Although it's easy to see that socialists are being intellectually dishonest when they reframe language in this manner, monopolies can indeed take place in a market economy. The question is; how does this happen? Socialists are incorrect to blame monopolies on an unregulated market - quite the opposite; state intervention allows monopolies to take place due to a *monopoly of force*. In other words, you cannot force people to frequent any business unless you use the threat of coercion. Imagine, if you would, a supermarket in your area. How could this business force you to buy its goods? Only two ways are possible; direct threat of harm, or indirect threat via an authority that has power over you. This, of course, is the state, with its many laws that must be obeyed, otherwise we risk fines, jail, or worse still – death if we evade and physically resist prosecution. Some would reply that non-state methods of forced compliance also exist, like protection rackets run by organised criminals. Not only is this illegal, thus receiving the full force of state opposition, but in a freer society we would be entitled to physically defend ourselves against this through private security and gun ownership.

States are such a monopoly on force that it's virtually impossible to oppose it without serious consequences extending way beyond organised crime or private criminals. This is why totalitarianism is so destructive – attempting to oppose state tyranny leads to millions of deaths because state monopolies are so well financed and entrenched. To create a force large enough to overthrow this comes at an extremely heavy cost, be it war between states, rebellion of citizenry, or civil war, making it a totally false juxtaposition to place state monopoly alongside any potential monopoly in an unregulated market.

The next objection will come with so-called natural monopolies, where certain natural barriers to entry prevent competition from taking place. To combat this, it's argued that these should be publicly owned. Utility companies are a major example of this, where the infrastructure for a service is controlled by the supplier that enters the market first. Since this entity creates the infrastructure that provides a service, no competitor can enter the market without permission from the first supplier. Be it electricity lines, water and gas pipes, or telephone and internet cables, these would all be considered natural monopolies. We can also see this with transport links like railway tracks and roads. However, every single one of these have been opened up to more competition over time, and it's certainly possible to argue that the initial cost for universally used infrastructure could be funded by the state, even in the most free market economy. Only anarcho-capitalists would generally object, as they perceive any state intervention into the market whatsoever as a violation of their principles. In response, I would argue that all free societies must have a certain amount of communal infrastructure that everyone can use, lest we're all trapped in private property prisons that we can't leave because we don't have access to the land around us. Obviously this is a form of tyranny in its own right, so some form of communal property has to exist, including parks and commercial districts that we can freely access.

No matter what argument you make against monopolies in a free market being inevitable, socialists will continue to argue that larger competitors will reduce their prices so much that others will be driven out of business. They state that larger businesses will have an advantage because they have a greater potential to raise capital and absorb losses. Lower or loss making prices will harm them, too, but as soon as their competitors are driven out of business, they can profit from the monopoly they created. The truth is that this can't happen in a genuine free market. Such a risky strategy will make a business extremely financially vulnerable, and without barriers to entry, as soon as local competitors are out of business, others can simply move into the market to take their place. It should be easy to notice that only one business is operating in an area that's charging very high prices, creating an attractive opportunity to competitors. Yet again we return to the fact that only state coercion can stop competitors entering the market, and in a free market, no such preventions can exist.

A major question will still persist when you refute the fundamental arguments socialists make about monopolies in an unregulated market; when considering how prone socialists are to suggesting that modern corporate corruption is a product of market monopolies, are corporations really free market entities at all?

What is a corporation?

To answer this question, we need to establish what a corporation is. A good place to start is how corporations originated. In the modern form we're now accustomed to, corporations began in around the 17th century, during the period of mercantilism. This practice involved aggressive militaristic protection and expansion of international markets by nation states, using corporations as proxies for trading ventures. The earliest corporations were maritime trading companies that would capitalise on colonies around the world, like India and Hong Kong. One of the earliest of these corporations was the Dutch East India Trading Company. These were publicly traded, much like many corporations today, where anyone can buy shares in the company to claim a stake in its potential profit, or loss if the company's profitability declines. In return for the protection that these corporations received from the state, they paid taxes. It might appear that this is some sort of early form of free market economics, but Adam Smith was very critical of this practice in The Wealth of Nations, such as when he wrote:

> *The exclusive privileges of corporations, statutes of apprenticeship, and all those laws which restrain, in particular employments, the competition to a smaller number than might otherwise go into them, have the same tendency, though in a less degree. They are a*

sort of enlarged monopolies, and may frequently, for ages together, and in whole classes of employments, keep up the market price of particular commodities above the natural price, and maintain both the wages of the labour and the profits of the stock employed about them somewhat above their natural rate.[7]

As Smith's view suggests, mercantilism was as disconnected from free market economics as socialism is today. Like socialism, mercantilism can operate in a market economy, but it isn't based on the kind of mutually beneficial interaction that free markets are truly about. Rather, mercantilism, like socialism, must have overall winners and losers, and is thus based on a win-lose, as opposed to win-win, dynamic. No one is supposed to lose in a free market economy. You want something more than what you are trading with, so you make an exchange. There are instances when people will pay more than they can afford for certain goods and services, but in a free market, the dynamics of supply, demand, competition and self-interest will limit negative outcomes. No one honest would suggest there aren't injustices from time to time in a market like this, but the indiscriminate nature of Adam Smith's invisible hand means that the human hand of corruption is far more restrained.

Under mercantilism you get little to no choice about the conditions of trade. A more dominant player forces you to trade under their terms, but given the weaker position of the other player, they get far less than what they could receive if the threat of force wasn't hanging over them. A well known historical example of this is what happened to Hong Kong during the Opium Wars[8] of the mid-19th century. The British East India Trading Company wanted to open up Chinese markets to Britain, though the Qing Dynasty was resistant to foreign trade. The British then began to smuggle opium into Hong Kong as a means to corrupt and weaken the local populace, making it susceptible to colonisation. What ensued were two wars that would eventually result in Honk Kong becoming a colony of Britain. As a result, Honk Kong was forced to trade at a significant disadvantage, allowing British interests to make a handsome profit. No credible economist would ever call this a free market. It's certainly a step up from slavery or serfdom, but Adam Smith's ideas transitioned us away from this destructive practice, and fundamentally opposed such exploitation.

Corporations have legal protections that would never exist in a free market, since these require the support of state law. Such arbitrary and artificial law is attributed to legalism and corporate legalese, wherein common sense is overridden by artificial protections from the state. A big criticism of current markets is very little protection for the consumer once a transaction has taken place. Because consumer guarantee is so poor, consumer fraud is a far bigger danger when there is a low legal standard for the quality of goods and services. This is perpetuated by limited liability that allows irresponsible business people to declare bankruptcy, whereby liability to creditors, suppliers, and customers is no longer an obligation. Any wealth is then protected from debt collectors, as long as it's not on the balance sheet for a business. A house you own in your own name would therefore be protected, though a property in the name of the business would not. In a free market, limited liability would never exist because the state wouldn't protect businesses with such laws, meaning that bad businesses would be liable, even if it meant personal assets of business owners being seized. As a result, people would be far less reckless in their business ventures - a significant moral hazard in the current system.

Also of note is what corporations morphed into in the 20th century. They became the primary economic driver for fascist economies, essentially acting like feudal lords under serfdom. Feudal lords would collect taxes for monarchs from peasants bound to the land they oversaw, in exchange for prosperity. Other obligations would be necessary, but this relationship was very beneficial to those higher up in the social hierarchy. Corporations under fascism fulfilled a very similar role, protected by state laws and regulations that kept competition at bay, receiving kickbacks like subsidies and tax breaks that would make their owners very powerful and wealthy. So symbiotic was this relationship that it's often said that fascism is the merging of state and corporate power. Some call this corporatism, but this is merely a relatively recent word that fails to consider that corporate legal protections and nepotistic arrangements between state and corporate interests are what make this possible, not to mention the prior history of mercantilism that this adapts for a modern world.

One final point for this chapter is legal protection called *corporate personhood*, where corporations are treated like individuals. On this basis, individuals within a corporation have limited liability when found breaking the law. Corporations are extended similar rights as individuals, like the right to lobby and fund politicians, while avoiding responsibilities for breaking the law that would lead to prosecution for individuals. Corporations often receive what amounts to a slap on the wrist by absorbing a fine that does little to dent its balance sheets, as executives that authorised an illegal decision get away scot-free. The 2008 banking crisis led to many examples of negligent investment that almost brought down the global economy, via subprime lending products that I covered in chapter 2. These hid bad loans so deeply within the market that no one could escape them, and yet prosecutions were limited to lower level employees.[9][10] It was suggested prior to this crisis that banks were 'too big to fail' – subsequently proven incorrect. Since then, a play on this folly has resulted in the saying that bankers are 'too big to jail', due to legal protections afforded by corporate status.

When we put all this together, it's easy to conclude that corporations, from their very inception, are a far cry from the economic ideas of Adam Smith, the true father of what would objectively be called free market economics. While corporate culture certainly should be questioned for its destructive influence on society, socialists wilfully spread falsehoods about free markets by unfairly associating them with corporations. If we recall the true definition of socialism as an all-encompassing social and economic ideology, corporations are actually in keeping with this given that their entire existence depends on the collective power of the state.

Chapter 19: Subversion of the Right

There is no truly right-wing choice in modern politics.

Thanks to left-wing subversion, modern politics provides no true alternative outside of different left-wing ideologies. British-American historian and poet, Robert Conquest, is believed to have written 3 laws that perfectly sum up why this happened. These are:

1. *Everyone is conservative about what he knows best.*
2. *Any organisation not explicitly right-wing sooner or later becomes left-wing.*
3. *The simplest way to explain the behaviour of any bureaucratic organisation is to assume that it is controlled by a cabal of its enemies.*

There are those that argue Conquest did not write these laws because no primary source is attributed to him. The second law is also sometimes attributed to John O'Sullivan, a British commentator and journalist. Since I would not want to take credit for these laws, mentioning the theory of their origins makes it clear that I did not write them. That being said, these laws are both insightful and prescient when it comes to the political climate we find ourselves in across the world, which is why I've reference them here. The laws demonstrate that organisations must ultimately be explicit about their values and goals. Otherwise they're at risk of being taken over internally by their opponents. In the case of politics, the very left-wing opposition of the right has systematically subverted groups, organisations and movements supposed to represent right-wing interests. It's this I am concerned with breaking down in this chapter, since it's essential to understand not only how this takes place, but the consequences within the political landscape.

First I'll clarify that the true right is always interested in the unalienable rights of the individual, as opposed to justifying absolute power to achieve political goals. Although some will argue that left and right were born out of the National Assembly of the French Revolution, using European continental politics to define left and right is a poor benchmark because this assembly was entirely reactionary and absolutist in nature.

My first personal experience with the subversive nature of the Left came by the summer of 2012. By now I was well on my way to realising how the

Left managed to take over society by using cultural Marxism. Since feminism was my first red pill, the men's rights movement became my initial contact with an online political community. As I learnt more about what was driving feminism, I began to piece together genuinely right-wing philosophical alternatives kept from the masses due to the dominance of socialism, but just as the men's rights movement began to take off, the movement started to become very hostile to these ideas. The flagship men's rights site, A Voice for Men, attracted the attention of people that blamed the rise of feminism on 'traditionalism' and 'conservatism' – or what they called 'TradCons' and 'SoCons'. Their hostility to Christianity also became abundantly clear, and though the site claimed to be apolitical, as did a growing number of new commenters and commentators that suddenly began to cause division in the men's rights community, it was anything but. The site was clearly veering in a left-wing direction, becoming a hub for subversion that adapted Marxist theory for men's rights. Whereas feminists speak of female objectification, this was replaced with male disposability. The latter has some credence in the way it was originally intended by Warren Farrell in The Myth of Male Power, but due to his left-wing credentials and ex-feminist past, this was was ripe for co-option by those that would capitalise on his belief that feminism was largely a good thing, and now it was time for men to receive the same professional victimhood status.

Some, like me, attempted to call out these bad actors, systematically deflecting any attention away from the fact that it was the left's hatred of family life that created the vitriol towards men in the modern world, not to mention radical socialist politics. But it was no good. The subverters gained editorial roles on A Voice for Men, and systematically picked off everyone that protested the new direction of the site.

To top it off, another online men's community closely associated with the men's rights movement was becoming even more radical – MGTOW. Standing for Men Going Their Own Way, it became a hotbed of radical egoists that saw no value in anything but their own happiness. At first this movement was about men learning how to live by values of individual sovereignty, but this began to change. Just as feminists see masculinity as inherently toxic, MGTOW inverted this by making female nature a destructive instinct that will always result in the betrayal of men. They attributed this to hypergamy, the natural instinct for women to marry up in society or gain the reproductive attention of the most successful males. Hypergamy can indeed be explained psychologically, but MGTOW describe it as a form of utter selfishness that prevents any women from true love, thus leading to the inevitability of divorce and child support for husbands and fathers.

In the case of A Voice for Men, two articles appeared on the site that made Marxist subversion obvious,[1][2] one of them flagrantly called MRM Marxism. As for MGTOW, the theories of Robert Briffault were where leftist ideology crept in. Briffault was a 19th Marxist[3] known for saying, "The female, not the male, determines all the conditions of the animal family. Where the female can derive no benefit from association with the male, no such association takes place."[4] As this gained momentum, MGTOW thought leaders singled me out because I sought to give men advice that would allow them to avoid toxic relationships with women. MGTOW became the most toxic online community imaginable, viciously brigading and vote bombing anyone who challenges them, including myself. What this taught me was how the Left take over groups and organisations that aren't explicit driven by opposition to the Left, and adamant about being a right-wing, just as the aforementioned laws stipulate. These patterns of subversion have been so successful that society is becoming more like the Soviet Union every day. Political dissent against the Left is becoming more and more dangerous, as censorship and repression continues to grow. To understand why the Left have been so effective in their subversion, we need to start with the development of liberalism in the 19th century.

Modern Liberalism

Modern liberalism is nothing like the original form it took. John Locke is a founding father of the original principles of liberal philosophy, covered in chapter 4 when I addressed natural rights. The other founding father of liberalism was Adam Smith, mentioned in the last chapter when I covered the origins of economics. Though there is some crossover between Locke and Smith in relation to moral and economic philosophy, both these philosophers laid out the core principles for liberalism that gained momentum in the 18th century. Sadly this was not to last, however. By the late 19th century, so many reactionaries sought to undermine liberalism that it became a shadow of its original self. This I covered when I talked about relativism in chapter 14, and postmodernism in chapter 15, though another significant aspect of this undermining was John Stuart Mill.

John Stuart Mill was an English economist, philosopher and civil servant, who had a major impact on the direction of liberalism in the mid to late 19th century. While Smith and Locke were critical in making liberalism a philosophy that limited state interference, Mill was far less principled in this regard. He believed that, though individuals should have certain protected rights, these weren't necessarily set in stone, leading to contradictions in his work. In one sense he set out the Harm Principle in his 1859 essay, On Liberty. In chapter 1 of this essay, he wrote:

> *The only purpose for which power can be rightfully exercised over any member of a civilized community, against his will, is to prevent harm to others. His own good, either physical or moral, is not a sufficient warrant.*[5]

Let's now compare Mill's view with the foundational social contract thinkers of modern political philosophy, starting with John Locke:

> *Their persons are free by a natural right, and their properties, whether large or small, are their own, to be dealt with by their choice and not by the conqueror's—otherwise they are not properties.*[6]

Thomas Hobbes believed in the absolute authority of the sovereign, demonstrated by the following passage he wrote in Leviathan:

> *He therefore to whom God hath not supernaturally revealed that they are His, nor that those that published them were sent by Him, is not obliged to obey them by any authority but his whose commands have already the force of laws; that is to say, by any other authority than that of the Commonwealth, residing in the sovereign, who only has the legislative power.*[7]

Likewise, Rousseau believed in a general will, set out in the following passage of his seminal work, The Social Contract:

> *To protect the social compact from being a mere empty formula, therefore, it silently includes the undertaking that anyone who refuses to obey the general will is to be compelled to do so by the whole body. This single item in the compact can give power to all the other items. It means nothing less than that each individual will be forced to be free.*[8]

If we contrast Mill with these foundational social contract thinkers, at first glance it would seem that Mill argued for similar moral limits to Locke that prevented harm to others, thus making him a liberal philosopher. Mill also appears very different to Hobbes, who is often considered an absolute monarchist, i.e., someone that believes the monarch has absolute power and authority. Hobbes wasn't necessarily this specific about the nature of the sovereign, however, making him very popular with many kinds of totalitarian thinkers. Unlike Hobbes, Locke believed the people had the right to break the social contract if there was an abuse of power, such as the following passage of his Second Treatise:

> *So when the legislators try to take away and destroy the property of the people or to reduce them to slavery, they put themselves into a state of war with the people, who are thereby absolved from any further obedience and are left to the common escape that God has provided for all men against force and violence.*[9]

The question thus remains, how did Mill deviate from Locke, if he did indeed corrupt liberal philosophy? Though he did not necessarily go as far as Hobbes' and Rousseau's totalitarianism, he was not as vehement about moral limits. Critical to this was his view of *utilitarianism* he adapted from his mentor, *Jeremy Bentham*. Utilitarianism is the ethical view that the greatest happiness for the greatest number of people is the best outcome for society. Already we see that Mill changed the original principles of liberalism by resorting to arbitrary notions of a greater good that cannot be attained without sacrificing some individuals along the way. The greater good has become the poisoned chalice that so many are tempted by, creating a brand of philosophical moral dilemma dubbed 'lifeboat ethics'. Under this system we must decide what's the best course of action by sacrificing others in the process, such as the fat man thrown out of the boat to stop it sinking, or choosing to flick a switch that allows a runaway mine cart to move onto a track that kills one person instead of two or more.

Particularly telling is the fact that another student of Jeremy Bentham was Robert Owen, a proto-socialist thinker that started out as a liberal philosopher in the same vein as Bentham and Mill. The trouble is that utilitarianism is totally incompatible with the roots of liberal philosophy in the 17th and 18th century when we compare them, becoming a sort of Trojan horse that married socialism and liberalism together. The fact that Robert

Owen then went on to become one of the first socialists tells you a great deal in this regard, but alas, it gets worse.

In 1869, 10 years after On Liberty, Mill wrote another essay that seriously damaged liberalism, called The Subjection of Women, where he adapted and finished the work of his deceased wife, Harriet Taylor Mill. In it he defended the notion of women's equality in a manner conducive with his utilitarian corruption of liberalism, doing further damage to moral limits espoused by Locke. Further tragedy can most certainly be found in the fact that Mill was arguing for so-called equality of the sexes, something I provided necessary nuance with in chapter 5. In one passage, he wrote:

> *I deny that any one knows or can know, the nature of the two sexes, as long as they have only been seen in their present relation to one another. Until conditions of equality exist, no one can possibly assess the natural differences between women and men, distorted as they have been. What is natural to the two sexes can only be found out by allowing both to develop and use their faculties freely.*[10]

Mill did a great deal to popularise some very flawed ideas about men and women that assumed their roles were not natural, but arbitrarily imposed by men. I already demonstrated the folly of such thinking in chapter 5. Many will point to universal suffrage as a legitimate example of women's inequality, though the vote was often restricted to one vote per household, or land and property owners, due to the danger of using the vote as a form of legalised theft against property owners, thus damaging the stability of society as a whole. Looking at the rise of socialism, the vote most certainly has been used in this fashion, and had we listened to Locke, perhaps some sort of democratic system could have been moral. What's more, in many instances women received the vote shortly after men, like the United Kingdom, where in 1928 women received the vote only 10 years after men. Is it a better system when no social responsibilities are expected of those that vote, like paying taxes for a certain number of years or being a home owner? I would argue that democracy is just another form of tyranny if it doesn't come with strong limits that don't allow socialism to take hold, which can be attained by implementing Locke's moral teachings.

Mill's key objections to the status of women in society were not only utilitarian, but based on another key objection he held – *the tyranny of the majority*. He argued in On Liberty that a majority can pursue its interests at the expense of a minority, stating that, "'the tyranny of the majority' is now generally included among the evils against which society requires to be on its guard," [11] and that "Protection, therefore, against the tyranny of the magistrate is not enough: there needs protection also against the tyranny of the prevailing opinion and feeling." [12] Mill therefore certainly laid the groundwork for the kind of absolute egalitarianism that gradually spread beyond economic socialism, and towards a cultural model outlined in chapter 10.

The Liberal Party

Now that the philosophical roots of the corruption of liberalism are set out, we can move onto how this affected the ballot box. Liberalism undoubtedly has English and Scottish roots, putting it in direct opposition to continental politics that formed not only radical French collectivism originating with Jean-Jacque Rousseau, but German reactionary idealism from the likes of Immanuel Kant and Friedrich Nietzsche. Certain exceptions should be noted, like Frédéric Bastiat of France or the Austrian economists in the late 19th to early 20th century, but as a rule, European continental philosophy was a catastrophic amalgamation of totalitarianism and relativism that utterly rejected classical liberalism. It should come as no surprise, then, that the United Kingdom had the earliest political parties to call themselves liberal in not only Europe but the world, particularly one party simply called The Liberal Party. It was founded in 1859, and born out of a loose parliamentary group called The Radicals, along with aristocrats from The Whig Party that sought to strengthen parliament and weaken the crown during the reign of Charles II.[13]

This origin should be very telling. The peace between the monarchy and aristocracy has always been a delicate one, causing many conflicts over the centuries. British aristocrats found a way to wrestle power into their hands by not only twisting liberal politics, but riding on the back of The Radicals, who helped turn Britain not into a liberal country in the original sense of the word, but a socialist one that put no true limits democracy, unlike classical liberalism. A good way to explain why democracy must have limits would be describing unrestrained democracy as mob rule. Just because a majority votes for something, it doesn't necessarily make it right. The majority could vote to make murder illegal, but this is still murder. This is why mob rule is often used to describe unrestrained democracy, with no moral framework or accountability. Democracy certainly has its value in certain instances, but this must be tempered with the kind of moral limits that John Locke set out.

It's thus apparent that The Liberal Party completely sidestepped the original enlightenment principles of liberalism embodied by Locke and Smith, moving immediately into the realm of utilitarianism that Mill and others set out. At the same time, socialism was beginning to gain momentum in the 19th century, forming a false choice between liberals on one hand and socialism on the other, both finding common ground in utilitarian ethics. By 1924, the socialist Labour Party began to win elections, and this created a struggle for the left of politics between Labour and the Liberal Party. The Conservative Party (full name being the Conservative and Unionist Party) became the party for the right of British politics, but in the end was built on the same platform of utilitarian democracy as Labour and the Liberals. Where were the classical liberal principles of John Locke, if these parties were indeed so very different from one another? The Conservatives were supposedly the party for the wealthy. The Liberals supposedly represented liberalisation of society (whatever that means in practice), and the Labour Party were born out of trade unions, though became so entrenched in communism that they were actually brought down less than one year after gaining power for the first time during a minority government with the Liberals, because it's sympathies to the Soviet Union were such a concern.[14]

Since liberalism is based on unalienable rights of the individual (or natural rights), which of these three parties represented that? The answer is none of them, and they pulled off this false choice through a combination of redefining political terms, and by making all politics utilitarian. Instead of making politics about principles, it became about voting for your group instead. Morals and ethics be damned - as long as you get more power for your bloc, that's all that matters – i.e., the greater good. This is *not* what classically liberal politics was about at all!

The Liberal Party developed a special name for their kind of liberalism by the end of the 19th century – New Liberalism,[15] whereby the state could intervene if it guaranteed more freedom and removed obstacles of unemployment and poverty. Others called this social liberalism, but euphemisms aside, the Liberal Party was always a socialist party in the end, always finding new euphemisms that hide this. By the 1980s the Liberal Party was in serious decline, having sat in government on numerous occasions and been the party of Winston Churchill from 1904 to 1924. This resulted in the party becoming the Liberal Democrats after merging with the

Social Democrats in 1988, a socialist party that hid behind one of the many labels that leftists have concocted to redefine them, when the former one becomes affiliated with atrocities. Is Communism becoming too toxic? Change it to social democrat, democratic socialist, liberal democrat, or more recently, progressive and social libertarian (also known as left libertarian). These are all the same utilitarian ethics in the end, and until people understand this they'll be stuck in a socialist paradigm.

The false political choice created by this bait and switch is sometimes called the *Hegelian dialectic,*[16] theorised by Georg Wilhelm Friedrich Hegel. He described two sides opposed to one another in some shape or form; one: the thesis, and two: the antithesis. As the two sides compete, the eventual outcome is a synthesis that creates a sort of hybridisation between these forces. Synthesis then becomes a new thesis that results in another antithesis, repeating the cycle indefinitely as synthesis after synthesis occurs. What we must also understand, however, is how the Left has managed to silence this co-option of true choice, or those exposing their subversion of our societies.

McCarthyism

Prior to the 1950s, people were too opposed to communism to simply allow it to run amuck in our societies, and although leftists were somewhat successful in deceiving the public to a degree, they couldn't get them to totally embrace hard left ideologies like communism in particular. After the Russian Revolution, a split between the USA and USSR immediately began to form, though it was too early to tell which country would win out. America became known as the champion of capitalism (despite the loaded connotations of that word), and of course the Soviet Union became the champion of socialism. After World War II it was clear that Stalin had manipulated the entire world into dancing to his tune, having taken over the entire of Eastern Europe, as described in chapter 17. What resulted is a standoff that, to this day, is still suffering with historical revisionism.

Having received a high school GCSE in history, I still recall how the Cold War was always taught in a way that frames the Soviets as just another side in a morally relative struggle. The same thing took place when I learnt about the Cold War at around 10 years old, and I still recall looking at maps in school that had the Soviet Union on them. To clarify, the Cold War was the military deadlock between the United States and the Soviet Union, supported by their corresponding allies. The US had the NATO countries in its corner, while the Soviet Union had the Warsaw Pact members. This military stalemate led to a vicious propaganda war that the West actually lost when we look at the direction of history and culture. Yes the Soviet Union collapsed by 1991, giving us the impression that communism was destroyed, but in chapter 10 I proved that communism shifted to a cultural dimension shaped not by classical Marxism but the Frankfurt School's critical theory, otherwise known as cultural Marxism. But how did the Left manage to fend off any criticisms of this subversion of our societies that became so deep-rooted that, even today, it's influence is all around us? The answer lies in the demonisation of Joseph McCarthy.

Ever since this took place, any attempt at exposing leftist subversion is labelled McCarthyism,[17][18] branding you a McCarthyite or a 'conspiracy theorist' in the process. History tells a very different story when we look at the declassified files that became available after the dissolution of the Soviet Union. Following the first red scare from 1917-1920, after the Bolshevik revolution, the second red scare occurred in the late 1940s to the early 1950s. Joseph McCarthy became a pivotal figure that stood up to the subversive activities of leftists within US society, fighting a hard battle he would ultimately lose.

On the 21st March 1947, President Harry S.Truman signed Executive Order 9835, requiring federal civil-service employees be screened for loyalty by a review board, with the aim of establishing whether these employees were unconstitutionally operating against the United States. The order specifically states that:

> *The loyalty Review Board shall currently be furnished by the Department of Justice the name of each foreign or domestic organization, association, movement, group or combination of persons which the Attorney General, after appropriate investigation and determination, designates as totalitarian, fascist, communist or subversive, or as having adopted a policy of advocating or approving the commission of acts of force or violence to deny others their rights under the Constitution of the United States, or as seeking to alter the form of government of the United States by unconstitutional means.*[19]

Note that this order does not purely target communists, mentioning totalitarians, fascists and others, therefore demonstrating how communists deliberately misrepresent history, not to mention dismissing the order's necessity when we consider the evidence. In January 1950, US official Alger Hiss became the focus of a growing concern for Soviet espionage within the United States when convicted of spying for the Soviet Union in 1948. He was in effect found guilty, but wasn't convicted of this crime because the statute of limitations resulted in the time limit for a conviction being passed. Instead he was convicted of perjuring himself when he denied an earlier testimony, serving three and-a-half years of a five year sentence. Perhaps the most far-reaching example of this espionage comes from the conviction and execution of Julius and Ethel Rosenberg in 1950, for stealing atomic-bomb secrets for the Soviets, and in the same year, Klaus Fuchs was convicted for the same crime in the UK. This information was part of the highly secretive Manhattan Project, though even this could not prevent the Soviet Union from acquiring the knowledge to build the atomic bomb. Were it not for this betrayal, history would have been very different given that the atomic bomb became the stalemate that allowed the USSR to spread its evil ideology throughout the world, as the US feared nuclear retaliation if it directly intervened.

We should further consider that Alger Hiss was involved in the establishment of the United Nations, an organisation that was rotten from its very inception thanks to the involvement of the USSR. And yet Joseph McCarthy is blacklisted by history as a paranoid, power mad lunatic. McCarthy himself became involved in the investigation by the US government on February 1950, when he said during his Lincoln Day speech that, "I have here in my hand a list of 205—a list of names that were made known to the Secretary of State as being members of the Communist Party and who nevertheless are still working and shaping policy in the State Department." McCarthy would subsequently become a scapegoat for the Left, whose life was totally destroyed in a campaign of slander. One such example is the claim that he was involved in Hollywood blacklists which, though certainly weren't meritless, he was not.

Ultimately history would vindicate McCarthy, first by post-war decodes of wartime Soviet radio, known as the Venona project. Much later on when declassified files became available once the USSR collapsed, we know that his suspicions were even more accurate – far too many to comprehensively list in this book, in fact. Owen Lattimore would become another example of Soviet collaboration, helping to derail attempts by the United States to prevent Stalin taking over territories in the years that followed World War II. His betrayal helped facilitate the loss of China to communism, and like Hiss, constant obstructions within the legal system resulted only in a prosecution of perjury.

And now we realise why the Left has managed to subvert our societies. By combining manipulation of language and historical revisionism with subversive activities, and demonising those that stand up to this, we find ourselves in a political vice with no way out. After the US Senate voted in 1954 to condemn Joseph McCarthy, reacting to a prolonged leftist campaign to sabotage his reputation and investigation, his career was ruined. McCarthy subsequently died in 1957 of symptoms that some believe to be alcohol induced, as he struggled to recover his life. History has proven that McCarthy was a hero whose warnings we should have heeded, for if we had, perhaps we could have prevented the Left's destruction of our societies. McCarthy would become the warning for all others that followed, reminding them never get in the way of the Left. Once the sexual revolution of the 1960s took place, we saw exactly why McCarthy's demise was such a catastrophe.

Chapter 20: The Smallest State Possible

Although the state is a moral hazard, it's still the most effective way to defend freedom from other states.

In the final chapter, I want to dedicate some time to an explanation of the best political system we can adopt, and what my extensive journey has led me to conclude in this regard. As I showed in chapter 12, anarchy is not realistic because it relies too heavily on wishful thinking and utopianism. That's not to say that the state shouldn't be limited in some way, and it's this that I hope to convey with this chapter. I hope that it's very apparent at this late stage in the book that the state is a significant risk to the freedom and prosperity of mankind, creating a type of conundrum called a *moral hazard.* This takes place when people assume they're secure, thus taking foolish risks that increase the likelihood of a disastrous outcome. Consider how the state gets people to believe that they have so much security they can make decisions that would ordinarily be perceived as reckless or irresponsible; the person with a state pension that doesn't save for retirement, the unemployed person that doesn't have any intention of finding a job because they receive welfare, the single mother than doesn't care about how they treat men when the state will always step in to subsidise her life, or the corporation that lobbies the government for economic advantage - the latter in particular requiring further explanation.

Regulatory capture

Far too few have the curiosity to ask why no matter how much state intervention we get, nothing seems to improve. If anything, things get worse, like the NHS in the UK – a money pit that requires ever more resources, while patient waiting lists continue to grow.[1] As I explained in chapter 3, the reason for this is that you cannot subtract and divide your way to prosperity. Despite the temptation of something for nothing being too attractive for many to resist, you can't fight cause and effect forever, hence why socialism creates shortages that are met with ever greater demands on individuals, until their very lives are a required sacrifice, as per the history of communist countries. While this danger applies to laws of all kinds, it's regulations that I will use to demonstrate this further, epitomised via a certain moral hazard known as *regulatory capture*.

A regulation is a kind of state law administered by government bodies. Regulatory capture takes place when parties supposedly restricted by these laws turn them to their favour. For example, a corporation lobbies the government to modify or create regulations that harm their competitors, facilitating the gradual formation of a monopoly, although this can also occur by co-opting pre-existing laws to your advantage. Corporations often use these tactics to squeeze out small to medium sized businesses, since smaller businesses will invariably find it more difficult to absorb the costs of mounting regulations incurred by the government. Meanwhile, corporations, already bolstered by advantages like corporate personhood mentioned in chapter 18, are large enough to outlast smaller competitors until they're driven out of business.

Part of this is attributed to economies of scale, where goods and services become cheaper as productivity increases. The industrial revolution was when the advantage of mass manufacture led to the understanding that the cost of producing goods reduces, the more that's produced, which is where the theory of economies of scale originates. Unsurprisingly, larger businesses are able to produce more than smaller ones, but we should always bear in mind that quality is not necessarily as high. Take the craftsman producing a meticulous product, like the sculptor, the joiner, or the mason. This will be a high quality product that's much scarcer, but far superior to a mass produced product if the creator is suitably skilled.

Barriers to entry are another major consideration here. The more costs the state imposes on starting a business, the harder it is to get off the ground. Regulations are what contribute to these barriers, and regulatory capture allows lobbyists to block any new entrants into their market sector. I will use the UK residential rental market to demonstrate how this occurs. In the mid to late 2010s, being a small private landlord with one or two properties in the UK became blighted by large growth in the number of laws that put all the advantage in the favour of tenants. If a tenant stopped paying rent it became difficult to evict them in a reasonable length of time, ultimately requiring a court order for forceful eviction that could take up to 6 months or more.[2] This is a significant cost to the landlord, who either has to maintain an adequate financial buffer to absorb non-payment of rent, or pay for landlord insurance.

Coupled with landlord licences and growing regulations for even more stringent safety standards than unrented homes, this caused further financial headaches. To top it off, a second property in the UK began to incur a further 3% stamp duty surcharge,[3] making the tax on a new purchase substantially higher. What this resulted in is a small landlord exodus from the sector to the benefit of corporations that capitalised on further profits, offset in ways unavailable to small landlords, along with investment boosts in the build to rent sector.[4] The exodus squeezed out competition, allowing corporations to grow their market share. An impression is given that bigger landlords will somehow be better for tenants than smaller ones, since small landlords are 'amateurs'.[5] However, big businesses are notoriously difficult to challenge when they make mistakes, sometimes requiring costly legal action. What you won't be told by those promoting corporate advantage is that the destruction of competition leads to increasing rental prices,[6] and the subsequent solution disingenuously presented by left-wing policy makers is yet more socialism that ruins the market further, like rent controls.

Another example of regulatory capture is taken from the aftermath of the 2008 financial crisis, where regulatory agencies set up to curtail irresponsible and corrupt practices actually benefitted banking firms. Recall that this banking crisis was covered in chapter 2, but it was regulatory capture that allowed banks to get away with almost bringing down the world economy. The actions of the Federal Reserve Bank of New York (New York Fed) is one such example of this,[7] albeit a significant one given that this is the most influential bank in the Federal Reserve system given its location and oversight in the financial heartland of the United States - New York, where it's assigned with overseeing Wall Street. When examining unfolding events, the New York Fed protected banks from irresponsible decisions that almost brought down the world economy, and this is believed to be the result of a board dominated by some of the chief executives of banks supposedly overseen by this agency. The president of the New York Fed is not only selected by some of these bank chief executives, but creates obvious conflict of interest by reporting to members that are also part of the very banks it oversees. During the years that Timothy Geitner was president of the New York Fed, this relationship became even closer, believed to be a catalyst for the catastrophe that followed.

Prior to the Emergency Economic Stabilisation Act of 2008 being put into effect, the New York Fed purchased $30 billion of credit default swaps from American International Group (AIG), which it sold to Goldman Sachs, Merrill Lynch, Deutsche Bank and Sociéte Générale. This amounted to a backdoor bailout of 100 cents on the dollar for these contracts, and had AIG been allowed to fail the bailout for the taxpayer would have been a great deal less. Not only did Geitner defend this decision, but the New York Fed refused to specify the counterparties that benefited from this bailout, and when it became clear that this information would become public, a legal staffer from the New York Fed sent an e-mail to colleagues that warned them in advance.

The two examples of regulatory capture I've provided demonstrate that this happens in two core ways; using regulations to destroy your competition, or capturing agencies charged with oversight, turning them to your advantage. As such, this is further evidence for the nefarious influence of the state, where intervention into any part of our lives can have unintended consequences that are dire for the liberty of mankind. That being said, sometimes these consequences *are* intended, as people with influence and power manipulate the state for their own ends. If the state is to exist at all, we must therefore ask ourselves how its power can be kept in check.

Positive and negative liberty

Freedom, liberty or rights can be put into one of two key categories; positive or negative. For the latter, we can only protect and preserve what people already have, life and property being two very obvious forms this takes. Chapter 4 made a distinction between natural and legal rights, showing that freedom is a birthright that extends from our liberties in a state of nature, minus the right to harm others. By each respecting this, we can have a peaceful coexistence where our rights are an unalienable part of who we are, just as John Locke expressed. Negative freedom, liberty or rights go hand in hand with a system of natural rights, and this allows the state to exist *only* to protect these unalienable aspects of our personhood.

When rights take on a positive form, a blank cheque allows you to do whatever it takes to increase freedom. The previous chapter covered the toxic influence of utilitarianism, with its condoning of anything for the greater good. Under this system, individuals become sacrificial lambs that can be disregarded whenever necessary. Hence this is one form that positive liberty takes, as we're told that we must sacrifice our freedom if it somehow increases liberty in the process. Obviously this is contradictory when someone must decrease their liberty for the benefit of others, so the first question we should ask is; increased liberty for whom? Can we truly calculate how much good has been created by expecting people to sacrifice their natural liberties for the greater good? The answer is an emphatic no, and we should be mindful of those that tell us otherwise. As proven by the bloody history of communism, regulatory capture, and indeed socialism as a whole, sacrificing freedom for security gives you neither, just as Benjamin Franklin warned. In fact, all you get is different degrees of chaos, and a modicum of order that inevitably crumbles into inhumanity.

Egoistic philosophies like nihilism and existentialism are also derived from positive liberty because moral limits are considered arbitrary, making will and consent the only moral standards. Either the will to get what you want is the only standard for what's right (just as Nietzsche described in his Ubermensche philosophy), or consent is the only moral limit. The former is no better than the rule of the jungle because only prowess matters, while the latter is basically an excuse to exploit those too naïve to understand what they're getting themselves into, such as children or the mentally disabled. For example, children could never consent to sex because their minds and bodies are not capable, and mentally disabled people are sometimes too cognitively impaired to consciously consent. That is not to say someone that advocates of positive liberty would always agree with will or consent as valid moral categories. Sometimes pure relativism is the entire basis for their moral system, creating incredibly contradictory ideas of morality like absolute democracy, where people think a vote can decide if anything at all is moral, as though this can possibly create a morally consistent outcome without objective limits akin to negative liberty.

The issue of gun ownership is a good way to distinguish between key differences with positive and negative liberty. Proponents of positive and negative liberty will both defend the idea that the state can protect us (barring anarchists), but this is as far as agreements will tend to go in this sense. Positive liberty proponents of the egoist variety will vary quite widely on this issue because their morals are so whimsical. On the other hand, those advocating for negative liberty will state that you always have the right to defend yourself, which includes the right to bear arms. This is a big no-no for the modern left, whose morals are entirely based on positive liberty, wherein they suggest that gun ownership is just as open to interpretation as any other morality. They'll justify the erosion of gun ownership through appeals to emotion, citing the risk of gun crime as too high a price. One big problem with this narrative is that no correlation between gun ownership and gun crime has been proven.[8] You'll certainly find examples of places with high gun ownership and higher gun crime, like the US states of Louisiana and South Carolina, though some states with low gun ownership have high gun crime, such as California and Ohio. Others have high gun ownership and low gun crime, like New Hampshire and

Idaho.[9] Going further by delving into countries, the homicide rate in the United States is higher than other Western countries, but Switzerland and Israel have much higher gun possession due to requirements for all citizens to bear arms, with a much lower homicide rate on average.[10]

As we can see by this snapshot of a country demonised by the Left as a trigger happy nation of gun owning nuts, many other factors contribute to violent crime that go beyond possession of firearms, though I will not delve any further here because I cannot provide a more dedicated analysis in the timescale of this book. What I can say is that rights should never be subject to arbitrary whims of any kind, and this includes the right to bear arms. We should always be mindful of attempts to make appeals of any kind to manipulate us into giving up our rights, whether it's easily misrepresented gun crime statistics or anything else. This is why negative liberty is always the morally correct choice. If we're convinced to go down a path of positive liberty, we'll quickly find that security in exchange for freedom will turn society into a dictatorship that traps us under the boot of tyranny. If you doubt this, you need only look at what happened under murderous communist regimes such as the Soviet Union[11] and Mao's China[12] - had people been armed, they might have been able to avoid the inhumanity that the government imposed. In every instance of democide, not least communism, citizens were always disarmed first. Could this have been possible if they were at least able to fight back? Possibly not, but at least the citizens would have had a chance, making it much less likely.

Minarchism

If government should be based on negative liberty, how should this occur? The answer is the smallest state possible, with strong limits on power, best served with a certain type of state called minarchism or minarchy. Neither a utilitarian state based on positive liberty, nor a form of anarchism, a minarchist state is based on pure negative liberty, its only legitimate purpose being to protect the natural rights and responsibilities of the individual. Sometimes called the night-watchman state and associated with libertarian philosophy, it's actually much closer to the original liberal ideals of John Locke and Adam Smith. This state would provide military, police and courts, upholding property rights and protecting against aggression, theft, breach of contract or fraud. I would not stop there, however, as classical liberals often agree that the state should provide basic universal infrastructure like roads and street lighting, which is absolutely essential if the individual is not going to become a prisoner on private land. Communal areas are also essential in society, not just for travel but for leisure and socialising. Parks, both national and local should therefore be included. Fire service is certainly another viable service of the state, although this could easily be replaced with a free market alternative when people are prepared to pay for it, with the added incentive of a tax break if they do. In the same vein, private security can replace police protection if that is what people prefer, although all legal cases should be handled by state courts that adhere to a universal legal system of natural rights and responsibilities. Prisons should also be handled by the state, since making these private would create the perverse incentive to increase the prison population for profit.

Such a state would be very inexpensive to run, leading to a massive reduction in tax. Looking at government spending throughout the world, around 50% of GDP is consistently spent on welfare and subsidies, meaning that removing these from the budget makes it perfectly possible to reduce tax to a range of 10-20%, depending on how many private alternatives you use. Obviously the state would need to provide military, communal and travel infrastructure, courts, prisons and border protection, but anything else could be private, although schools, fire services and police should be a state based option. State police may still have to arrest those that aren't paying for this service, but state courts would universally judge who is innocent or guilty, irrespective of whether you rely on private security or public policing for protection. If we take the UK as an example, government spending was between 41.9% of GDP from 2016 to 2018,[13] while consistently half of this is spent on healthcare and welfare.[14] The USA tells a similar story, exceeding 37.5 of GDP as government spending from 2016-2018,[15] around half also taken up on healthcare and welfare.[16] It's thus perfectly possible to slash government to the services I mentioned, just by removing welfare spending.

Bearing all this in mind, along with tax obligations I've extensively covered in this book, it's not unreasonable to suggest that by the time we pay all forms of direct and indirect taxes like sales tax, VAT, income tax, capitals gains, council tax, or federal tax, that people give up well over 50% of their income to taxation of some kind, creating a massive burden on the taxpayer that's brushed aside by people that rely on this revenue for their income. This is not only a serious injustice in itself, but the way that people who depend on that income rally to oppress the majority into never being able to reform this system is yet another aspect of this injustice. Certainly the minarchist system I propose is a very good solution to this problem, although it would be a battle of monumental proportions to enact. Since modern politics is mired with egoism and utilitarianism - all forms of positive liberty, it's very difficult for people to so much as fathom such a political direction. However, as explained in the prior chapter, utilitarian ethics was a reaction to the growth of liberalism, so the aristocracy could maintain relevance in a post-feudal world. Aristocrats used this opportunity to create a new order that would indeed weaken the crown, but usurp liberal ideas by turning them into a new form of oligarchical and autocratic control.

The economy would also work very differently under minarchism. No state intervention would be allowed, making it impossible for regulatory capture to enable corporations to dominate under what's sometimes called *crony capitalism*. This is when the government actually helps certain businesses thrive, through a nexus between selected business interests and the political class. Since corporate personhood and limited liability would be abolished as well, the market would operate entirely through competition and merit, making it an even playing field where the customer is king, not corporate largesse. More satisfying is that socialism would be impossible under this system, putting an end to any form it takes, be it market socialism like the economic fascism that we see in every country in existence today, or the centrally planned and communist models that proliferated and then subsided in the 20th century.

Leftists will protest indignantly at this possibility because they've done everything they can to blame and demonise market economics, not least associating it with fascism. Although I've already gone into some depth about the similarities between communism and fascism in chapter 16, it's worth reinforcing the key economic difference because this is how people have been convinced that market (let alone free market) economics akin to what I describe under minarchy is the ultimate evil. Aside from a focus on economic class in Marx's original communist theory, as opposed to race in fascism, there is a centrally planned economy under communism and a market economy under fascism. Communist apologists will misrepresent this by suggesting that fascism is a 'capitalist' system because it operates in a market economy, but nothing could be further from the truth. Just because a socialist system operates in a market economy it hardly makes it free market economics. As chapter 16 showed, Pierre Leroux coined the term 'socialism' in 1834, not Karl Marx, whose journalism and early work only really began after 1836. In his Individualism and Socialism essay, Leroux wrote:

We are all responsible to one another. We are united by an invisible link, it is true, but that link is more clear and more evident to the intelligence than matter is to the eyes of the body. From which it follows that mutual charity is a duty. From which it follows that the intervention of man for man is a duty. From which follows finally a condemnation of individualism. But from that follows as well, and with an equal force, the condemnation of absolute socialism.[17]

Leroux was talking here about common bond being the basis for what he called 'socialisme'. In fact, he actually criticised the kind of absolute socialism that Marx later popularised. Earlier in the same essay, Leroux states:

But let the partisans of absolute socialism come to outline their tyrannical theories, let them speak of organizing us in regiments of scientists and regiments of industrials, let them go as far as declaring against the liberty of thought, at that same instant you feel yourself repulsed, your enthusiasm freeze, your feelings of individuality and liberty rebel, you start back sadly to the present from dread of that new papacy, weighty and absorbent, which will transform Humanity into a machine, where the true living natures, the individuals, will no longer be anything by a useful matter, instead of being themselves the arbiters of their destiny.[18]

There can be no doubt, then, that the communist theories of Marx hold no monopoly on socialism whatsoever, and convincing the masses otherwise is one way we find ourselves in the absurdly dishonest predicament of Marxists defining socialism as *only* communism, with *any* market economics associated with their favourite pejoratives of capitalism and fascism. However, fascism as an economic theory is a form of market socialism that allows individuals to own the legal title to property, controlling the economy and siphoning productivity through regulation and taxation. Dominance of corporations we see in the modern economy was a big part of fascist economics, hence the reason that corporatism is sometimes called *corporate fascism*. No, this isn't a completely centrally planned economy, but then again, even Vladimir Lenin abandoned this for his new economic policy that ushered in some market reforms. What many leftists fail to grasp is that, on paper, their theories may seem plausible, but every single time they're put into practice, market reforms are essential for the aversion of the typical catastrophes associated with their ideology. China proved once again that this is the case after Deng Xiaopin's economic reforms, post-1978,[19] leading to the Chinese economy we have today which, while far from perfect, is a significant economic improvement than under Mao.

What we must begin to accept is that the market is not our enemy. Quite the opposite; it is our path to freedom and prosperity that has its flaws, but unlike communism and socialism, its proponents do not pretend that they are trying to create a utopia. As it stands, the idea that minarchism could ever be in our future seems too unlikely to contemplate, but I truly hope that someday enough people will see how much they've been lied to by the powers that be, completely besotted with socialism in some shape or form because it allows them to move perpetually towards absolute power.

Conclusion: The Journey Continues

If there's one thing that surprised me about writing this book it's how difficult it was to include everything I wanted to cover. At first I was honestly concerned that I might not be able to substantially fill a book, but I soon began to realise that I had to limit what I wanted to say. At the risk of sounding arrogant, since starting my YouTube channel in October 2010, it's clearer to me than ever that I've learnt so much that I could easily write a series of books, let alone one. What this book ultimately covered was my very early journey away from left-wing dogma, starting with feminism but eventually leading to the realisation that socialism was the heart of the political problems in society, and that limited government was the solution, at least in a material sense. I'm not pretending that I have nothing else to learn - far from it. My work continues to delve into new areas, as I'm always looking for another piece of that big picture I'm putting together. That being said, the tapestry of truth I'm compiling would need at least two other books to do justice to it, but I honestly don't know if this would also be enough.

For the purpose of this book, however, I feel I've adequately addressed the false narrative of feminism, how socialism is the root cause of our socioeconomic destruction, and what we can do to resolve these problems if we return to the original values of classical liberalism. I cannot say that classical liberalism alone will help us defeat the evils we face in our morally relativist order, but it's a good start. There are other problems that feminism accompanies, adding to the leftist corruption in our societies – environmentalism, gender ideology that delves into sexuality, and multiculturalism to name the more prominent examples. In no way could I address these areas within this book without cutting too many corners, but I trust that this makes it obvious where subsequent books could delve.

Regardless, this book has proven that feminism is based on deeply exaggerated and simplistic distortions of history, making us think that the only reason women weren't as influential in the past is because men kept them down. Sometimes there were legitimate reasons for women *not* to have as much power as men because people formerly expected leaders to direct from the frontlines, or at least practice what they preach – a far cry from the type of leaders we have today, who never actually get their hands dirty at all. The respected warrior kings of old may be long gone, but that doesn't mean we should revise history by suggesting that anything other than our modern world could ever accommodate the amount of liberty that women have today. Furthermore, what is the cost of this liberty to our families and communities? Should they become secondary concerns because women are supposedly modern slaves if they're stay-at-home mothers and housewives, as though they're any freer if they have to go to work every day instead? Pure logic alone proves how absurdly over-simplistic this is. And what about the way men are treated when feminism is institutionalised, with fathers denied their parental rights yet forced to adhere to their parental responsibilities? We must begin to realise that broken families create broken people, meaning that the state is expected to intervene.

Once we make this connection to the state, we can begin to piece together the true reason feminism is pushed on society so aggressively, with a picture of history that actually does the vast majority of men a serious injustice. Imagine going to a medieval peasant and telling him that he's a misogynist when he's neck deep in mud and dirt, as he works the land for his lord. If people want a conversation about the corruption of the ruling class of society that is a far better place to start, but dividing people up into their sexes, and expecting this to create an accurate picture of oppression is nothing but demagoguery, and socialist demagoguery at that, which brings me onto socialism itself, another big part of this book.

We should now be able to see that socialism is a con – a ruse to make us think we can have something for nothing, and give up what truly have in return. No decent person is unconcerned about poverty, but this will always be with us, and anyone that says otherwise is either lying or ignorant. There's a million miles between theory and practice, as socialism proves. All the sentiment in the world about shared ownership and every need being met will not change the fact that socialism in practice just doesn't work. On a small scale (far smaller than anything we have today) it may work when people are prepared to sacrifice for those they immediately known and love, but we already have something like this – family! How interesting that socialists constantly try to tear down this natural safety net in society, or not so interesting when we realise that this is one of many characteristics of a cult that socialism shares. Feminism is the original attempt to cripple the family, becoming the foundation for everything that came later. What we do see very clearly with socialism is what happens when people give up their natural rights to an absolute authority, trading negative for positive freedom in a suicidal exchange that caused more rapid death and destruction than any other time and place in history. If we're asking the right questions we quickly find ourselves asking why this happened after atheism started replacing Christianity in Europe. Why did the state atheism of communist societies lead to the eradication of all the moral limits that even the injustices of feudalism held in place? This book explained that this decline was due to relativism, both moral and epistemological, ushering in the postmodern society we now have.

Throughout this book, I've documented my journey away from socialism to truly liberal or libertarian values, with John Locke and Adam Smith being the founders of these principles in a modern academic sense. It was this that allowed me to see that natural rights, free markets and small government is the closest thing we have to the security of our liberties, constantly wrestled away from us by demands for absolute security and no objective moral limits – yet another foolish yearning pushed by demagogues in our society – the Vladimir Lenin's that tell us we'll be set free from tyranny if we pool all our freedoms into one big pot that they'll be in charge of, of course. It's all for the greater good, you see! Utilitarianism is the heart of this all corrupting temptation, which is why communism, fascism, and socialism are all part of the same left-wing totalitarian entity. No matter how upset this makes proponents of those ideologies, the fact is that values, not policies, define belief systems in the end. Thus it doesn't matter whether communists want a post-private property anarchist world, fascists want to create a form of socialism based on corporatism and race, or other socialists want to create another interpretation of this ideology. As long as this is based on positive rights, aka utilitarianism or the greater good, they all stem from the same totalitarian roots.

Before concluding, I would like to add some remarks about the censorship I touched on in the introduction. Since writing this book, censorship has indeed gotten a lot worse, just as I predicted. The reasons for this are tied to the essence of the totalitarian nature of the left, and its growing subversion that's behind the hegemony we now see, also addressed in this book when I went into cultural Marxism manifesting in society. What this tells me is that reliance on social media or the internet alone is not a sustainable policy. Work must be preserved in a variety of mediums that are out of reach of gatekeepers, and the internet is proving surprisingly vulnerable for takedowns of whole bodies of information. Make no mistake, this is a modern day book burning that is no better than the Nazis creating pyres of literature, but we can fight back by not only moving towards a decentralised internet based on blockchain technology, but with literature that isn't stored online. I hope this book can help with this endeavour and that there are enough people out there that appreciate this timeless format. Equally, I hope that this will not be the last book I write, and that I can continue to archive my work in this age old fashion.

References

Introduction

1. https://en.wikipedia.org/wiki/Replication_crisis
2. https://www.cnet.com/news/us-internet-control-ted-cruz-free-speech-russia-china-internet-corporation-assigned-names-numbers/

Chapter 1

1. https://en.wikipedia.org/wiki/Republic_(Plato)#Book_V
2. https://www.youtube.com/watch?v=BA3uryDJzI0&t
3. https://www.telegraph.co.uk/news/uknews/1532012/Day-nursery-may-harm-under-3s-say-child-experts.html
4. http://www.nber.org/papers/w21571
5. https://www.nber.org/papers/w14969
6. https://www.youtube.com/watch?v=4HRUEqyZ7p8

Chapter 2

1. https://en.wikipedia.org/wiki/Northern_Rock
2. https://en.wikipedia.org/wiki/Financial_crisis_of_2007%E2%80%9308
3. https://en.wikipedia.org/wiki/Emergency_Economic_Stabilization_Act_of_2008
4. https://en.wikipedia.org/wiki/Fractional-reserve_banking
5. https://en.wikipedia.org/wiki/Nixon_shock

Chapter 3

1. https://www.dailymail.co.uk/debate/article-6223205/TOBY-YOUNG-stop-teachers-brainwashing-children.html
2. https://www.foxnews.com/politics/by-the-numbers-teachers-union-political-contributions-in-2016
3. https://www.breitbart.com/tech/2018/10/09/the-good-censor-leaked-google-briefing-admits-abandonment-of-free-speech-for-safety-and-civility/

4. https://www.breitbart.com/tech/2017/08/07/google-fires-viewpoint-diversity-manifesto-author-james-damore/
5. https://www.dailymail.co.uk/news/article-3606562/Facebook-changes-policies-Trending-Topics-activist-claimed-accused-site-Right-wing-censorship.html
6. https://www.breitbart.com/tech/2018/05/09/twitter-is-banning-conservatives-for-posting-facts/
7. https://en.wikipedia.org/wiki/Slavery_in_ancient_Greece#Historical_views
8. https://en.wikipedia.org/wiki/Slavery_in_the_United_States#Justification_in_the_South
9. https://en.wikipedia.org/wiki/National_Health_Service#Funding
10. https://www.dailymail.co.uk/news/article-2865479/Britain-spends-1-000-welfare-person-rest-Europe-FOUR-times-Romania.html
11. https://en.wikipedia.org/wiki/List_of_countries_by_social_welfare_spending

Chapter 4

1. https://plato.stanford.edu/entries/hobbes/
2. Thomas Hobbes, Leviathan, XIII.9
3. https://en.wikipedia.org/wiki/Two_Treatises_of_Government
4. https://en.wikipedia.org/wiki/Natural_and_legal_rights
5. https://en.wikipedia.org/wiki/Labor_theory_of_property
6. https://plato.stanford.edu/entries/rousseau/
7. https://en.wikipedia.org/wiki/Discourse_on_Inequality
8. Jean-Jacque Rousseau, Discourse on Inequality, the First Part, Paragraph 9
9. Jean-Jacque Rousseau, The Social Contract, Book 3, Chapter 1
10. Jean-Jacque Rousseau, The Social Contract, Book 1, Chapter 7

Chapter 5

1. https://en.wikipedia.org/wiki/List_of_Olympic_records_in_athletics
2. https://en.wikipedia.org/wiki/List_of_world_records_in_Olympic_weightlifting
3. https://www.dailymail.co.uk/sport/football/article-4389760/USA-women-s-team-suffer-5-2-loss-FC-Dallas-U-15-boys.html

4. https://www.theguardian.com/observer/osm/story/0,,543962,00.html
5. http://emilkirkegaard.dk/en/wp-content/uploads/Men-and-things-women-and-people-A-meta-analysis-of-sex-differences-in-interests.pdf
6. http://iqcomparisonsite.com/SexDifferences.aspx

Chapter 6

1. https://www.ncbi.nlm.nih.gov/pmc/articles/PMC3247300/
2. https://www.dailymail.co.uk/health/article-1303395/Hormone-rush-turns-man-father.html
3. https://www.theguardian.com/news/datablog/2010/jan/28/divorce-rates-marriage-ons
4. https://www.washingtonpost.com/news/wonk/wp/2015/06/23/144-years-of-marriage-and-divorce-in-the-united-states-in-one-chart/
5. https://www.cdc.gov/nchs/data/databriefs/db18.pdf
6. https://www.ncbi.nlm.nih.gov/pmc/articles/PMC1802108/
7. https://link.springer.com/article/10.1007/s10508-017-0953-1
8. https://www.lshtm.ac.uk/newsevents/news/2019/declines-sexual-frequency-seen-among-over-25s-and-married-couples
9. https://ifstudies.org/blog/counterintuitive-trends-in-the-link-between-premarital-sex-and-marital-stability/
10. https://ifstudies.org/blog/does-sexual-history-affect-marital-happiness
11. http://www.ucd.ie/geary/static/publications/workingpapers/gearywp201320.pdf
12. https://www.dailymail.co.uk/sciencetech/article-4563512/Religious-people-regret-casual-sex-slightly-more.html

Chapter 7

1. http://ftp.iza.org/dp4200.pdf
2. https://www.familyfirst.org.nz/wp-content/uploads/2012/01/WHO-CARES-Report-2012-Executive-Summary.pdf
3. https://www.dailymail.co.uk/health/article-2462801/Does-daycare-turn-children-monsters-Kids-childminders-likely-behavioural-problems.html

4. https://www.dailymail.co.uk/health/article-4257458/Sending-toddlers-childcare-make-stressed.html
5. https://allthatsinteresting.com/james-bulger-killers-robert-thompson-jon-venables
6. https://www.theguardian.com/uk/2000/nov/01/bulger.familyandrelationships
7. http://www.civitas.org.uk/archive/pubs/experiments.php

Chapter 8

1. https://en.wikipedia.org/wiki/No-fault_divorce
2. http://www.dailymail.co.uk/news/article-1346603/Britains-fatherless-families-1-5-children-lose-touch-parent.html
3. https://www.telegraph.co.uk/women/sex/divorce/6575997/Third-of-family-break-up-children-lose-contact-with-fathers-in-failing-court-system-poll.html
4. https://www.dailymail.co.uk/news/article-2253421/1-3-US-children-live-father-according-census-number-parent-households-decreases-1-2-million.html
   https://www.dailymail.co.uk/news/article-2540974/Britain-fourth-highest-number-single-parents-EU.html
5. https://www.dailymail.co.uk/news/article-1033661/Second-Fathers-4-Justice-roof-protest-Harriet-Harmans-house-month.html
6. https://en.wikipedia.org/wiki/Children_Act_1989
7. https://www.dailymail.co.uk/news/article-2005402/David-Cameron-Absent-fathers-bad-drink-drivers.html
8. https://assets.publishing.service.gov.uk/government/uploads/system/uploads/attachment_data/file/319134/how-is-child-maintenance-worked-out.pdf
9. https://www.theguardian.com/money/2013/feb/15/divorce-what-happens-to-the-family-home
10. https://www.ons.gov.uk/employmentandlabourmarket/peopleinwork/earningsandworkinghours
11. https://www.gov.uk/income-tax-rates/previous-tax-years
12. https://www.gov.uk/government/publications/rates-and-allowances-national-insurance-contributions/rates-and-allowances-national-insurance-contributions

Chapter 9

1. https://legaldictionary.net/preponderance-of-evidence/
2. https://www.dailymail.co.uk/news/article-2540919/At-Victory-secret-courts-Rulings-family-cases-public-Mail-campaign.html#comments
3. https://www.telegraph.co.uk/news/uknews/law-and-order/11166564/Father-wins-custody-battle-after-being-falsely-accused-of-sexually-abusing-his-daughter.html
4. https://abc13.com/news/child-custody-battle-ends-with-charges-against-mother/1202079/
5. https://publichealth.arizona.edu/sites/publichealth.arizona.edu/files/JCCP1987.pdf
6. https://www.city-journal.org/html/campus-rape-myth-13061.html
7. https://en.wikipedia.org/wiki/Mary_P._Koss#Career
8. https://www.justice.gov/archives/opa/blog/updated-definition-rape
9. https://en.wikipedia.org/wiki/False_accusation_of_rape
10. https://www.bbc.co.uk/news/uk-25964991
11. https://www.theguardian.com/society/datablog/2015/oct/22/one-in-four-women-has-experienced-domestic-violence-at-partners-hands
12. https://ncadv.org/learn/statistics
13. https://en.wikipedia.org/wiki/Duluth_model
14. https://www.theguardian.com/society/2010/sep/05/men-victims-domestic-violence
15. https://www.independent.co.uk/news/uk/home-news/women-are-more-violent-says-study-622388.html
16. https://www.avoiceformen.com/feminism/government-tyranny/primary-aggressor-listings-by-state/
17. http://www.ejfi.org/News/Table_4.htm

Chapter 10

1. https://en.wikipedia.org/wiki/Critical_theory
2. https://en.wikipedia.org/wiki/Historical_materialism
3. https://en.wikipedia.org/wiki/Cultural_hegemony
4. https://en.wikipedia.org/wiki/Fabian_Society

5. https://en.wikipedia.org/wiki/Antonio_Gramsci#Imprisonment_and_death
6. https://en.wikipedia.org/wiki/Hungarian_Soviet_Republic
7. https://en.wikipedia.org/wiki/Frankfurt_School
8. https://en.wikipedia.org/wiki/The_Authoritarian_Personality
9. https://en.wikipedia.org/wiki/Dialectic_of_Enlightenment
10. Erich Fromm, Escape from Freedom, pp. 36–37
11. https://en.wikipedia.org/wiki/New_Left
12. https://en.wikipedia.org/wiki/Eros_and_Civilization
13. https://en.wikipedia.org/wiki/One-Dimensional_Man
14. https://www.marcuse.org/herbert/pubs/60spubs/65repressivetolerance.htm

Chapter 11

1. https://www.hawaii.edu/powerkills/20TH.HTM
2. https://en.wikipedia.org/wiki/The_Gulag_Archipelago
3. https://en.wikipedia.org/wiki/Sukhanovo_Prison
4. https://en.wikipedia.org/wiki/White_Sea%E2%80%93Baltic_Canal
5. https://en.wikipedia.org/wiki/Holodomor
6. https://en.wikipedia.org/wiki/Great_Leap_Forward
7. https://www.marxists.org/archive/marx/works/1853/03/04.htm
8. https://marxists.catbull.com/archive/marx/works/1849/01/13.htm
9. https://en.wikipedia.org/wiki/Karl_Marx
10. Richard Wurmbrand, Marx & Satan, pp. 20-21
11. https://hubpages.com/politics/KARL-MARX-ABUSED-HIS-CHILDREN
12. https://en.wikipedia.org/wiki/Helene_Demuth
13. https://en.wikipedia.org/wiki/Blat_(favors)

Chapter 12

1. https://www.hawaii.edu/powerkills/MURDER.HTM
2. https://en.wikipedia.org/wiki/World_population
3. https://www.hawaii.edu/powerkills/20TH.HTM
4. https://en.wikipedia.org/wiki/Slavery_in_antiquity
5. https://en.wikipedia.org/wiki/Tax_protester_Sixteenth_Amendment_arguments
6. https://freedomain.blogspot.com/2006/11/gun-in-room.html
7. https://en.wikipedia.org/wiki/New_Economic_Policy

8. https://en.wikipedia.org/wiki/Dictatorship_of_the_proletariat
9. https://en.wikipedia.org/wiki/Communism
10. https://en.wikipedia.org/wiki/Marx%27s_theory_of_alienation
11. https://www.marxists.org/archive/marx/works/1845/german-ideology/ch01a.htm
12. https://en.wikipedia.org/wiki/Labor_theory_of_value
13. https://en.wikipedia.org/wiki/Commodity_fetishism

Chapter 13

1. https://www.theguardian.com/education/2018/nov/30/record-number-of-uk-children-excluded-for-racist-bullying
2. https://www.stopbullying.gov/at-risk/groups/lgbt/index.html
3. https://en.wikipedia.org/wiki/Ordination_of_women_in_the_Anglican_Communion
4. https://en.wikipedia.org/wiki/New_Atheism

Chapter 14

1. https://www.marxists.org/archive/marx/works/1848/communist-manifesto/ch02.htm
2. Friedrich Nietzsche, The Gay Science, Section 125, tr. Walter Kaufmann
3. https://en.wikipedia.org/wiki/%C3%9Cbermensch
4. Friedrich Nietzsche, Beyond Good and Evil, Section 195, tr. Helen Zimmern
5. https://en.m.wikipedia.org/wiki/Thus_Spoke_Zarathustra
6. https://en.wikipedia.org/wiki/The_Will_to_Power_(manuscript)
7. https://plato.stanford.edu/entries/kant/
8. Arthur Schopenhauer, Studies in Pessimism, The Essays
9. Arthur Schopenhauer, Studies in Pessimism, The Essays
10. https://en.wikipedia.org/wiki/The_World_as_Will_and_Representation
11. https://plato.stanford.edu/entries/sartre/

Chapter 15

1. https://en.wikipedia.org/wiki/Modernism

2. https://www.ons.gov.uk/peoplepopulationandcommunity/birthsdeathsandmarriag-es/lifeexpectancies/articles/howhaslifeexpectancychangedovertime/2015-09-09
3. https://en.wikipedia.org/wiki/Life_expectancy#Variation_over_time
4. https://en.wikipedia.org/wiki/Claude_Monet
5. https://en.wikipedia.org/wiki/Pablo_Picasso
6. https://en.wikipedia.org/wiki/Romanticism
7. https://en.wikipedia.org/wiki/Fountain_(Duchamp)
8. https://en.wikipedia.org/wiki/My_Bed
9. https://en.wikipedia.org/wiki/Chris_Ofili#The_Holy_Virgin_Mary
10. https://www.khanacademy.org/humanities/global-culture/identity-body/identity-body-europe/a/chris-ofili-the-holy-virgin-mary
11. https://www.tate.org.uk/whats-on/tate-britain/exhibition/turner-prize-1998/turner-prize-1998-artists-chris-ofili
12. http://www.importanceofphilosophy.com/Metaphysics_Identity.html
13. https://en.wikipedia.org/wiki/Theory_of_forms
14. https://plato.stanford.edu/entries/sartre/
15. https://plato.stanford.edu/entries/beauvoir/
16. https://plato.stanford.edu/entries/foucault/

Chapter 16

1. https://www.etymonline.com/word/socialism
2. https://en.wikipedia.org/wiki/Pierre_Leroux
3. https://en.wikipedia.org/wiki/The_Road_to_Serfdom
4. https://www.etymonline.com/word/nazi
5. https://en.wikipedia.org/wiki/National_Socialist_Program
6. https://en.wikipedia.org/wiki/Fascist_Manifesto

Chapter 17

1. https://en.wikipedia.org/wiki/New_Soviet_man
2. https://en.wikipedia.org/wiki/Molotov%E2%80%93Ribbentrop_Pact
3. https://en.wikipedia.org/wiki/Operation_Barbarossa
4. https://en.wikipedia.org/wiki/Shtrafbat
5. https://en.wikipedia.org/wiki/Dmitry_Pavlov_(general)
6. https://plato.stanford.edu/entries/egoism/

7. https://plato.stanford.edu/entries/ayn-rand/

Chapter 18

1. https://en.wikipedia.org/wiki/Local_knowledge_problem
2. John Meynard Keynes, A Tract on Monetary Reform (1923), Chapter 3, p. 80
3. https://wikieducator.org/KEYNES%27S_THEORY_OF_AGGREGATE_DEMAND
4. Adam Smith, The Wealth of Nations, Book 4, Chapter 2, Paragraph 9
5. Adam Smith, The Theory of Moral Sentiments, Part 4, Chapter 1
6. Ludwig von Mises, Socialism: An Economic and Sociological Analysis, Part 2, Chapter 1
7. Adam Smith, The Wealth of Nations Book 1, Chapter 7, Paragraph 28
8. https://en.wikipedia.org/wiki/Opium_Wars
9. https://www.channel4.com/news/factcheck/factcheck-how-many-bankers-were-jailed-for-their-part-in-the-financial-crisis
10. https://en.wikipedia.org/wiki/Too_big_to_fail

Chapter 19

1. https://www.avoiceformen.com/feminism/mrm-marxism/
2. https://www.avoiceformen.com/mens-rights/political-dyslexia/
3. http://www.unz.com/print/MarxismToday-1962may-00154
4. Robert Briffault, The Mothers, Vol. I, p. 191
5. John Stuart Mill, On Liberty, Chapter 1
6. John Locke, Second Treatise of Civil Government, Chapter 16, Paragraph 194
7. Thomas Hobbes, CHAPTER 33, Their Authority And Interpretation
8. Jean-Jacque Rousseau, The Social Contract, Book 1, Chapter 7
9. John Locke, Second Treatise of Civil Government, Chapter 19, Paragraph 222
10. John Stuart Mill, The Subjection of Women, Chapter 1
11. John Stuart Mill, On Liberty, Chapter 1
12. John Stuart Mill, On Liberty, Chapter 1
13. https://en.wikipedia.org/wiki/Liberal_Party_(UK)#Origins
14. https://www.britannica.com/topic/Labour-Party-political-party

15. https://en.wikipedia.org/wiki/Liberal_Party_(UK)#Rise_of_New_Liberalism
16. https://plato.stanford.edu/entries/hegel-dialectics/#HegeDescHisDialMeth
17. https://en.wikipedia.org/wiki/Joseph_McCarthy
18. https://en.wikipedia.org/wiki/McCarthyism
19. https://teachingamericanhistory.org/library/document/executive-order-9835/

Chapter 20

1. https://www.health.org.uk/news-and-comment/blogs/nhs-performance-and-waiting-times?gclid=Cj0KCQiAyKrxBRDHARIsAKCzn8xdArl_dut7PUoydh_wfJmS38S2wP8Es0xAu4fbSF7gW0hDWxDByl0aAsDKEALw_wcB
2. https://www.propertyinvestmentproject.co.uk/blog/how-long-evict-tenant/
3. https://www.pricebailey.co.uk/blog/stamp-duty-additional-property/
4. https://propertyindustryeye.com/corporate-landlords-earning-two-times-more-from-buy-to-let-than-private-owners/
5. https://www.bbc.co.uk/news/business-43324486
6. https://www.dailymail.co.uk/property/article-7911943/How-fast-rents-rising-near-Biggest-hikes-seen-three-years.html
7. https://en.wikipedia.org/wiki/Regulatory_capture#Federal_Reserve_Bank_of_New_York
8. https://www.heritage.org/crime-and-justice/commentary/here-are-8-stubborn-facts-gun-violence-america
9. https://en.wikipedia.org/wiki/Gun_violence_in_the_United_States_by_state
10. https://en.wikipedia.org/wiki/List_of_countries_by_intentional_homicide_rate#By_country
11. https://en.wikipedia.org/wiki/Gun_control_in_the_Soviet_Union
12. https://en.wikipedia.org/wiki/Gun_control_in_China
13. https://www.heritage.org/index/country/unitedkingdom#government-size
14. https://en.wikipedia.org/wiki/Government_spending_in_the_United_Kingdom
15. https://www.heritage.org/index/country/unitedstates

16. https://en.wikipedia.org/wiki/Government_spending_in_the_United_States
17. Pierre Leroux, Individualism & Socialism, Part IV
18. Pierre Leroux, Individualism & Socialism, Part III
19. https://en.wikipedia.org/wiki/Chinese_economic_reform

About the Author

Cid Lazarou is a vlogger and writer with a Greek Cypriot heritage, from the United Kingdom. Born and raised in Cardiff, Wales, where he lives with his Welsh wife and two daughters, he spent his twenties teaching, composing and performing music, honing his writing skills, and developing a passion for philosophy. Since then he's gone on to establish a philosophy based blog site called Rocking Philosophy, stemming from a YouTube channel under the same name. He uses the online alias of RockingMrE.

www.rockingphilosophy.com

Printed in Great Britain
by Amazon

37703060R00115